ENGLISH LANGU

Language and Creative Illusion

ENGLISH LANGUAGE SERIES
General Editor: Randolph Quirk

LANGUAGE AND CREATIVE ILLUSION
Walter Nash

ADVERBS AND MODALITY IN ENGLISH
Leo Hoye

CREATING TEXTS: AN INTRODUCTION TO THE STUDY OF COMPOSITION
Walter Nash and David Stacey

THE ENGLISH INFINITIVE
Patrick J. Duffley

RHYTHMIC PHRASING IN ENGLISH VERSE
Richard D. Cureton

GOOD ENGLISH AND THE GRAMMARIAN
Sidney Greenbaum

THE LANGUAGE OF HUMOUR
Walter Nash

THE RHYTHMS OF ENGLISH POETRY
Derek Attridge

STYLE IN FICTION
Geoffrey N. Leech and Michael H. Short

AN INTRODUCTION TO MODERN ENGLISH WORD-FORMATION
Valerie Adams

COHESION IN ENGLISH
M.A.K. Halliday and Ruqaiya Hasan

A LINGUISTIC GUIDE TO ENGLISH POETRY
Geoffrey N. Leech

INVESTIGATING ENGLISH STYLE
David Crystal and Derek Davy

Language and Creative Illusion

WALTER NASH

LONGMAN
London and New York

Addison Wesley Longman Limited
Edinburgh Gate
Harlow, Essex CM20 2JE
England

and Associated Companies throughout the world

Published in the United States of America
by Addison Wesley Longman Inc., New York

First published 1998

ISBN 0 582 29164-X Paper
ISBN 0 582 29163-1 Cased

British Library Cataloguing-in-Publication Data
A catalogue record for this book is
available from the British Library

Library of Congress Cataloging-in-Publication Data
Nash, Walter.
Language and creative illusion / Walter Nash.
p. cm. — (English language series)
Includes bibliographical references and index.
ISBN 0–582–29163–1 (cased). — ISBN 0–582–29164–X (paper)
1. Rhetoric. I. Title. II. Series.
P301.N37 1998
809—dc21 97–46988
CIP

Set by 35 in Bembo
Produced by Addison Wesley Longman Singapore (Pte) Ltd.,
Printed in Singapore

All knowledge is foredoomed, forlorn –
Of inmost truth and wisdom shorn –
Unless imagination brings
Its skies wherein to use its wings.

(Walter de la Mare, *Dreams*)

It is of the essence of knowledge that it should consist of the bringing together of a subject and an object. The subject is not only modified by the object; he is modified in such a way that some characteristic of the object becomes part of his consciousness.

(Sir Russell Brain, *The Nature of Experience*)

Contents

Preface

My theme is the playful effort of writing; or, more expansively, the process that leads out of reflection and daydreaming, into the formal processes of composition, and finally to the business of fixing a text on paper. Each of the chapters in which this theme is explored might be taken as an essay in its own right, but two strands of argument run connectively throughout the book. One is expressed in a recurrent phrase 'the look of the page', referring to the 'conscious', editorial phase of composition, the creation of a place of encounter between writer and reader. The other is the theme of the mind entranced, the mind at play, the mind observing and recollecting, always searching for ways of telling its dreams.

In shaping these themes I have at times been indebted to my earlier work. The essays on Tennyson and the 'Morte' (Chapter 7), on the translation of Horace (Chapter 9), on Chestertonian argument (Chapter 10) and on Scott Fitzgerald's 'The Cut Glass Bowl' (Chapter 11) are adaptations of pieces previously published in *The Cambridge Review*, in *Language and Literature (Journal of the Poetics and Linguistics Association)*, in *Literature and Language – Theory and Practice; A Tribute to Walter Grauberg* (Nottingham University, 1989) and in *The Nottingham Linguistic Circular.*

My thanks are due to friends and colleagues who have expressed interest in the book and have given me the benefit of their supportive comment; to the Canadian poet Martin Gray, to Dr David Stacey of Missouri Western State College, and to Professor Peter Verdonk of the University of Amsterdam I am particularly grateful.

WN.

Acknowledgements

We are grateful to the following for permission to reproduce copyright material:

Jonathan Cape on behalf of the Estate of Robert Frost and Henry Holt & Co. Inc for an extract from the poem 'Mending Wall' from *The Poetry of Robert Frost* edited by Edward Connery Lathem © 1958 by Robert Frost, © 1967 by Lesley Frost Ballantine, Copyright 1930, 1939, © 1969 by Henry Holt & Co. Inc; A P Watt Ltd on behalf of The Royal Literary Fund for extracts from 'The Wind and the Trees' from *Tremendous Trifles* by G K Chesterton; Faber & Faber Ltd and Harcourt Brace & Company for an extract from the poem 'The Waste Land' from *Collected Poems 1909–1962* by T S Eliot; Ernest Hemingway Literary Rights for an extract from *The Snows of Kilimanjaro* © Hemingway Foreign Rights Trust; The Society of Authors as the Literary Representative of the Estate of A E Housman and Henry Holt & Company Inc for the poem 'Diffugere Nives' from *The Collected Poems of A E Houseman* by A E Houseman. Copyright 1939, 1940, © 1965 by Henry Holt & Company Inc, © 1967 by Robert E Symons; the author's agent for an extract from the poem 'Prayer Before Birth' by Louis MacNeice from *Collected Poems 1924–1948* by Louise MacNeice; W W Norton & Company for the poem 'insu nli gh t' from *Complete Poems 1904–1962* by E E Cummings, edited by George J Firmage, © 1991 by The Trustees for the E E Cummings Trust and George James Firmage; Scribner, a Division of Simon & Schuster for extracts from 'The Baby Party' from *The Stories of Scott F Fitzgerald* edited by Malcolm Cowley. Copyright 1925 by Hearst's International Magazines, Inc. Copyright renewed 1953 by Frances Scott Fitzgerald Lanahan and 'The Cut-Glass Bowl' from *Flappers and Philosophers* by F Scott Fitzgerald. Copyright 1920 Charles Scribner's Sons. Copyright renewed 1948 by Zelda Fitzgerald; the author's agent for an extract from *The Prime of Miss Jean Brodie* by Muriel Spark; Rosemary G Thurber for an extract from 'The Dog That Bit People' from *My Life and Hard Times* by James Thurber (HarperCollins) Copyright © 1933, 1961 James Thurber.

Preliminaries: on illusions and creations

When Lord Fairfax, sometime commander of the New Model Army, decided to quit soldiering and retire to his house at Nun Appleton in Yorkshire, he offered to one Andrew Marvell the position of tutor to his daughter Mary; and rarely in the history of patronage can a modest private appointment have been so felicitously made. At Appleton House, far away from London and politics, Marvell was free to write poems, memorable poems, among them 'The Garden', surely one of the most enchanting, and wittily mysterious, of seventeenth-century lyrics.

Deeply involved in this delightful piece is the theme of creativity. The garden, a thing planned by man to be propagated by nature, is astonishingly and intricately fruitful, lush with plants and flowers and vegetables, the very image of a paradise whose easy fertilities mock the barren achievements of human beings as they vainly strive for honour and distinction. Merely to look at the garden, to walk in it, is a bemusingly voluptuous experience; but for Marvell there is something more, a retreat into a state within a state:

Meanwhile the mind from pleasure less
Withdraws into its happiness;
The mind, that ocean where each kind
Does straight its own resemblance find;
Yet it creates, transcending these,
Far other worlds and other seas,
Annihilating all that's made
To a green thought in a green shade.

The poet's theme in these lines is the creative trance which other writers have occasionally described; a condition proper to poets, indeed, but not altogether unknown to others, less gifted, who nevertheless seek access, at times, to worlds within worlds. We know something of this; it is a not uncommon experience that the daydream, or 'brown study', is a source of revelations, understandings and solutions.

Three words in particular suggest stages in a creative process: *resemblance*, *transcending* and *annihilating*. As to the first of these, Marvell makes playful reference to a contemporary belief that the sea contained creatures corresponding in form or function to those found on land. The poetic implication of this bold image is that the mind, containing in its depth and restless motion the ideational forms of whatever the senses observe, can thus conceive of similitudes, metaphors, symbols. *Resemblance* – 'A looks like B', 'X *puts me in mind* of Y' – is a preliminary stage of withdrawal into creative illusion. It suggests a reporting of what we know and see, an acknowledgement of 'reality' and actual experience. Each stimulus, as a behaviourist might put it, prompts a response. But in a subsequent phase, contemplation withdraws from the immediate stimulus, the observation of resemblances. The observer becomes the dreamer, lost in a reverie that seemingly has no basis in immediate or objective experience. The reverie may make sense in its own way, but it is not an 'everyday sense', the apparent sense of non-oceanic realities; it *transcends* these, is not dependent on external stimuli and frames its own structures and plausibilities.

What then follows, if the withdrawal into the mind is continued, is the *annihilation*, the complete shutting-out, of external reality. Perhaps it is not wholly clear what Marvell means by 'annihilating' or by that lovely phrase 'a green thought in a green shade'. We might attempt paraphrase: 'everything is reduced to this one radiant moment, here in this garden', or possibly 'an intense spiritual experience supersedes for a time the pleasurable awareness of the garden and its plants', but such clumsy prosaic attempts at conveying a poetic meaning leave unresolved a potential ambiguity. Does the poet's 'annihilation' mean simply that the perception of external reality is expunged, as the dreamer withdraws more deeply into his reverie?; or is there something more? Are the dream-visions themselves annihilated, brought to nothing, or perhaps to nothing more expansive than a point of focus, a phrase, a mantra, a colour, a musical interval, an elegantly powerful mathematical formula?

A disturbing thought, this, that we can lose control, lose possession, lose touch with it all; a thought not easily accepted by those of us who, as everyday egoists, want to make something of ourselves; who selfishly cling to what we have in this world, to our ideas and perceptions and visions no less than to our bank balances, to the places we visit in dreams no less than to our real residences. If there is illusion, it must become, we insist, a *creative* illusion; it must make a new sort of sense. There is in us the persistent impulse to recover something of this creative illusion before it fades and is lost, as dreams are so often lost. We seek lines of retrieval, to bring the dream into shape, to anchor the fugitive notion. It is then that the painter reaches for his pigments; the musician devises patterns of notes; the mathematician proposes the formulae that specify the abstractions of his thinking; but the rest of us, less particularly gifted, have to rely on language to help us make something of our musings. For us, it is language that accredits the creative illusion. Its operations establish the belief that the illusion is no longer illusory; there is something in the air, or better, something on the page, something ostensibly real, inviting observation and interpretation.

The writing on the page is an attempt to reconstitute two complementary forms of creative vision: Marvell's poem prompts us to call them illusions of resemblance and illusions of transcendence. Illusions of resemblance arise as the mind contemplates actual experience, or moves through memories of having been there, seen it, heard it, done it. Illusions of transcendence imply possibilities and plausibilities, conceptions of a parallel world; here are the inventions of the poet and story-teller, here also the elaborate explorations of argument and meditative discourse.

These two creative types are not mutually exclusive; in many pieces of writing, especially in fictions, they are interrelated or – more accurately – 'synergetic'. They work together. It is this interplay that makes good writing so persuasive, exercising an authority no less powerful, no less convincing, for being illusory. Somewhere in his *Rhetoric* Aristotle speaks of 'the corruption of the hearer', meaning the power of the orator to secure assent to an argument, even a dubious argument, by giving his audience pleasure. On this precedent, one might then speak of *the induction of the reader*, meaning the imposition, through skilful writing, of certain illusions, not the least of which is that the text has complex meanings, secrets pleasurably accessible to those who will pay attention to details.

Among illusions of resemblance, one of the most powerful must be the recollection of speech. Not of 'hearing voices' as the schizophrenic allegedly hears them, but rather of having, from daily experience, an imprinted memory of intonations, phrasings, a generalised idea of how people speak. A writer of fiction creates for his characters the illusion of conversation, its emphases and variations of pitch, recoverable from the page by a reader who can respond to conventional signs, much as a reader of music can retrieve a melody by observing the patterns of notation. For the reader of fiction, there is a pleasure in 'overhearing' conversations, as characters assert, question, expostulate, ironise. There is a further pleasure in realising the significance of the conversational exchange as an episode in the structure of narrative – but that carries the illusion beyond the merely mimetic, the simple incidental resemblance of people speaking, and into the transcendent domain of a whole fictional world taking shape. The conversations of everyday life are transmuted into the 'episodic dialogue' of the novel, the extended passages of conversation that establish a development in the story.

Non-fiction also has its voices. As I sit writing these pages, I am aware of an unremitting drive to imitate an idea of speech: not to mimic my own speaking voice, for I am not at all sure that I would know how to do that, but rather, to present 'how I want to sound' to my readers, on this occasion, for this compositional purpose. In effect, I try to script the role I have allotted myself. This is a matter of such importance that I am prepared to write some passages again and again – to correct them, restore them, correct them again, sleep on them, think about them as I clean my teeth, return to them – until I am satisfied that a rhythm is perceptible, a change of pitch implied, an emphasis clearly scripted. This I can only do if, underlying the words I put down in print, there is a notion of talking to someone.

This 'notion of talk', however, is not quite the same thing as the transcription of naturally occurring conversation. My 'talk' in writing is an artifice, frequently compromised by the need to interrupt the flow of address with phrases that qualify, reformulate, allude in explanatory fashion to things occurring elsewhere in the text. Constant qualifying and expansion of the text, repeated editorial activity, must eventually cancel any claim of mine to write as I speak. That illusion is nullified, or neutralised. The illusion to which I still remain committed is essentially an illusion of scripted address. I write as though I might seem to be speaking; I cultivate the pleasant assumption that a text can somehow be made to 'talk'.

The perception that the text is 'talking' is promoted in the first instance through some familiar visual indices. Marks of punctuation suggest pauses and intonations, the phrasings of vocal performance; other typographical devices – underlinings, changes of typeface and case, insets, line-breaks – further suggest the affective tone, the vocal gestures, the 'paralinguistic features' of speech.[1] These same punctuations have an additional value, over and above the transcription of talk. They may quite subtly present to a reader the illusion of different discourse types – the typical procedures of the learned journal, of the scientific report, of legal argument, of scenic descriptions, and so forth; but this, like the illusion of 'episodic dialogue' mentioned above, involves more than simple resemblance of people talking. The point, for a novelist, of imitating styles variously representative of the lawyer, the scientist, the politician and others, is not to display a talent for parody (though that may be involved), but, beyond that, to create the perception of a self-contained world of personalities and actions, a world like our own and yet not our own, a world of 'virtual reality' reduced to the printed page.

The layout of the printed page, the arrangement of its text, most commonly in the form of paragraphing, promotes one of the oddest, yet most powerful and persistent, of creative illusions. This is the impression that the text is somehow a picture, a visual semblance, of an ideational content. In an extreme form, the illusion can take the shape of a variety of *rebus*, or game with letters laid out in near-graphic design, as in 'concrete poetry' or typographic verse like that of E.E. Cummings.[2] In such cases, the verbal references of the text, the meanings associated with its words, may be all but 'annihilated' as the typographical design imposes – or superimposes – another level of meaning.

That, however, is a special instance of the text as picture, or pictogram. A more usual management of visual illusion is often apparent in quite ordinary layout and paragraphing. One way of sampling this is to look at the editorial or leader columns in broadsheet newspapers and tabloids, preferably on a day when some important issue is in the news. Broadsheets argue their way through long discursive paragraphs; tabloids as a rule present their theme in much shorter typographical blocks, covering essentially the same content as the broadsheet, but presenting to the eye a different textual shape and with it the illusion of a different 'slant' on the reported material. More precisely, what broadsheet 'shapes' and tabloid 'shapes' embody are attitudes of writers to readers. The broadsheet editor writes as though presenting a case to a jury, or to a captive audience in the calm of the lecture theatre; the tabloid writer stands up like a salesman and makes his hustling pitch to punters going about their daily business.

Broadsheet editors, it might be added, use different words, a range of descriptive and affective vocabulary somewhat unlike the usual lexicon of tabloid journalists. (The *Telegraph* perceives 'corruption' where the *Mirror* prefers to detect a 'scam'; the *Times* 'reproves' where the *Sun* 'raps'.) This is a recurrent instance of the workings of yet another illusion of resemblance: the conventional assumption that words, phrases, idioms, metaphors, etc., make a difference in their encoding of 'things', and in their stimulation of feelings and perceptions associated with those 'things'. A consequence of this illusion, as practised by writers on readers, or even as practised by writers on themselves, is that changing a word modifies a perception: as when 'vigorous debate' becomes 'stormy confrontation' or 'firm economic measures' become 'ruthless cost-cutting'.

This practice, known to publicists and admen as 'loading' or 'putting on a spin' will doubtless appear crude and risible when we detect it in the columns of the Daily Beast, but cuts a more respectable figure in the work of literary authors struggling endlessly to find the right word and lodge it in the right place. Often, this is not so much a matter of reporting as of reminiscing; a poet's intention, ostensibly to define the sense of how it *is*, is quite frequently a pursuit of the illusion of how it *was*. The retrieval of the creative illusion is essentially a retrieval of a moment past. Voices come back to us, bringing the names of times and places and vanished faces.

'Voicing' (representing speech) and 'naming' (making descriptions) are illusions of resemblance, which, if pursued, induce creations of much larger psychological scope. The story-teller's art is a dreamer's art that goes far beyond the reporter's brute realism, or the feature-writer's entertaining reflections on current affairs. When a great poet tells his dreams, it is in a dream-language which we do not speak, though we are convinced of the possibility of understanding it. A great novelist, observing this world, creates 'other worlds and other seas'; the illusions out of which a *Bleak House* or a *Moby Dick* are bred, are indeed transcendent. Fiction presents us with passages vividly and credibly describing places and persons we have never seen, and never expect to see, in 'real life'; includes passages couched in language we approve though we have never previously read anything quite like it; gives us accounts of actions common sense might deem impossible, made wholly plausible in the very terms of ordinary likelihood; incorporates sequences of dialogue simulating speech yet quite unlike any natural conversation ever heard – 'unlike', because in common with descriptions of persons, of places, of actions, dialogues are components in a developing narrative, blocks of significance in an ever-expanding aesthetic structure. By and by, the narrative moves plausibly to its own otherworld music, and the reader, unresisting, puts aside any lingering objection that, really, this state of affairs is quite impossible, that nobody ever spoke like this, that such things could never happen. It is all done by legerdemain and mirrors; the illusion triumphs; there is no argument about it.

Yet argument – meaning exposition, discussion and debate, formal rhetoric or any discursive presentation of ideas – has more in common with narrative than is generally suspected, at least in its structure. It exploits the illusions of resemblance – for example, in its not infrequent resort to metaphor and similitude – and it makes a persuasive appeal, evoking emotions and feelings of pleasure, in passages that begin with something recognisable, something 'given', and entice the reader step by step into some little realm of transcendent thought, moving out of the known and heading purposefully towards the conceivable. Like narrative, argument has a beginning, a middle and an end; like narrative, it has its digressions. It has a central thread of significance, in effect, a plot. What it lacks are human actions and characters (and even they may sometimes be introduced, as casual agents in a philosophical fable). Otherwise there is not a huge difference between telling a tale and putting a case, though scholars, philosophers and critics may not like to think of themselves as mere story-tellers. Politicians know they are, as do their public relations officers. There is such a thing as the narrative of policy. What do spin-doctors spin, if not a yarn?

But poetry, as Marvell so commandingly demonstrates, is all transcendence. If there is no transcendent illusion there is no poetry; only verse at best, at worst doggerel. Coleridge makes this point in his *Biographia Litteraria*, where he notes a crucial distinction between *poesis*, 'creating', and *morphosis*, 'constructing'.[3] Yet the recording of the poet's creative conceptions requires a good deal of craft-work with solid schoolroom materials like layout, punctuation and grammar. One chapter of this book (Chapter 5) turns on the proposition that a classic English poem, Gray's *Elegy*, depends for its almost hypnotic illusory power on repetitions and variations of the patterning of elements in the simple English sentence, creating a grammar of baroque enchantment. How can that be? How can ordinary grammar become poetic substance? Yet this is so. Poets share a grammar with the rest of us; but they use it more inventively, possibly with greater licence, in the service of the creative illusion.

Now it may be asked whether 'illusion' is the appropriate word and, further, if there is not something shifty about the way it is used here? As to the first of these queries, the critical reader might suggest that 'imagination' is as good a word as any for what has so far been described. And so it is, and yet it is not; for there is a meaning in 'illusion' which 'imagination' does not reach. Principally, it is the sense of something involuntary, something *received*. Imagination 'acts', illusion 'abides'; we 'exercise' the imagination, but simply 'have' or 'experience' illusions. Imagination plans and disposes: we speak of rooms imaginatively furnished, imaginative flower arrangements, imaginative settings, imaginative decor. Illusions are not arranged. They come into the mind by drift or impulse or casual association or, in sad instances, morbidly through the action of hallucinogenic drugs – the kind of illusion we would rather our children avoided. We may all dream and have daydreams, but no one can have an imaginative dream, plan a reverie or arrange the interior of what used to be known as 'a brown study'. Imagination has little to do with these experiences, though it may be vitally important in organising the transient vision, in directing the scenery of revelation. Illusion necessarily precedes the fulfilling work of the imagination; and then, its work fulfilled, imagination creates, or *re-creates*, the illusion.

The second imputed charge, that the word 'illusion' is used here in ways that elude a single definition, invites a plea of guilty. It covers, in fact, several stages of a phenomenon, there being at least three related types of illusion, namely:

(a) The movement of mind; whatever takes shape as the writer sits and thinks – his conviction that, like the creatures coming out of the sea-caves in Robert Graves' poem *Welsh Incident*, 'things never seen or heard or written about' are emerging from the depths of his consciousness.
(b) The text on the printed page, an illusory record of illusion; it being an illusion that print can represent the vagaries of musing and the accents and tones of speaking, or convincingly present, through its visual arrangement, the inherent structures of discourse.
(c) What readers take out of the text; their 'interpretation'; their conviction that the text, however strange, must have a 'meaning', one meaning alone or one meaning above all others; their supposition that through the text they are in touch with the mind of the writer.

It is possible to talk about 'creative illusion' with simultaneous or overlapping reference to these three types; and indeed, the assumption that one thing may be implied in another runs throughout the pages of this book, even through those chapters which appear to focus exclusively on some particular aspect of creativity in language.

The book has its agenda, or at least a *direction*, conducting a diversified argument through sections entitled 'The induction of the reader', 'The formation of the text', 'Modes of composition' and, finally, 'Means to an end'. This final section, devoted to a long essay on the relationship between composition and the technology of writing, takes up a question which is not so much 'How do we compose?' as 'What do we compose *with*?' Anyone who does much writing will at some time be seized by the conviction that it goes better, or more controllably, with certain materials and instruments at hand. There is always that favourite pen, that paper, that notebook, or their equivalents in modern writing technology. Do these things matter? Do they affect the writer's art, or the writer's view of composition? That my word processor induces habits of composition different from those formed by my old typewriter may be just another kind of illusion, yet it compels investigation, especially now, as the mechanics of writing grow ever more sophisticated – as, indeed, the mechanics of writing are giving place to the electronics of transcription. Who knows how, in fifty years' time, the functions of *script* will be performed, or if script in the strictest sense will continue to exist? Perhaps, as machines learn to render our very mumblings into text, 'writing' will become less and less laborious and more and more societal. Our descendants will no longer retire to a quiet corner to write their letters; they will convene at the cybercafé or the virtually real pub.

Then perhaps composition will change, abandoning such images of solitude as are evoked from time to time in the chapters of this book: Lemuel Gulliver on the alien strand; Thomas Gray alone and benighted in his country churchyard; the boy Wordsworth enraptured and terrified on the moonlit lake; Bedivere on the last battlefield; Chesterton on a park bench; Browning's madman in his wretched cottage; Marvell in the green heaven of his master's garden. Images all of visionary withdrawal; and yet not to be conveyed, not transmitted from mind to mind, from heart to heart, without the scribal effort, the necessary and absorbing drudgery of writing things down. Without this labour – the struggle for a reading, a transcription, a punctuation – there is no creativity; the imagination is spent, the great illusion annihilated.

In the *Aeneid*, at the close of the great sixth book, which describes Aeneas's visit to the underworld, there are some enigmatic lines on the status of dreams.[4] Sleep has two portals, Virgil tells us, one made of horn (workaday, commonplace stuff), the other of smooth and shining ivory. Through the Gate of Horn true visions make their way into the world; but false dreams escape through the Ivory Gate, and are lost. In the context of the poem, this little fable is indeed enigmatic; but if we are allowed to read it as an image of creativeness it presents a clearer purport. Language and the labouring imagination create the common texture that retains and gives shape to the illusion. The dreams that we cannot tell, that have eluded the memory or the power of articulation, have escaped almost irretrievably through the exotic and slippery Gate of Ivory, the portal of lapsed consciousness. We have little hope of recovering them (except, perhaps, under hypnosis or on the psychotherapist's couch); but the devices of writing are homely forms that detain the fugitive dream. Given that gloss on Virgil's lines, this book might be called a guide to the Gate of Horn.

NOTES

1 'The laryngeal, pharyngeal, oral, and nasal cavities [passages of the throat, the mouth, the nose] can all be used to produce "tones of voice" which alter the meaning of what is said. These effects are sometimes referred to as effects of "timbre" or "voice quality", and studied under the heading of vocal *paralanguage* . . .'(Crystal, 1987: 169). Getting the paralanguage convincingly onto the page is a recurrent problem for the poet and the story-teller. It is not easy to put into writing, for example, the 'creaky' voice often adopted by English speakers in making dismissive or disparaging remarks; or the nasal, 'down-the-nose' timbre of some upper-class speech.

2 But *rebus* means, literally, 'with things', a true *rebus* being a punning representation of things implying words; for example, a picture of an eye standing for the pronoun 'I', or of a sheep representing 'you' (ewe), or of a water jug (ewer) to stand for 'your'.

3 'Could a rule be given from *without*, poetry would cease to be poetry, and sink into a mechanical art. It would be *morphosis*, not *poesis*. The *rules* of the IMAGINATION are themselves the very powers of growth and production. The *words* to which they are reducible, present only the outlines and external appearances of the fruit' (Coleridge, 1907: ch. XVIII).

4 *Aeneid*, VI, 893–6:

> sunt gemini Somni portae: quarum altera fertur
> cornea, qua veris facilis datur exitus umbris,
> altera candenti perfecta nitens elephanto,
> sed falsa ad caelum mittunt insomnia Manes.
>
> 'Sleep has two gates, of which the one, made of horn, gives ready exit to true visions; the other is perfectly formed from shining white ivory, but through it the Spirits send false dreams up into the daylight.'

The lines are not 'enigmatic' in themselves, but in their application to what follows: Aeneas, who in the course of his visit to the underworld has been shown the future of Rome, is described as being guided back to the upper world *through the Gate of Ivory* – the portal of *false* visions. By this means, presumably, the *manes* protected the secrets of their realm, and also no doubt protected Aeneas from the certain knowledge of his own future; it was only a dream. Horace (*Odes* I.xi) tells us it is *nefas* – unlawful – for human beings to know what the gods have in store for them.

REFERENCES

ARISTOTLE. *The 'Art' of Rhetoric*, ed. and transl. J.H. Freese. London: Loeb Classical Library, 1926, repr. 1947, III.i.6.

COLERIDGE, S.T. *Biographia Litteraria*, ed. J. Shawcross, 2 vols. London: 1907.
CRYSTAL, DAVID. *The Cambridge Encyclopaedia of Language* Cambridge: University Press, 1987.
MARVELL, ANDREW. 'The Garden', in John Hollander and Frank Kermode (eds) *The Oxford Anthology of English Literature: The Literature of Renaissance England*. New York: Oxford University Press, 1973.
VIRGIL. *P. Vergili Maronis Opera*, ed. F.A. Hirtzel. Oxford: Clarendon Press, 1900.

Part I

The Induction of the Reader

One

On writing for reading's sake

Oh that my words were now written! oh that they were printed in a book!
(*Job*, 19: 23)

Consider the plight of Harry, the doomed, self-destroying hero of Hemingway's *The Snows of Kilimanjaro.* A writer who has neglected writing, rejecting the disciplines of his craft, promising to write later – later – some day – he finds himself in the unhappy position of being laid up with a gangrenous leg and unable to write at all. In this mortal predicament Harry has time for recollection and repentance, a kind of redemptory self-communing that he would like to put on record, if only he could get it written down; but he is bedridden and the woman, his companion, never learned to take shorthand. No matter; he begins to think of his ruminations as the essential part of writing. Writing gets done in the head. Writing is how you speak to yourself before you finally reach for the A4. 'I've been writing,' he tells her, on the night of his death – and adds, 'but I got tired.'

It must be a hard-hearted reader who cannot accept, as a matter of special pleading, that what Harry does in the last days of his life deserves to be called 'writing'. Nevertheless, a pedantic doubt creeps in. Is this not a misuse, however pardonable, of the word? Was Harry writing in the fullest sense? Could he really make that claim, without having something palpable to show for his efforts? Can there be writing, if not for reading's sake? Anyone with any experience of writing knows the urge to get the words down onto the page, to see how they look, to free them from the subjective clutter in the skull, to view and judge them in an objective, revelatory dimension.

Writing begins in the head, as Harry rightly supposes; but then it continues with a pencil, with a biro, with a keyboard, onto sheets of paper, onto a computer screen. To write is *scribere* as well as *componere* – inscription as well as composition – and between those two things there is a reciprocal relationship. This means, for the writer, a continual monitoring of one against the other. Show me how it looks on the page, and I will know if it is right, or if I need to change it. Show me how it looks on the word-processor screen, but no, better, just show me how it looks on the page – for despite the undoubted technological superiority of the word processor, its screen still shows me my composition in a glass, darkly, whereas a page of typescript, given into my hand, is a real object where I see all my words set out in defining borders of space.

A feeling for the look of the page is essentially a product of what Marshall McLuhan used to call the print culture; it is the envisaged format of the *book*, an ordered gathering of leaves, uniform in size, regularly imprinted with text that never extends to the extreme limits of the available surface, but is confined within a border of white paper. The look of the printed page is the look of a picture. Ancient manuscripts often have a different look from modern books, and not least in this, that they invite the eye to travel *across* the leaf, rarely *down*. They are to be followed horizontally, and seldom scanned, or vertically 'conned'. A familiar example from Early English literature is the *Beowulf* manuscript, BM Cotton Vitellius A15, in which the scribes have ignored – or perhaps have had no pressing sense of – the convention that the poetic page reads downward as well as across. Their MS shows no attempt to reflect the prosodic measures of the poem, but sets out the whole epic in continuous form, like a prose text. For them, presumably, one thing mattered above all: to have a record of the poem's content. They may have supposed that any reader who knew an *arsis* from a *thesis* could be relied on to supply the prosody.[1]

This is possibly an extreme instance of the supposition that the text goes on reading from left to right, without gaps, with no downward skips, artful breaks or what word-processing manuals call 'hard returns'. Of course the poets of the Middle Ages arranged their pieces (or instructed their scriveners to arrange them) in layouts that reflected their concepts of line and form. But the printed book powerfully affirmed these notions of the aesthetics of composition – notions of spacing, pattern, punctuation, typography, all those things that constitute the visual dimension of literature.[2]

The arts of advertisement and publicity have helped to confirm modern writers and readers in their sense of the value of the space surrounding the text. For the copywriter, the layout makes the message. Spacings and indentations speak significantly; the text reads down the page, as well as across, the eye making a vertical scan of typographically highlighted words; phrases are placed between margins in ways that make a picture without making a speech. This is adman's business, but its resources are not for the adman alone, and do not originate with him. The copywriter is the legatee of the poet; or rather, of a longstanding tradition, that what appears on the page is a portrait of the poem, a silent form making its visual contribution to the message we read out of the text.

Any committed reader of poetry, anyone for whom this art has something more than a peripheral or decorative role in life, will testify to the importance of the poetic text as something *seen*, if seen in order to be *heard*. Think of a lyric you know well, perhaps a poem that you once memorised. How did you commit it to memory? What were the clues that subsequently prompted a recall of the words? Was it not important to see, in your mind's eye, the layout of the words on the page? And having thus learned the poem from a particular text, did you never feel that text to be the *right* text, the only layout, a shape not to be violated in the slightest degree without seriously impairing the tenor and true meaning of the poem?

There are some poems – old, sedate anthology citizens – that are quite surprisingly affected by the look of the page. It might seem, for example, that there could be nothing less controversial, typographically, than the rhymed (abab) quatrain, as we find it, for example, in Thomas Gray's *Elegy written in a Country Church Yard.* Yet Gray worried about the layout of the Elegy. He apparently shared a view, current in his time, that the decasyllabic quatrain was an appropriate measure for elegiac poetry. His original title – *Stanza's wrote in a Country Church Yard* – suggests that he had made up his mind about the form the poem was to take in print. It would be a sequence of 'Stanza's', spaced one from another. Yet he evidently began to feel, as he prepared to go to press with the poem, that its regular sectioning into quatrains would be in some places misleading.

Of the text in the so-called Eton Ms, one of Gray's editors observes, 'The quatrains are carefully written, with uniform spaces between.' He then adds:

> Gray's wish at first publication, to have the poem printed without 'any Interval' between stanzas because 'the Sense is in some Places continued beyond them', developed later than this manuscript, or may have begun to develop as he was drafting the last part of the poem. Even in the continuation, however . . . where the intervals are less obvious, they can be seen to exist. In the Pembroke and Wharton Manuscripts they have gone. The quatrains there are marked by the more consistent indenting of their first lines.[3]

This 'indentation of their first lines' was adopted for the printing of the quatrains in the first (1751) edition of the *Elegy*. There, the second and third stanzas of the poem look like this (the first stanza, of course, is not indented):

    Now fades the glimmering Landscape on the Sight,
And all the Air a solemn Stillness holds;
Save where the Beetle wheels his droning Flight,
And drowsy Tinklings lull the distant Fold.
    Save that from yonder Ivy-mantled Tow'r
The mopeing Owl does to the Moon complain
Of such, as wand'ring near her sacred Bow'r
Molest her ancient solitary Reign.

Here, the sense is certainly 'continued beyond' the first four lines of the passage (the clause beginning 'save that from yonder Ivy-mantled Tow'r' is dependent on 'holds', three lines previously), and the absence of space between the stanzas accords with this; on the other hand, the indented lines point to the quatrain-division. It seems that in this first edition Gray enjoys the benefit of two options. The text says, on the one hand, 'read me as continuous discourse'; and, on the other, 'observe the division into stanzas'.

Modern editors have not felt Gray's anxiety about the continuity of the text, and so have not followed the practice of the 1751 edition. In a current standard edition, the two stanzas cited above read like this:

Now fades the glimmering landscape on the sight,
And all the air a solemn stillness holds,
Save where the beetle wheels his droning flight,
And drowsy tinklings lull the distant folds;

Save that from yonder ivy-mantled tower
The moping owl does to the moon complain

Of such as, wandering near her secret bower,
Molest her ancient solitary reign.[4]

Now the quatrains are seen *as* quatrains, duly spaced, and any difficulty about 'sense continued', or the syntactic flow breaking its stanzaic banks, is solved by a little punctuational shoring-up – the relocation of the semi-colon formerly placed after 'holds', now after 'folds'. But there is a further editorial option, namely this (from another modern edition):

Now fades the glimmering landscape on the sight,
  And all the air a solemn stilness holds,
Save where the beetle wheels his droning flight,
  And drowsy tinklings lull the distant folds;

Save that from yonder ivy-mantled tower,
  The moping owl does to the moon complain
Of such as, wandering near her secret bower
  Molest her ancient solitary reign.[5]

In that case, the appearance of the quatrain is broken by indentations of the second and fourth lines, suggesting a semantic subdivision into distiches or couplets – something readily perceptible in the composition of a number of stanzas in the *Elegy*, but not particularly obvious here. Why does the editor do this with the text, when it seems there is no warrant for it in the MSS and earliest editions? Perhaps with motives quite averse from Gray's own intention of presenting the text as continuous discourse – perhaps to break up the visual impression of the text, to make it more inviting?; to ease the burden of reading?; to prettify it?; or merely to follow a convention, that in lyric stanzas alternate lines are commonly indented?

Whatever the answer to these questions, there is one near certainty: that readers will have a preference, will regard one of these versions of layout as more agreeable than the others, aesthetically preferable, perhaps truer to the spirit of the poem as they understand it. That preference need not be governed by scholarly considerations of what the poet originally wrote, or intended. Readers generally nurture in themselves the illusion that there is a right way for a poem to look on the page, a way that is somehow intrinsic with whatever message the poem has to express. Poets in their compositions occasionally practise this same illusion upon themselves – a graphological illusion, identifying the visual pattern of the poem with its flow of feeling.

There can be few more striking instances of this than Louis MacNeice's 'Prayer before Birth' (MacNeice 1949: 215), a poem in which the 'speaker' is an unborn child pleading for the chance to live in a world blessedly free from all the permutations of nightmare and evil. The poem opens thus:

> I am not yet born; O hear me.
> Let not the bloodsucking bat or the rat or the stoat or the
> club-footed ghoul come near me.
>
> I am not yet born, console me.
> I fear that the human race may with tall walls wall me,
> with strong drugs dope me, with wise lies lure me,
> on black racks rack me, in blood-baths roll me.

There are two dimensions of visual interest in the typographical picture of this poem. One is, that the second stanza, or section, as quoted above, is slightly 'deeper' (i.e. longer) than the first – four lines succeeding three. This 'deepening' goes on progressively throughout the poem. The other is that, after the first two lines in each section, there begins a progressive indentation or 'staggering' of lines from the left-hand margin. This also continues throughout the poem, the sections getting generally longer (or 'deeper'), the indentations straying catty-cornered down the page until we come to this, the longest passage in the poem, and its greatest typographical mass:[6]

> I am not yet born; O fill me
> With strength against those who would freeze my
> humanity, would dragoon me into a lethal automaton
> would make me a cog in a machine, a thing with
> one face, a thing, and against all those
> who would dissipate my entirety, would
> blow me like thistledown hither and
> thither or hither and thither
> like water held in the
> hands would spill me.

No one reading 'Prayer before Birth' can pretend that the poem would be anything but damaged – dissipated in its entirety – if the staggered lines were vertically justified to the left-hand margin. The indenting is a part of the total perception of the poem; it is a part of the discourse of the unborn, the stammering irruption of anguish and fear into the tumbling eloquence of pleading words. If the child had language, it might speak like an adult, but still feel and kick and fret like a child. So the illusion goes as, reading *across*, we follow its words, and reading *down*, we discern the image of its pulsing anxiety.

In MacNeice's poem, what we see on the page is important; but it is still in a sense subordinate to what we hear as we read the words to ourselves. The layout offers a poetic image, but that visual image is only a part of the 'meaning' of the poem. Take the illusion one stage further, into the realms of *poésie concrète*, and the printed image *becomes* the meaning, a *Gestalt* to which words and their references are subordinate. Look, for example, at this poem by E.E. Cummings (1944: no. 24):

```
insu nli gh t

              o
              verand
              o
              vering

A

              onc
              eup
              ona
              tim

e ne wsp aper
```

The poem can be read aloud – 'in sunlight over and overing a once upon a time newspaper' – but the hearing of it makes something less than a poem. The poetry here is in the seeing; what we read out of it is only a theme which the text on the page embellishes, *draws*, with playful, quasi-mathematical symmetries. Let the reader forget the dictionary and pay attention to the letter. The poem's first 'line' is a sequence of letters in diminishing clusters, beginning with 4 (insu), then 3 (nli), then 2 (gh), then 1 (t). The last 'line' reverses the arithmetical sequence, thus: 1 (e), 2 (ne), 3 (wsp), 4 (aper). Lodged in mid-image, at the left-hand margin, is a single letter, the capital A. Above that, to the right of the upper half of the text thus divided, is a vertical sequence of letters and letter-groups; there are four items in the downward sequence, in the symmetrical proportions 1 (o), 6 (verand), 1 (o), 6 (vering). In the lower half of this verse-diagram, correspondingly at the right-hand margin, is another vertical sequence, a series of groups of three letters, 3 (onc), 3 (eup), 3 (ona), 3 (tim).

The total effect of this is not to reinforce the meanings of words, but rather to break words down into their strange componential fragments. Words are teased and bantered by the wind; this is no longer a text, only a once-upon-a-time newspaper, its pages riffled by the breeze as it sprawls in the sun, flashing, to the observing eye, messages in a half-penetrable letter-code. The 'poem' is a drawing – of discarded letterpress lying outdoors somewhere, on the ground, on a table, on a bench. It can be decoded, but not altogether demystified. The reader is left to decide, for example, whether there is anything to be discerned in the shape the poem makes on the page; and whether the capital A (capitals are unusual in cummings) has any significance in the poetic diagram.

To these questions readers find answers that sometimes verge on the fanciful – suggesting, for instance, that the text is a picture of a door, the gap in the middle (the 'A' line) being its letter-box. Or, picking up a hint from the cluster 'verand', that the literal image is of railings on a veranda, seen from above, where the discarded newspaper lies. (These interpretations were offered by students in a university seminar.) Quaint though such fancies seem to me, I am not prepared to reject them outright while I have a fancy of my own; which is that the diagram presents the first two letters of the alphabet, A in the middle, at a focal point, and B as the total shape or design of the text.[7] This too is fanciful, no doubt, but that is arguably the point of cummings' typographical playfulness. The look of the page here allows the reader some licence of interpretation, freeing the imagination, allowing the possibility of renovating things as familiar and banal as the printed letters of the alphabet.

This is nevertheless a special instance of a special kind of writing. Usually, the visual pattern of the text on the page is an ancillary (albeit an important one) to something larger, a 'content', a 'reading'. Poetic texts are set out in ways that specify a focus here, an accent there, a junction or a disjunction – and hence give shape to an interpretation. As readers we may be familiar almost beyond familiarity with the opening lines of Eliot's *The Waste Land*:

April is the cruellest month, breeding
Lilacs out of the dead land, mixing
Memory and desire, stirring
Dull roots with the spring rain.

I say *familiar almost beyond familiarity* not only because that example turns up quite often in discussions of poetic metre, but also because the lines have become, for most of us, almost acquaintances whose names we pronounce with privileged assurance. When we speak them to ourselves, or repeat them aloud from memory, do we not linger for an instant over 'breeding', 'mixing', 'stirring', as though it were the most natural thing in the world, a matter of everyday usage, to pause on a participle, in contemplation of the following object or complement? (Do it in burlesque: 'Billy is the greediest boy, stealing – crumpets out of the breadbin, eating – caramel for dessert, feeling – full up with his baked beans.') It is not in the least 'natural'. To deliver the lines so is an instruction taken from the page, bidding us depart from our common understanding of the groupings of grammar. With a different look, the text would invite a different delivery:

April is the cruellest month,
Breeding lilacs out of the dead land,
Mixing memory and desire,
Stirring dull roots with spring rain.

That presents a way of speaking it, but it is not Eliot's way, or our understanding of Eliot's way.[8] We have made a mental record of how the lines should sound; and that record is closely associated with a long-ingrained sense of how the lines *look*.

In prose composition, the look of the page is possibly less dramatic, less crucially important than in poetic texts, but the writer is not wholly excused from the struggle to create, in print, the phenomena of *seeing* that promote illusions of *hearing*. A recurrent problem is that of typographical representation. My word-processor, for example, allows me the choice of normal type, underlining, and bold type, and I must make shift between these to create a text that appeals to the understanding through the eye, distinguishes between styles of discourse, and also, on due occasion, suggests a vocal delivery, a 'scoring' of the text. These are (for me) essentially academic problems, arising out of my wish to be understood by my readers as a person not professorially cold or constipated; but they are not unknown to writers of fiction, who sometimes need to 'orchestrate' significantly contrasting styles in their works.

Italics are commonly used in such orchestrations; in *The Snows of Kilimanjaro* (Hemingway 1974), Harry's meditations are set in italic type, and this is of some importance to the reader, since the changes from roman to italic give visible notice of transitions from an 'outer world' state – the scene of the action, its personnel, events, material facts – to an 'inner world' condition – the world of memory, random juxtapositions, surreal imagery. As Harry's story proceeds, the visible balance of the narrative shifts towards the typography of the 'inner world', and the look of the page tells the reader what is happening as the passages in italic type grow longer. Harry is retreating, memory by memory, into the palisade of the soul; Harry is dying. So much can be conveyed by the simple act of changing a type-font.

Devices of spacing, connection and division can have a significant effect on the look of a page of prose; whether textual space is controlled and expressed by various marks of punctuation and their implications of contrasting value – as between a comma and a semi-colon, between a semi-colon and a colon, between a bracket and a dash, between this and that mark of segmentation, between any pointings that govern the visual piecing-out of the text – or whether the spacing appears most obviously in the act of breaking off and beginning a new line. It is a frequent experience that a page of text, though lucidly expounded with all its connectives precisely in place, will look discouragingly heavy until it is visually lightened by division into paragraphs. Such divisions in expository prose show a becoming consideration for the reader, and incidentally allow the writer to view the text in segments that make revision easier. In scholarly texts there can be too much reading across and too little opportunity for reading down, for scanning. Paragraphing is often an act of mitigation.

In prose fiction or in belles lettres, the paragraph-break can be as important, expressively, as the line-end break or stanza-break in poetry. Here, for example, is the text at the close of John Updike's essay 'The Bankrupt Man' (1991: 662):

> He ascends because he transcends. He deals from the bottom of the deck. He builds castles in the air. He makes America grow. His interests ramify. He is in close touch with Arabian oil. With

> Jamaican bauxite. With antarctic refrigeration. He creates employment for squads of lawyers. He gets on his motorcyle. He tugs a thousand creditors in his wake, taking them over horizons they had never dreamt of hitherto.
>
> He proves there is an afterlife.

Thus the essay ends, with one fairly short paragraph followed by another, very short, indeed a mini-paragraph, a mere sentence doing a paragraph's job. The first paragraph is rhetorically constructed, principally around the figure of *anaphora* (i.e. the repetitive pattern of 'he ascends', 'he deals', 'he builds') but also round a device of sentence-length, controlling the rhythm of the passage with short sentences (nine in all, of between 3 and 8 words in length) until the rhythmic stride at last broadens into the long sentence (18 words) beginning 'He tugs a thousand creditors in his wake.' (Thus *short–short–short–short–short–short–short–short–short–LONG*.) One might expect the final short sentence ('He proves there is an afterlife', 6 words) to follow on directly, returning emphatically to the short-sentence rhythmic norm, and so concluding the piece. But Updike's essay, which parodies the manner of a fable or folk tale, evidently requires an emphatic sign of ending, something equivalent to *they all lived happily ever after* or *then they all went home*; and that sign is provided by the paragraph-break, a vertical shift leading to the short sentence standing in its own space, proclaiming an end to continuity, declaring that there is nothing left to be said. And shall we not agree? If there were anything more to add, the look of the page would presumably tell us so.

For a reader the look of the page has important implications, beyond the feeling that the book is meanly or handsomely printed. (Even that feeling, ostensibly an incidental matter, is not to be discounted; it has its part to play in the induction of the reader; it can make all the difference between an eager willingness to read and an irritable, unreceptive approach to the text.) Arrangements of print control the speed of reading; draw attention to this feature or that; promote – or inhibit – the grasp of a concept, the acceptance of an image; even give the brain a peripheral task to play at while central powers of concentration are engaged in the task of decoding messages and constructing meanings.

For the writer, the look of the page records the alternations of the creative process: between musing, a formless reverie, and editing, an imposition of form on the ideational flux, an operation of intellect on the imagination; between *explaining*, through linkages of punctuation and grammar, through the logic of linear sequences, and *showing*, through the management of space on the paper, the positioning of words and sentences, the fragmentation of the text, the imposition of a 'vertical' reading on the 'horizontal' frame.

When Harry said he had been writing, he can only have meant that he had started to write, had taken the first, indispensable, most important step of yielding to the emergent daydream, the half-hypnosis in which possibilities of selection, ordering, relationship, are vaguely perceived. But there is so much beyond that, as Harry must have known. There is labour here, hard work, spade work, piece work. There is a pain in writing, like the pain of waking, of struggling into plain worldliness out of the unworldly dream. So the page struggles into its morning life, and after many rituals and exercises puts on its morning look, which drudging authors hope may last an hour or two, perhaps a day or two, perhaps even into next week . . . ; well, we can always hope, or try again.

NOTES

1 R.W. Chambers, noting that 'The lines of the MS do not correspond to the lines of the poem' adds: 'This does not, however, cause any serious trouble, for so uniform is Old English metre that cases where there can be any real doubt as to the division of the lines very seldom occur' (Chambers 1948: xiii).

2 There is an excellent treatment of 'all those things that constitute the visual dimension of literature' in David Crystal's *The Cambridge Encyclopaedia of Language* (Crystal 1987).

3 From Alastair Macdonald's Introduction to the facsimile reproduction of the Eton Manuscript (Gray 1976: 10).

4 See Lonsdale (1969).

5 The 'modern' edition here is in Richard Aldington's *Poetry of the English-Speaking World* (Aldington 1947). This layout is not specifically Aldington's, however; it occurs in more than one anthology.

6 Although it is not misleading to describe the sections of the poem as 'getting generally longer', there is one short section that breaks (or 'brakes'!) the progression, and immediately precedes the 'greatest typographical mass'; a kind of recoil before the last and greatest impetus. This, too, seems to me to be important in the look of the page.

7 My fanciful B may recommend itself to the reader who will take the trouble of writing out the text as shown here, and then drawing connecting lines in pencil round the periphery: that is, from i(nsu) to A to e; from aper to tim; from onc to A; from A to vering; and from o to t. This is hardly conclusive as an argument, but at least it demonstrates the plausibility of a perceived shape.

8 The poet Jon Silkin, commenting on these lines at the beginning of *The Waste Land*, characterises them as supplying 'a good working example . . . of Eliot's proposition that the reader is given a sop, so that the poetry can get to work on him/her. Here it seems that it is the rhetorical structure that engages the reader so that evocation and meaning may work on the mind' (Silkin 1997: 74).

REFERENCES

ALDINGTON, RICHARD (ed.). *Poetry of the English-Speaking World*. London: Heinemann, 1947.

CHAMBERS, R.W. *Beowulf with the Finnsburg Fragment* ed. A.J. Wyatt. New edn revised Chambers. Cambridge: University Press, 1948.

CRYSTAL, DAVID. *The Cambridge Encyclopaedia of Language*. Cambridge: University Press, 1987; pp. 72, 75, 182–84.

cummings, e.e. *73 poems by e.e. cummings*. London: Faber & Faber, 1944, no. 24.

GRAY, THOMAS. *An ELEGY wrote in a Country Church Yard*. The Eton Manuscript and the First Edition, 1751. Reproduced in facsimile with an Introduction by Alastair Macdonald. London: The Scolar Press, 1976.

HEMINGWAY, ERNEST. *The Snows of Kilimanjaro*. Harmondsworth: Penguin Books, repr. 1974; p. 15.

LONSDALE, ROGER (ed.). *The Poems of Thomas Gray, William Collins, Oliver Goldsmith*. London: Longman, 1969.

MACNEICE, LOUIS. 'Prayer before Birth', in *Collected Poems 1925–1948*. London: Faber & Faber, 1949.

SILKIN, JON. *The Life of Metrical and Free Verse in Twentieth Century Poetry*. London: Macmillan Press Ltd, 1997.

UPDIKE, JOHN. 'The Bankrupt Man', in John Gross (ed.) *The Oxford Book of Essays*. Oxford: University Press, 1991.

Two

Speech in writing

But all symbolism harbours the curse of mediacy;
it is bound to obscure what it seeks to reveal.
(Ernst Cassirer, *Language and Myth*)

Drudging authors grumble, of course, about their blocks and inexplicable hindrances, the obstacles that send them on fool's errands and present them with repetitive chores; but in practice they know what the matter is. They know that they are engaged in the absorbing task of attempting to make bridges or channels between the invisible, interior world of cogitation and reverie, and the visible, audible, palpable exterior which we share with our fellows and which we commonly call 'experience'. This is exacting, certainly, often elusive, commonly frustrating, even desperate, but it cannot truly be called drudgery, let authors grumble as much as they will. In it there is always an element of play. The 'bridges' and 'channels' – solid metaphors for semi-substantial things – are words or schemes of words, infinitely mutable, indefinitely meaningful in the pattern of the verbal game, like moves in chess. There is pleasure in this. The play is dictated, however, by certain conventions, familiar to students of literary style, and it is in the conventionality of writing that its problems and frustrations, paradoxically, are rooted. Stylistic conventions can hinder even as they help; they offer an access to reality – a representation of the experiential world – leading only to the realisation that such 'reality' is ultimately inaccessible.

For anyone who writes, and is concurrently aware of the *process of writing*, this realisation involves questions of stylistic method – 'How do I set about doing this?' – shadowed by a questioning of the legitimacy of any assumption we make about style – 'But does it really work?' In such self-awareness the playful spirit is compromised and humbled. Every confident act is dogged by some doubt; doubt lowers vitality; with the loss of vitality comes a sense of mental toil; and the product of that phantom labour is something in which we have little confidence, less pleasure, diminished recognition of whatever we had hoped to represent. This, indeed, is Cassirer's 'curse of mediacy', and it calls for the examination of some common stylistic assumptions.

One of the most obvious is the supposition that writing represents speech. Here is the most usual intuition about writing, a questionable position, perhaps, but still a belief upon which many ideas of literary style are founded. We do not easily free ourselves from the conventional assumption that literary composition is a raising of the voice. To write is to *say*, in an extended sense. Common usage affirms this idea: 'You *say* in your letter . . .', 'This author has nothing to *say*', 'Shakespeare *tells* us', 'Virgil still *speaks* to us'. I sit at a keyboard and watch the emergence, on an illuminated screen, of words I have the illusion of *speaking* – in my head. I cancel a sentence, or change its word-order, because it does not 'sound' right. I have an image of myself listening attentively to the promptings of an inner voice, and I suppose that others, as they write, must be similarly disposed. All instinct – perhaps we should say all honest superstition – urges upon the author the conviction that writing is a transcription of silently conceived speech.

But, in truth, this belief is one that cannot be held without a good deal of qualification. There are writings that speak, and there are others that have little accent and no melody. This line of verse, for example, is obviously writing-as-speech, or speech-in-writing:

> *For God's sake hold your tongue, and let me love.*

That was written nearly four centuries ago (by John Donne, in his poem 'The Canonisation') and the implied sound of it, as the sort of thing an actual person might credibly say, is as strong as ever. But here, by way of contrast, is a modern utterance rather less powerfully dictated by the speaker within:

> The cash value of this certificate at the end of the second or subsequent certificate years shall be (i) the excess, if any, of the then net single premium for the face amount of this certificate over the then present value of a series of annual nonforfeiture factors payable continuously from such date to the end of the premium payment period specified on the first page hereof, each

> such nonforfeiture factor to be based on the face amount of this certificate and determined from the Table of Values herein plus (ii) the then present value of any outstanding paid-up additions.[1]

There is no pretence of colloquial inflection, no grace of phrasing, not the echo of an echo of speech in this typical piece of actuarial prose. It is not spoken, it is laboriously spelled out; and the absence of any feeling for speech makes it all the harder to read and understand. The reader's mind cannot store the sense of it; again and again we drop the meaning and have to go back and pick it up. But then, we may say, this speechlessness and consequent lack of literary grace is a question of categories, for surely we would never mistake an insurance contract for a specimen of literary English?

No; but then consider another sentence, one that, by virtue of its content alone, must have some claim on the adjective 'literary':

> Certainly the first half of *Lord Jim* is one of the most breathtaking exercises in nonstop textual production that our literature has to show, a self-generating sequence of sentences for which narrative and narrator are mere pretexts, the realization of a mechanism of well-nigh random narrative free association, in which the aleatory and seemingly uncontrollable, unverifiable generation of new detail and new anecdotal material out of the old – all the while filling in the exposition, so that it ends up presenting the narrative content as exhaustively as any representational aesthetic – obeys a logic of its own, as yet unidentified in this text taken by itself, but which in the hindsight of the emergent textual aesthetic of our own time we can clearly see to be textuality born fully grown up.
>
> (Jameson 1981)

That is a single sentence of one hundred and twenty-nine words, a textual career ungoverned, one might well think, by the whisper of any controlling voice. Where is 'speech' in this contrivance? Whatever faculty it is that monitors the 'sound' of a text and adjusts it to a semblance of intoning, breathing, grouping, pausing, accentuating, seems here to have gone into recess. Commas and dashes and pronominal connectives ('for which', 'in which', 'but which') lay out the text in whorls and patches, making, it seems, a problem for the eye, only casually addressed to the ear. It is conceivable – just – that this extraordinary process of phrasing-on-the-page is indeed representative of somebody's speech; it may be a miming of vocal mannerisms recognisable by the author's acquaintances. Strangers, however, are debarred from such recognition. We only see the unvocal clutter, and we may well wish for that designing of cadences, that elegant-haphazard pretence of speech which is, after all, not speech but a most carefully calculated artifice of scripting, or 'scoring'.

But it seems indeed (glancing back to the poet and the actuary) that the cultivated illusion of speech in writing is a matter of categories; that there is a gradation, or what some linguists might call a *cline*,[2] of different species of composition, variously demanding or inhibiting the sense of a vocal, personal presence. Let us suggest that the potential 'speakers' in acts of writing are:

- lyric poets;
- characters in fiction or dramatic poetry, the 'actors', whose speech is presented verbatim;
- fictional narrators ('internal' narrators, characters in charge of the narration, telling the story from the inside);
- authors of fictional works (the creators of characters and narratives, telling the story from the outside);
- expositors (commentators, *causeurs*, critics, essayists);
- regulators (taxmen, businessbodies, guide-writers, etc.).

The 'cline' runs down through poets–characters–narrators–authors–expositors–regulators.

There is no type of writing in this list, except, perhaps, the regulatory sort that is quite devoid of some sense of speech, and in the middle of the cline the categories may often merge; 'expositors', for example, may assume the role of 'authors' presenting small fictions in which they adopt the style of 'narrators' (e.g. in relating an anecdote). But intuition acknowledges the extremes of the cline; in general, we think, the poet speaks and the insurance man writes, and the people in between variously write speech or speak writing.

It is in works of fiction that the representation of speech is at its most elusive, illusory, delusive – because of the variety of speech types and speakers, the reflection of things spoken and unspoken by 'I' or 'the other' or 'they', the *ego*, the *alter ego*, the *ille* of the unfolding tale. Authors may assume a 'neutral' style, which, however, is necessarily coloured by the judgements they make on the fictional world they create. Narrators speak (and think, aloud or otherwise) in styles created for them by their shadowing, puppeteering authors. Characters are allotted styles of speech in which they converse and in which they also meditate on their own actions and motives:

> You kept from thinking and it was all marvellous. You were equipped with good insides so that you did not go to pieces that way, the way most of them had, and you made an attitude that you cared nothing for the work you used to do, now that you could no longer do it. But, in yourself, you said that you would write about these people; about the very rich; that you were really not of them but a spy in their country; that you would leave it and write of it and for once it would be written by someone who knew what he was writing of. But he would never do it, because each day of not writing, of comfort, of being that which he despised, dulled his ability and softened his will to work so that, finally, he did no work at all.

That is subtler than it may seem at first, because it involves or complicates the speech of the character (Harry, in *The Snows of Kilimanjaro*) with that of the overseeing author. The style is that of free indirect speech, or rather, free indirect *thought*, a way of representing a character's communings with himself. What it conveys to us, however, is something a little more complex than *Harry talking to himself*; it conveys the sense of *someone listening in to Harry talking to himself.* The pronouns 'you' and 'he', in Harry's self-scrutinising thought, are equivalent to 'one' (i.e. the impersonal *you*) and 'I': thus 'You kept from thinking' means 'One kept from thinking', and 'But he would never do it' represents 'But I would never do it.' This is Harry reflecting on himself.

But Harry's reflections are also the author reflecting on Harry, and for the reader those pronouns become a little shifty. The final sentence of this passage (beginning 'But he would never do it') could be read – or 'heard' – as Harry's voice, saying 'I'; equally, it could be taken for the authorial voice of Hemingway, saying 'he'. It is, so to speak, vocally neutral. The preceding sentence (beginning 'But, in yourself, you said . . .') looks like Harry-speech, mainly because the 'you'-pronoun has not yet shifted to 'he'; yet we must note how artfully that sentence is cadenced, with its parallel 'that'-clauses and the semi-colons that invite the reader to assume a rhythm and a tempo like that of formal rhetoric, not the language of a person speaking, but the language of a writer composing speech.

Presently, under repeated scrutiny, the supposedly naturalistic style of the character appears to be overtaken by the controlling artifice of the author using the device of 'internalised' speech as a vehicle for 'external' commentary.

Characters in fiction have conversations; or, to be more precise, 'speak', in conversational style, words assigned to them by dialogue-designing authors. Alice thought that a book should have pictures and conversations, and Alice was within her innocent reader's rights; but really there are no conversations in literature. Literary speech is not conversational speech; it is dialogue-speech, a semblance of speech wrought to a governing design, even in seemingly 'naturalistic' passages such as the following, where the headmistress of a girls' school is seen quizzing some of her pupils about the habits of their class teacher, Miss Brodie, to whom they are cunningly and stubbornly loyal:

> Then she began to pump them. Miss Brodie took them to the theatre, the art galleries, for walks, to Miss Brodie's flat for tea? How kind of Miss Brodie. 'Does Miss Brodie pay for all your theatre tickets?'
>
> 'Sometimes', said Mary.
>
> 'Not for all of us every time,' said Jenny.
>
> 'We go up to the gallery,' Sandy said.
>
> 'Well, it is most kind of Miss Brodie. I hope you are appreciative.'
>
> 'Oh, yes,' they said, united and alert against anything unfavourable to the Brodie idea which the conversation might be leading up to.
>
> 'That's splendid,' she said. 'And do you go to concerts with Miss Brodie? Miss Brodie is very musical, I believe?'
>
> 'Yes,' said Mary, looking at her friends for a lead.
>
> 'We went to the opera with Miss Brodie last term to see *La Traviata*,' said Jenny.
>
> 'Miss Brodie is musical?' said Miss Mackay again, addressing Sandy and Jenny.
>
> 'We saw Pavlova,' said Sandy.
>
> 'Miss Brodie is musical?' said Miss Mackay.
>
> 'I think Miss Brodie is more interested in art, ma'am,' said Sandy.
>
> 'But music is a form of art.'

'Pictures and drawings, I mean,' said Sandy.

'Very enlightening,' said Miss Mackay. 'Do you girls take piano lessons?'

They all said yes.

'From whom? From Mr Lowther?'

They answered variously, for Mr Lowther's piano lessons were not part of the curriculum and these three girls had private arrangements for the piano at home. But now, at the mention of Mr Lowther, even slow-minded Mary suspected what Miss Mackay was driving at.

This 'conversation' (taken from Muriel Spark's novel, *The Prime of Miss Jean Brodie*) is a narrative device for informing readers, or reminding them, about the story's characters and the circumstances of the plot. Miss Mackay is formidably persistent in her effort to find grounds of complaint against her subversive colleague, Miss Brodie. She wants, as the saying goes, to 'get something on' her junior; perhaps a hint that the pupils' loyalties are being corruptly purchased, or, failing that, some guileless intimation of an affair between Miss Brodie and the music teacher, Mr Lowther. To elicit this revelation is the purport of the repeated 'Miss Brodie is musical?'; and the question-and-answer pairing of Miss Mackay's 'Miss Brodie is musical?' and Sandy's 'I think Miss Brodie is more interested in art' might be decoded in the form 'Is Miss Brodie having an affair with Mr Lowther?' – 'No, she is more interested in the art master, Mr Lloyd.'

The participants, or 'interactants' in this conversation make exchanges in a code, to which, of course, the reader is privy. Miss Mackay is engaged in 'pumping' the girls, in a clumsily oblique way. The obliquity of it does not deceive them. They know they are being pumped, and in their responses are more or less skilfully evasive – less in the replies of Mary, more in Jenny's, most in Sandy's. Sandy is Miss Mackay's most intelligent and teasingly inventive opponent, a fact which the headmistress acknowledges with her deadpan 'Very enlightening', in response to the girl's cryptic observation 'Pictures and drawings, I mean'.

The 'conversation' is, in sum, the portrait of a situation, the diagram of a subliminal conflict, the staging of an interaction with incidental revelations of character (Miss Mackay's obdurate, brooding malice, Mary's good-natured obtuseness, Jenny's social competence, Sandy's perception and cunning). In all this, the representation of speech certainly has a part to play, and Muriel Spark manages the techniques of representation with typical skill. Her report of the 'pumping' process begins with Miss Mackay in free indirect speech, presently shifting into direct speech (i.e. with quotation marks – 'Does Miss Brodie pay for all your theatre tickets?'). From that point onwards she supplies brief stage-directive comments, denoting a brief movement or the catching of an eye ('looking at her friends for a lead', 'addressing Sandy and Jenny'), but she avoids the adverbial or participial tags (*defensively*, *scratching her head in exasperation*) that litter the texts of lesser writers.

It is indeed this refusal, on the author's part, to describe an intonation or a gesture that gives peculiar stylistic power to Miss Mackay's repeated question about Miss Brodie's musicality. The control of the text is here tacitly surrendered to its readers. They are left to supply for themselves the appropriate tone of voice for this situation, this person, this intention. Does it remain implacably, patiently the same throughout the repetitions, or do Miss Mackay's reiterated questions shift their intonations, through subtle nuances of impatience? It is the reader's knowledge of the probabilities of speech and paralanguage ('tone of voice') that is called on at this point; but also the reader's interpretation of character and text.

To savour the episode in full, we must draw on that primitive storage, in our own memories, of the characteristic speech patterns of our native language, heard for years in a thousand-and-one commonplace encounters: the options of intonation, emphasis, etc., now evoked for us by a skilled writer who knows just what signals to make in order to prompt, in the reader's mind, the work of imaginative recall. But, in addition to that, and more than that, we must be able to decode a design, a pattern in language presenting a narrative mode. There are many ways of telling a story, and dialogue is one of the ways. An alternative 'narrative mode' would be straightforward description, the obvious choice if scenes are to be depicted or if actions are busily going forward. But in this episode from *The Prime of Miss Jean Brodie* (Spark 1965: 64–5) there is no scenery and no action – though much is happening on the psychological stage. To describe those happenings and their implications might take up pages. Conversation – or, let us insist, *dialogue* – does it better.

'Conversation' is a linguistic category, 'dialogue' a literary mode; and though the one must seem to be reflected in the other, there are great differences between them. As far as the linguist is concerned, conversation is a purely *auditory* phenomenon, and therefore its content is limited to whatever can be readily managed in the interactions of speech, and stored in the minds of the participants. Natural, or 'real-life' conversation is governed by a social sense that prohibits the development of long, complex, abstract utterances. Because it is auditory and social, and because it is therefore impromptu – for no one can plan a conversation in advance – it is full of 'hesitation phenomena' (*ums* and *ers*), incomplete utterances, distortions of syntax, 'phatic communion' (stereotyped phrases – *well, well!*, *you don't say!*, *know what you mean!*) conveying no message other than the assurance of sympathetic attention), gestures which variously admit others to the conversational exchange, or debar them from it. A conversation generally involves more than the conveying of a message; it is also a social game of power and control, in which the 'situation', whatever it might be, is a field of play where individuals struggle for mastery or enter into team-like alliances. (This is adroitly evoked by Muriel Spark in the dialogue cited above.) In sum, natural conversation is *auditory*, *impromptu* and *social*.

Some of this is incorporated into the artifice of written dialogue; yet dialogue is a very different matter. For the writer, it is not limited by the constraints of 'auditoriness', though he or she will naturally hope to convey some sense of the immediacy of speaking. Dialogue permits, if the writer wants to use them, long sentences, with subordinate clauses, with parentheses, with the rhythmic parcellings of elaborate punctuation. There need be no struggle among fictional characters to hold the conversational floor. Participants wait patiently for the speaker to finish his or her turn, and then set off on their own course of well-rounded sentences. Being 'of the page' rather than 'of the moment', dialogue is not subject to the vagaries of the incomplete or malformed utterance, unless the writer deliberately chooses to work into the script, for the sake of realism, a selection from that stuttering thesaurus that includes *but what on earth* . . . and *I . . . er* and *why . . . why you . . . you!*.

Apart from such scriptings of conversational lameness, the language of dialogue is usually complete and well-formed. It is 'social' in the sense that it reflects the social interactions of a story, but its overriding value is structural: it has a chosen place (chosen by the author, planned in advance) and a function in the process of literary composition. The writer's concern is compositional, not conversational. Authors evoke conversational tones and turns of phrase, and readers like it best when characters appear to speak after the fashion of 'real people', but good conversation, after all, does not necessarily make good dialogue. The first business of dialogue is not to sound natural, or to be decorative, but to promote the reader's understanding of a narrative process. It is an artifice which involves by the way the imitation of an idea of common speech.

The idea is in the reader's mind as much as the writer's; or it is an idea the writer may reasonably hope the reader has in mind. This is notably apparent from some types of semi-formal expository prose, for instance the humorous discourse of which James Thurber was an unrivalled master. Here (see Thurber 1983: 191) he describes the personality of the indomitable Airedale called Muggs, 'The Dog that Bit People':

> But the Airedale, as I have said, was the worst of all my dogs. He really wasn't my dog, as a matter of fact: I came home from a vacation one summer to find that my brother Roy had bought him while I was away. A big, burly, choleric dog, he always acted as if he thought I wasn't one of the family. There was a slight advantage in being one of the family, for he didn't bite the family as often as he bit strangers. Still, in the years that we had him he bit everybody but mother, and he made a pass at her once, but missed. That was during the month when we suddenly had mice, and Muggs refused to do anything about them. Nobody ever had mice exactly like the mice we had that month. They acted like pet mice, almost like mice somebody had trained. They were so friendly that one night when my mother entertained at dinner the Friraliras, a club she and my father had belonged to for twenty years, she put down a lot of little dishes with food in them on the pantry floor so that the mice would be satisfied with that and wouldn't come into the dining room. Muggs stayed out in the pantry with the mice, lying on the floor, growling to himself – not at the mice, but about all the people in the next room that he would have liked to get at. Mother slipped out to the pantry once to see how everything was going. Everything was going fine. It made her so mad to see Muggs lying there, oblivious of the mice – they came running up to her – that she slapped him and he slashed at her, but didn't make it. He was sorry immediately, she said. He was always sorry, she said, after he bit someone, but we could not understand how she figured this out. He didn't act sorry.

For some readers the illusion of speech so powerfully created in this text will have been prepared through the reading of other texts by the same author. It is hardly possible for a devotee to come to any piece by Thurber, even one not previously read, without some anticipation of the typical quirks of his humorous style. He is an author whose writings have remained popular; we know him well, we admire him for – among other things – his apparently inexhaustible gift of elegantly translating ways of speaking into styles of writing. In short, we expect Thurber to show us how words printed on the page are made to stand up and *say*; and in that expectation much of the illusion of speech may be accomplished almost as soon as we begin to read. We presuppose a degree of artful talkativeness. But Thurber in his writings leaves nothing to chance or presupposition. He regularly and explicitly suggests to the reader that his comic fantasies are to be conceived as *recitals*. Here, for example, he frames his reminiscences of his mother and Muggs with reminders of the verb *say*: 'But the Airedale, as I have said . . .' (at the beginning of the anecdote), 'He was always sorry, she said' (at the end). Thus the presentation of the story, first and last, points to the idea of *saying*.

Tokens of saying, emblems of the speaking voice, are distributed throughout the text. The contraction of verb + negative (wasn't, didn't) is an obvious symptom. Another sign is the resolute chattiness of vocabulary and idiom, designedly avoiding any expression that might suggest book-language: 'she slipped out to the pantry', 'everything was going fine', 'it made her so mad', 'how she figured this out', 'he didn't act sorry'. This, we might readily agree, is a plausible representation of how people *speak*. They are rather less likely, in relating domestic happenings, to say 'it angered her greatly', or 'what led her to this conclusion' or 'he did not behave as though he were sorry'; the folks at home *say* – by writerly suggestion and readerly consent – 'it made her so mad', 'how she figured this out', 'he didn't act sorry'.

This structure of casual talk is nevertheless not wholly secure from comic intrusions of bookishness – for example, *choleric* (in 'a big, burly, choleric dog') and *oblivious* (in 'oblivious of the mice'). Thurber might easily have written 'a big, burly, bad-tempered dog' – with the incidental advantage of alliteration – or 'taking no notice of the mice'; but *bad-tempered* and *taking no notice* would have lacked the pointed stylistic effect of *choleric* and *oblivious*. That effect is in essence the old comedian's trick of not keeping a decorum – a level of style – but incongruously blending formal and informal, bookish and colloquial, making readers laugh by unsettling the sense of stylistic propriety.

In this particular context, the blending of book-words with talk-words also suggests something of the narrator's self-awareness and self-mockery. This is a family chronicle absurdly unravelling into anecdote. We laugh at the mother, solicitous for the human rights of mice and Airedales, and meanwhile Thurber laughs a little at himself, striving after the dignity of a literary recital but repeatedly falling back on household phrases. Once again, it seems, the representation of speech in writing is not a simple act of imitation. It is more complex, especially in humorous writing; it reaches beyond the immediate location of the joke, the one-liner, the witty remark, the particular moment of laughter, and enters into the broader *texture* of comic discourse.

From beginning to end, however, this writing of Thurber's cultivates the *pretence* of speech, immediate and spontaneous. It begins with one of those little scraps of concessive or corrective phrasing that so often occur in spoken communication – 'as a matter of fact'. A similar impression of speech annotating speech is made by 'still' at the beginning of the third sentence. ('Still, in the years that we had him'; 'still' rather than 'however', 'nevertheless', or 'despite that', the habitual conjuncts of written composition.) This casual metacommentary is accompanied by the *deixis* of anecdote, a raconteur's way of alluding specifically to unspecified persons, exactly recalling inexact times, giving location to the more or less unlocated event – the precisely imprecise, impersonally personal use of *that* and *this*.[3] Thurber's deixis is briefly temporal; it frames his story in a time which is never more definite than 'that summer', 'that month'. He does not overplay the device by writing, for example, 'There was that month when we had these mice and my parents gave a party for this club, the Friraliras.' As with the metacomments ('as a matter of fact', 'still'), the brief touch of a recognisable colloquial device is enough to suggest a way of speaking, an anecdotal manner, that brings the audience closer, into an immediate circle of address.

The habit of a speaker is further suggested by touches of deliberate redundancy and designed awkwardness. Some sentences or sentence-sequences have the air of having eluded the monitoring process that normally checks and trims language on its way to the page: 'That was during the month when we suddenly had mice, and Muggs refused to do anything about them. Nobody ever had mice exactly like the mice we had that month. They acted like pet mice, almost like mice somebody had trained.' A comic style that is wickedly skilful – a pattern of careful phrasing and studied rhythms – but it plays on our general intuition that speech is full of repetitions and expansions. The usual instinct of the prose expositor, conditioned by the advice of preceptors and manuals, is to tighten and reduce – to write, for example, 'Nobody ever had mice quite like those we had that month. Their behaviour was almost that of trained pets.' But that sort of revision would merely lame the text, impair the sense of speech, rudely destroy the delicate balances of the comic style.

Those balances appear again and again, in alternations of what seem to be the impromptu phrasings of a speaker and the repeated emergence, under the rambling talk, of a writer's feeling for rhythm and rhetoric. 'She put down a lot of little dishes with food in them on the pantry floor' lays out its word-order in common talkative progression (what pedant would demand 'She put down on the pantry floor some little dishes of food'?). The interposed 'they came running up to her' is an afterthought parenthesis, a rough intrusion of a sort common enough in speech, but in writing usually smoothed away into some more elegant structure, e.g. a relative clause: 'oblivious of the mice, which came running up to her', or, for emphasis, 'oblivious of the mice, which actually came running up to her'.

But in such instances the apparent roughness of the writing is a matter of humorous design; the comedian's rough is silky-smooth. And periodically the inherent spirit of comic calculation breaks in with juxtapositions which actually suggest the parallels, antitheses and repetitions of traditional rhetoric: 'to see how everything was going – everything was going fine'; 'she slapped him and he slashed at her'; 'He was sorry immediately, she said. He was always sorry, she said'. All comic writers – to risk a large generalisation – are rhetoricians; and the particular source and playground of their rhetoric is an amused consciousness of how talk is talked and how writing gets written; a consciousness of *writing as speaking as writing*, an odd, reverberant interplay of two modes of language.

All compositions, other than the figments of bureaucrats, lawyers, insurance agents and tax collectors, embody to some extent the complex illusion of speaking. The dominant illusion, cultivated with the help of a small repertoire of linguistic devices (personal pronouns, contractions, elisions, marked syntactic forms, familiar phrase-forms, etc.), is that writing can translate or 'transpose' speaking. But if that were wholly true, it would be the death of literature, the downfall of humour, the paralysis of poetry; a piece of unpremeditated 'real life' talk, or an 'actual' conversation, faithfully transferred to the printed page with every hiatus and hiccup in place, might well baffle and repel everyone but the dedicated discourse analyst. The notion of 'writing as speaking' becomes a little precarious under close examination. It is a little like the invitation to come to a party 'as you are – nobody will mind, nobody will notice'; everybody notices and everybody minds.

Writers, however, may sustain themselves with a companion illusion: that there is a special kind of speaking, 'internal' speaking, which is the true basis of writing. Sentences are formed in the head, their constructions monitored, their rhythms criticised, their accents adjusted, their connections with other sentences anticipated, the possibilities envisaged of a kind of emergent *marriage* with the outward sense of speech, with those colloquial tricks and turns which the author casually edits into the text. But this internalised 'speaking as writing' is not wholly convincing either, because we can never know whether, for every writer, there exists a truly separate 'pre-transcript' stage of composition, or whether, in most cases, the act of transcribing is part of an extended monitoring process that makes its orderings, inclusions, and exclusions in accordance with diffuse, impressionistic criteria, including the way the text looks on the page.

All that an author can really achieve is 'writing as speaking as writing', an illusion compounded of illusions: one, the illusion that writing imitates speech; but two, the further illusion that an abstract idea of speech may inform the conventions and devices of writing so effectively that readers will impute to a text a convincing power of *saying*, and will be satisfied that a beloved author is somehow 'talking' to them. It is a phantom, that 'talking', that 'power of saying', an artifice, an agreement struck between writer and reader for the duration of the text. It is not the writer who speaks; it is the text that is assumed to speak, under the direction of the writer, according to the interpretation of the reader.

We come no nearer than that, and for no longer than that, to the truth of how people speak to each other; still less, perhaps, to the truth of how we speak to ourselves as we think about speaking. The mind of the writer is baffled in the circles of its own reflection. Cassirer's *curse of mediacy* attends this, as it attends all other ventures in symbolism. Writing is bound to obscure what it seeks to reveal; and that is why writers come to their labours again and again, grumbling, hapless, endlessly seeking the satisfaction of being dissatisfied, inescapably caught up in the fascinations and servitudes of their literary game.

NOTES

1 From the text of a life insurance policy issued (in 1964) by the Independent Order of Foresters.

2 Of the concept of *cline*, the 'systemic' grammarian Margaret Berry (1975: 26) observes:

> A cline is a scale on which all the points shade into each other. One end is quite different from the other end but it is impossible to tell exactly where one merges into the other. Systemic linguists often say of two categories that they are on a cline. When they say this they are recognizing that some items of language fall quite clearly into category A and that some items fall quite clearly into category B, but that some items fall at various points along the scale between A and B.

Miss Berry is speaking of linguistic categories, but the notion of *cline* is readily applicable to varieties of style.

3 *Deixis*, meaning 'pointing out', 'indicating', is a linguist's term. Some typical *deictic words*, pointing to the persons, times, places, etc., involved in a text are 'they', 'that', 'then', 'there'.

REFERENCES

BERRY, MARGARET. *Introduction to Systemic Linguistics, 1: Structures and Systems.* London: Batsford, 1975.

CASSIRER, ERNST. *Language and Myth*, transl. Susanne K. Langer. New York: Dover Publications Inc., 1946; p. 7.

JAMESON, F. *The Political Unconscious: Narrative as a Socially Symbolic Act.* Ithaca, N.Y.: Cornell University Press, 1981; p. 219.

SPARK, MURIEL. *The Prime of Miss Jean Brodie.* Harmondsworth: Penguin Books, 1965.

THURBER, JAMES. 'The Dog That Bit People' in *Vintage Thurber; A Selection of the Best Writings and Drawings*, Vol. 2. Harmondsworth: Penguin Books, 1983.

Three

Ludus litterarius; or games writers play

A likely impossibility is always preferable to an unconvincing possibility.

(Aristotle, *Poetics*)

Does 'game' seem quite the appropriate word for any species of literary composition? Someone may protest that Literature (with a capital L, to denote its consecrated status) is not to be called a game; that whatever it does is done in sober earnest and moral commitment. Possibly, and yet there is no Literature without playfulness, for story-telling (or the making of verses or the creation of dialogues plausibly rehearsing what this one says and that one replies – in short, the whole business of devising words for literary ends) is essentially *ludic*. Imagination may rise above the prescriptions of known fact, and yet, in coping with what we have called 'illusions of resemblance' (see p. 3), it relies unremittingly on fact, raids it, rearranges it. We playfully infer what is plausible from our knowledge of what is possible. We devise new combinations of combinable things, and cultivate imaginary gardens with real toads in them (Marianne Moore's playful and unforgettable phrase).[1] We coax reverie into logic, and create in writing a simulacrum of speech. We invent the harmonics of rhyme and the dancing counterpoint of metre. We manipulate 'ordinary' language until it seems to acquire a power of illusion – spellbinding, symbolic, self-referential, beyond the everyday power of words to say what words need to say. And all this and more is involved in the *ludus litterarius*, the playing of the literary game.

Literature may be called a game in this particular meaning, of a serious craft learned by playing. (Note in passing: for the Romans, one of the meanings of *ludus* was 'a school'.) But then it might be still more appropriate to speak of *games*, in the plural, for literary creativity, or *poesis* in the age-old sense, demands several kinds of exercise in self-forgetfulness and other-worldliness, only to be perfected by players adept in the sport of lifting their heads into the clouds while they keep two feet planted squarely on the ground. These are the disciplines of the imagination, implemented by certain verbal skills, or devices, that draw the bounds and make the bridges of apprehension between this, our everyday world in which we act, suffer and pay our taxes, and those other worlds of infinite possibility, where we can experience all the passions, endure all the trials, enter all the heavens and have all wisdoms without stirring from our chairs. Here is a *virtual reality* – in the modern technological phrase – which is created, let us suggest, in three interrelated forms of literary game: games of personality, games of place and games of progression.

OF PERSONALITY

I have been told of a Swedish poet who suggested for himself a witty epitaph: *Här ligger en annan* – 'here lies another'. The point of the joke is that in Swedish, 'en annan' means 'another', but in genteel usage can also mean 'one', 'I myself'. Thus *här ligger en annan* means 'here lies another', but also 'here I lie'. This poetic invention may serve for texts as well as for tombstones. If my text, as I sit producing it, is a sort of plot where my personality is interred, I may indeed say, 'Here lies another', for though all lively writing is governed by a *persona*, it will not necessarily reflect or express the personal characteristics of the writer. Of myself, as I get about the business of writing, I can say that I mutter and fidget, that I lapse into stultified trances, that I am often lost for words, that I bumble and lose track of my discourse, that even when I can see the point at which I am driving, I commonly have difficulty in grasping it, that my logic is often as suspect as my fantasy is clownish.

How much of this will appear from my finished text? How much will I allow to appear? Now that I have described myself in that way, in that long sentence with its parallel ranks of *that*-clauses, six in all, I ask – is this really me, or is it *one* displaying *another*? The fact is that from the moment writers sit down to create the most ordinary text – the most commonplace report or routine history, the most dutifully objective recital of unexciting circumstances – they commit themselves to the masquerade of sentence-building and sentence-balancing, creating points of emphasis and focus, looking for the effective word, moving as swiftly as possible towards that point at which, mysteriously, the text begins to assume its own destiny and apparently speak for itself. Then here one lies, indeed. And lies. And lies. For this patient shaping of a text, following the time-honoured prescriptions of compositional craft, always brings the writer farther from the fact of 'I' and nearer to the fiction of 'another'.

Students of composition – freshmen doing their stint in rhetoric, young tee-shirted poets, fierce, crop-haired Maenads taking the Creative Writing option – commonly refuse to accept that one of the most powerful motives of writing is to escape from 'I'. Theirs is the angry pursuit of self-expression. They write about their blisters and malfunctions, about the hell of being who they are in a world that gives them hell for being who they aren't. It is difficult to persuade them that this is something they must go through before the study of writing can begin; and unavailing to remind them that T.S. Eliot, no less, said that he wrote to escape from a self rather than to express one. The cult of 'I' obstructs the progress to 'another', and 'I' must be banished.

The writer's 'I' may be no more than a property of the text, an aspect of the struggle to make something that has a shape and carries conviction. The subject pronoun need never be mentioned. There is an 'I' in this, the first aphorism of Hippocrates:

> Life is short, the craft long, the crisis sudden and dangerous, experience deceptive, diagnosis difficult.

Likewise, there is an 'I', unmistakably, in the first sentence of *Pride and Prejudice*:

> It is a truth universally acknowledged, that a single man in possession of a good fortune, must be in want of a wife.

What those instances have in common (apart from their assumption that there is a world beyond the page, with things to be known and judged) is the sense of a voice conveyed, an impression made on the reader of 'overhearing'. We overhear Hippocrates briskly laying out his theme, we overhear Jane Austen's sweetly ironic drawl – or think we overhear them, for, of course, *here lies another*. The illusion of an 'I' arises in each case from the management of the style; from the *brachylogia* of the Hippocratic text – the composition in brief phrases

– and, in Jane Austen, from the devices of grammar, sentence-rhythm, and even punctuation, that suggest a living voice, and will go on suggesting it, thank heaven, whenever we open the book to begin again our acquaintance with the middle-class Bennets and the vertically structured Mr Darcy.

The delicious paradox of this opening is that the syntactic form of the so-called 'extraposition' (i.e. 'It is universally acknowledged that . . .', rather than 'Everybody acknowledges'), the cautious parenthetic qualification ('in possession of a good fortune' – well, but of course) and the accent of justifiable inference ('must'), collectively suggest the professor expounding his theme rather than the young lady about to pass on some engaging gossip. But, as we all realise in an instant, this 'professor' is the 'other', the authorial role Jane Austen playfully assumes for one brief moment at the beginning of her novel, to make all the more striking, even shocking, the stylistic entry of that doyenne of all vulgarian prattlers, Mrs Bennet. The concealed 'I' of that famous opening sentence is only one instance, albeit a striking one, of a fairly common literary device.

But novelists and poets also make use of an explicit 'I', a pronoun-in-the-text; whether it is the 'I' of a narrator recounting something witnessed – the 'I'/'eye'/'aye' of a reporter – or whether it is the 'I' of a narrator who is also a participant, a central or an attendant character.[2] An example of a story discreetly conducted by a narratorial 'I' is John Fowles's *The French Lieutenant's Woman* (Fowles 1976); the narrator comments from time to time on the narrative, makes asides to the reader and at one point even interferes with the progress of his own story to present an alternative resolution of the plot. That is one instance of the 'I' as seeing, or overseeing 'eye'. In contrast to that, fiction has numerous instances of the 'I' narrating as a participant in the story: Stevenson's *Kidnapped*, for example, or Raymond Chandler's *Farewell, My Lovely*. (A glance at my bookshelves suggests the examples at random.)

What a random survey also suggests is that authors experiment freely with possible interminglings of 'I external' and 'I internal'. The first chapter of George Eliot's *The Mill on the Floss* (Eliot 1979) presents the case of a narrator apparently involved in her narrative, standing *inside* the scene which will immediately (and rightly) be the location of her story, viewing the prospect from a stone bridge, on the balustrade of which she is leaning. But she is not leaning on the bridge; the pressure on her forearms comes from the armchair in which she has fallen asleep. She has been dreaming – dreaming about the proposed scene of her narrative; and she describes her dream *in the present tense* until she reaches that point at the end of the chapter when she announces, 'Before I dozed off, I was going to tell you what Mr and Mrs Tulliver were talking about, as they sat by the bright fire in the left-hand parlour, on that very afternoon I have been dreaming of.' Chapter Two then sets in train what is ostensibly a third-person narrative, now couched in the past tense. The author stands external to her story; but her first chapter puts in a claim for herself as insider.

In other classic instances, some play with the narratorial 'I' is evidently necessary to establish the credentials of the tale. How are we to believe the epic/mythic events of that stormbound tale, *The Nigger of the Narcissus* (Conrad 1957)? We believe because a trustworthy narrator is there, discreetly masquerading as one of the crew. We do not meet him at first; then presently the pronoun 'we' begins to mingle with 'they' in descriptions of the ship's company; finally – and not until the book's penultimate paragraph – the pronoun 'I' designates the narrator. The presentation of narratorial credentials is somewhat differently managed in Emily Brontë's *Wuthering Heights* (Brontë 1965). The narrating 'I'of that story is at first the newcomer to the district, Mr Lockwood; but Lockwood, as newcomer, cannot know the history of Heathcliff, the Earnshaws and the Lintons, and the 'I' role is ceded to an insider, Mrs Dean, who keeps it through most of the narrative until the final page, when Lockwood's 'I' re-emerges. The transition from Lockwood's 'I' to Mrs Dean's 'I' takes place at the beginning of the fourth chapter, so quietly that the reader is barely conscious that the narrator has changed, from the visiting gentleman to the personage described by Emily's sister Charlotte (in her Preface to the New [1850] Edition of *Wuthering Heights*) as 'an example of true benevolence and homely fidelity'.

Experienced readers, or those who do not need to be instructed in the difference between 'literary' and 'literal', are prepared to accept the 'I' of fiction as a personality not identical with the person of the author.[3] The 'I' of poetry, on the other hand, is generally supposed (except in dramatic poems) to identify the poet. Reading 'My heart leaps up when I behold/ A rainbow in the sky', or 'I leaned upon a coppice gate/ When frost was spectre-grey', we unquestioningly assume that 'I' means, respectively, William Wordsworth and Thomas Hardy. When Masefield says 'I must go down to the sea again', or when Yeats declares 'I will arise and go now, and go to Innisfree', we do not take them so literally as to suppose them immediately committed to making travel arrangements with Horizon Holidays, but we do assume that these are the expressed desires of John Masefield in person or William Butler Yeats and no one else.

Yet there are poetic instances not so clear-cut as the personal lyric, on the one hand, or, on the other, the dramatic recital that invents a *persona* (such as the madman in Browning's 'Porphyria's Lover', or the murderous autocrat in his 'My Last Duchess'). There are poems that bespeak a personality, apparently expressing 'myself', but also *design* a personality, projecting 'another'. There is, for example, Robert Frost's 'Mending Wall' (Frost 1976). A curious and significant title, this; note, not 'Mending *a* wall', or 'Mending *the* wall', but 'Mending Wall', without an article, like 'catching fish', or 'chopping wood', or 'baking bread', just another routine chore for everyday country folk. The poem describes how a New Hampshire farmer, supposedly Robert Frost himself, goes out every springtime with his neighbour to mend the dry-stone wall that runs between their properties. The business of wall-mending is described in some detail: how they keep the wall between them as they walk the line, how each takes charge of the stones that have fallen on his side, how the stones vary in shape and size and are sometimes so tricky to fit that the workers 'use a spell to make them balance'.

This quite interesting account of New Hampshire farming practice is not, however, the whole substance of the poem. Frost the farmer – 'I' – is disturbed by the reflections of Frost the poet – 'another' – who finds it strange that sections of the wall tend to collapse for no obvious reason. It occurs to him that there is some mysterious force at work, that dislikes divisions and will destroy them if there is nothing essential to divide. Farmer Frost observes that the wall between his property – an apple orchard – and his neighbour's – a pine wood – is not strictly necessary. Walls on farms are for keeping livestock away from crops. 'My apple trees will never get across/ And eat the cones under his pines, I tell him.' The poet Frost elaborates this notion, but his companion is unconvinced, and keeps doggedly repeating the folk-wisdom, 'Good fences make good neighbours'. 'He will not go beyond his father's saying.' Frost remarks. It is borne in upon the reader that in this poem the wall is an image of the restricted imagination, a monument to the unexamined ideas that separate mind from mind, soul from soul. It is not really 'the wall' that is being mended, but Wall, with a capital letter, a patriarchal deity of primitive man. When that is perceived, the poem lies open to numberless personal, social and political interpretations. (Not too long ago, the classroom consensus was that Wall suggested the Berlin Wall, and 'his father's saying' the dogma of communism.)

Now it is interesting to see how the poet's 'I' figures in what is seemingly a text capable of interpretation at more than one level. All the talking in the poem is done by this garrulous 'I'. The dim neighbour is represented by a single speech, a proverbial maxim which he trots out twice. The complex 'I', on the other hand, farmer-poet-philosopher, speaks in a medley of styles, ranging from colloquial directness to literary circumlocution. Speech-style appears in lines like these:

Why do they make good neighbours? Isn't it
Where there are cows? But here there are no cows.

One can accept that Farmer Frost, the poem's ordinary 'I', might talk like this (though freed from the constraints of metre he would probably say 'there are no cows here'). Yet the 'ordinary' speech of those lines continues in a style that is something less than colloquial:

Before I built a wall I'd ask to know
What I was walling in or walling out,
And to whom I was like to give offence.
Something there is that doesn't love a wall,
That wants it down.

Now is this quite so farmerly? This 'I' is a little pedantic about grammar (not 'who I would be offending', but 'to whom I was like to give offence'), and portentous in idiom ('I'd ask to know' for 'I'd try to find out', 'was like to give' for 'might give'). The impression of cultivated literariness is even stronger in the line 'Something there is that doesn't love a wall'. What sort of dialect is this for a homeloving 'I' to speak? It is an existential sentence – 'There's something that doesn't love a wall'; but more than that, it is an existential sentence with a 'fronted theme' – '*Something* there is . . .' – and such fronting, for the purpose of emphasis, is an old device of the practised rhetorician.[4] But this rhetorically turned clause in Frost's poem has an important structural role. It is the line with which the poem opens; it occurs twice, like the neighbour's 'Good fences make good neighbours', and might be read as an antiphonal counterpart to it.

The opening lines of the poem further illustrate the shiftiness of a style that drifts between the impression of a man speaking and the idea of a man recalling the language of books:

> Something there is that doesn't love a wall,
> That sends the frozen ground-swell under it,
> And spills the upper boulders in the sun,
> And makes gaps even two can pass abreast.
> The work of hunters is another thing:
> I have come after them and made repair
> Where they have left not one stone on a stone,
> But they would have the rabbit out of hiding,
> To please the yelping dogs. The gaps I mean,
> No one has seen them made or heard them made,
> But at spring mending-time we find them there.

Speech ('doesn't', 'is another thing', 'The gaps I mean, no one has seen them made') blends into a bookish, almost stilted idiom ('made repair', 'not one stone on a stone') and a syntax that the writer appears almost to have invented for himself (for example, the *but*-clause in 'Where they have left not one stone on a stone/ But they would have the rabbit out of hiding').[5] Such a stylistic blending, the deliberate formation of an idiomatic hybrid, precludes the easy identification of 'I' with a 'real' person, duly listed in the telephone directory and the electoral register as Robert Frost. Style in this case is not the man, or not *that* man. Style is the assumption of a role. Here lies another.

OF PLACE

In literary texts, the necessary fooling with 'I' is commonly accompanied by a play of 'where' (or 'where-and-when'). Even in non-literary texts, everywhere is likely to be elsewhere. Consider, for example, the business of writing a few descriptive lines on the back of a holiday postcard. I write, let us say, from Muddville-on-Sea: 'Staying here for a fortnight! This is *almost* the view from our room. Beautiful sunsets, except when it rains, which it has for the last three days, wouldn't you know. The picture shows the esplanade and the Spa. The man covered in pigeon-droppings is the famous Dr Mudd.'

Now, the postcard picture in itself is one step removed from the abstract idea of Muddville-on-Sea (or at least, the idea in the visitor's mind), and the text written on the back is one further step away from the representation in the picture. So we have a 'here', a place called Muddville-on-Sea; then a photographic view of part of Muddville-on-Sea, made at a particular hour of a certain day in a given season of a historical year; then a jocose commentary on the photograph, made on some other day, in some other year, perhaps many years after the time when the photograph was taken. The writer may say, 'staying here for a fortnight', but in the transmutations of postcard fiction, 'here' has become elsewhere. Nobody sends holiday postcards from 'here'. The message always comes out of a possible location in the not inconceivable distance.

Then put the case – which is the case indeed – that 'Muddville-on-Sea' is a complete invention. There is no such place, although experience tells me there *are* such places. I dream up a resort called Muddville, pictured in imaginary postcards the like of which I have seen in kiosks on a dozen-and-one real esplanades. I locate, in fancy, a modest hotel in which I have never stayed, of the sort in which, given my modest resources, I am always staying. I design the outlook, the weather, the furnishings of the street; and then I imagine an 'I' who comments typically on the typical experience of staying in a place like this on a typical summer holiday. Now I have a 'here' constructed in reverie, a plausible 'here' which begins 'there', in the otherwhere of dreams.

It is a necessity of the soberest, most realistic fiction, even of what is currently called 'docufiction', or 'faction', that the author's postcards come from elsewhere. What is called 'realism' is an elaborate accommodation of fantasy:

> . . . we were driven by a violent Storm to the North-west of *Van Diemen's* Land. By an Observation, we found ourselves in the Latitude of 30 Degrees 2 Minutes South.

This is Jonathan Swift, in the realistic role of that fact-loving seaman Lemuel Gulliver, at the beginning of the first voyage, and Gulliver is lying with cool plausibility (Swift 1944). The exactitude of the navigator's 'observation' is thoroughly bogus. It would have been clear to anyone who consulted a good atlas – though perhaps there were not too many of those available in Lemuel's 1699 or Jonathan's 1726 – that Jonathan Swift/Lemuel Gulliver had no more than the barest notion of where Van Diemen's Land (Tasmania) might be found.

Furthermore, this documentary narrator supplies only one of the coordinates – the latitude; for the longitude we are left guessing, or trusting.[6] And indeed we trust – for what else should we do, and what else could Swift's first readers have done? 'Van Diemen's Land' must have sounded convincing enough to eighteenth-century stay-at-homes, and that finicking '30 Degrees *2 Minutes*' clinches the conviction that Gulliver starts from a thoroughly respectable, credible, identifiable 'here'. And so we gullibly follow Gulliver, bit by realistic bit, as he sails, and rows and swims, until at last:

> . . . when I was almost gone, and able to struggle no longer, I found myself within my Depth; and by this time the Storm was much abated. The Declivity was so small, that I walked near a Mile before I got to the Shore, which I conjectured was about Eight o'Clock in the Evening. I then advanced forward near half a Mile, but could not discover any Sign of Houses; at least I was in so weak a Condition, that I did not observe them. I was extremely tired, and with that, and the Heat of the Weather, and about half a Pint of Brandy that I drank as I left the Ship, I found myself much inclined to sleep. I lay down on the Grass, which was very short and soft; where I slept sounder than ever I remember to have done in my Life, and as I reckoned, above Nine Hours; for when I awaked, it was just Daylight.

He is indefatigable in his vague exactitude; '*near* a Mile', '*about* Eight o'Clock', '*near* half a Mile', '*about* half a Pint of Brandy', '*above* Nine Hours'. We can count the paces with him, we know just where we stand, more or less; and when he awakes here, he is elsewhere, and we are all in Lilliput.

One property of the fictional elsewhere is that it forestalls disbelief; once we are in Lilliput, or Illyria, or Erewhon, the houses may be thus and the costumes so, and the manners whatever they please – we are abroad, and they are bound to do things differently there. But there is another important characteristic, in that the plausibility of 'here' generates the perception of a shadowing 'elsewhere', a place not *this* place, but co-present, co-existent, with transcendental, symbolic significance.

We do not have to search out current examples of Sci-Fi or surreal narrative to illustrate this. There is a powerful instance in Charles Dickens's story *The Signalman* (Dickens 1975), a tale of the supernatural which has for its setting that most robustly modern of nineteenth-century technological marvels, the railway system. The gist of the narrative is that the railway signalman who is the subject (or perhaps the object) of the tale keeps receiving supernatural warnings of disaster, which he cannot report to his superiors, since in the rational age of the Victorian engineer no one is likely to give much credit to apparitions and spiritual sensations. The story ends with the death of the signalman – a man trapped in a 'here', desperately conscious of bad news from 'elsewhere'.

When it begins, its narrator is gazing down into a deep railway cutting, where he sees the portal of a tunnel, and close by, a signal box. This inquisitive 'I' is what we might now call a railway buff, or, as he puts it, 'a man who had been shut up within narrow limits all his life, and who, being at last set free, had a newly-awakened interest in these great works'. So we find him peering down into the 'narrow limits' where another man is ominously 'shut up'. Presently he seeks, and is reluctantly granted, permission from this man, the signalman, to take the zig-zag path down into the cutting:

> The cutting was extremely deep, and unusually precipitate. It was made through clammy stone that became oozier and wetter as I went down. For these reasons, I found the way long enough to give me time to recall a singular air of reluctance or compulsion with which he had pointed out the path.
>
> . . . His post was in as solitary and dismal a place as I ever saw. On either side, a dripping wet wall of jagged stone, excluding all view but a strip of sky; the perspective one way, only a crooked prolongation of this great dungeon; the shorter perspective in the other direction, terminating in a gloomy red light, and gloomy entrance to a black tunnel, in whose massive architecture there was a barbarous, depressing, and forbidding air. So little sunlight ever found its way to this spot, that it had an earthy deadly smell; and so much cold wind rushed through that it struck chill to me, as if I had left the natural world.

He has indeed 'left the natural world'; for, as a literary student might reflect, this is Hell, nor is he out of it. The vocabulary bespeaks the topography of Avernus: the place is a 'great dungeon', it is solitary and dismal', its walls are 'dripping and jagged', it draws the traveller's eye towards the 'gloomy entrance to a black tunnel', which has a 'barbarous, depressing and forbidding air'. And out of this cavern-chasm blow the cold, earth-fusty, chthonian winds. What could be more Hellish? Recall the *Aeneid* (Virgil 1900):

> spelunca alta fuit vastoque immanis hiatu,
> scrupea, tuta lacu nigro nemorumque tenebris,
> quam super haud ullae poterant impune volantes
> tendere iter pennis: talis sese halitus atris
> faucibus effundens supera ad convexa ferebat.
>
> (*Aeneid VI, 237–41*)

> (There was a deep, jagged cave, huge and gaping, protected by a lake of black water and the gloomy forest. Over the lake no birds could directly fly without harm, such was the breath that blew out of those black jaws and up to the sky above.)

The railway cutting is like a dream of Virgil's dream. And yet it is not Hell-mouth; it is only a railway cutting, one of those 'great works' of the Victorian engineers, a state-of-the-art technological marvel, a plausible, matter-of-fact setting for the story. The reader's perception of the place is made to shift uneasily between an illusion of resemblance and an illusion of transcendence (for these expressions, see p. 3); between the recognition of an ordinary if rather dispiriting workplace, and the *locus malum*, the 'bad place' of traditional literary rhetoric, an abode of mishap and false seeming. The sense of a plausible, explicable 'here', haunted by the apprehension of a half-perceived 'elsewhere', comes to the reader through the story's narrator, its other-personal 'I', a most methodical and level-headed man, observant, rational, unready to believe in the visitant that besets a desperate signalman with phantom (and accurate) warnings of disaster. Even this sensible citizen is caught up in the dilemma of the place, between the knowledge that some things cannot happen in the world of everyday and the tingling conviction that this is not the world of everyday, that here is elsewhere. It is a dilemma that persists, questioning the nature of perception, to the very end of the story and even beyond, as the reader who studies its final paragraph may discover. Dickens' compelling story of *The Signalman* depends for its power on the author's adroit conduct of a Game of Place; the topography of the story is the scenic plan of nightmare, and its logic, consequently, the irrational but compelling progression of a dream.

OF PROGRESSION

The constructions of imaginative fiction are not so far removed from the experience of dreaming. The narratives of our dreams are juxtapositions of scenes linked by prompts that seem logical and inevitable while the dream is in progress: it follows compulsively that the cow jumps over the moon shining on the water where the boat is waiting to take us over the hills and far away, or that the kettle sings in the gutter while we steal an umbrella from the fat soprano. In the tickover of sleep the mind goes on devising those patterned visions that look absurd in the light of day.

The patterns of writing, governed and edited by our waking reason, are not so obviously absurd, but they nevertheless originate in a mental tickover. In all so-called 'creative' writing there is a phase of reverie, or meditation, which is followed by an attempt to realise, sequentially and 'logically', the meditator's tumbling, trance-induced perceptions, to trace a path leading out of *thus* – this occurrence, this state of affairs – and into *therefore* – what duly follows. (An ordinary example of this is the recital at the breakfast table and the attempt to make narrative sense of one's dreams.) The most realistic narratives bear traces of this process of retrieval, begun in a half-dream (or what the Scots expressively call a *dwam*) and ending in the establishment of key points in a text.

Scott Fitzgerald's short story *The Baby Party* (Fitzgerald 1984) affords a typical example of this narrative game of progression, a game of verbal stepping-stones. The story describes neighbourhood rivalries in small-town America; doting and jealous parents are so absurdly infected by the combative antics of their children that women quarrel hysterically and grown men actually come to blows. Here, from the central episode of the story, is a moment of 'thus', from which a crucial 'therefore' will inexorably develop. Edith Andros has taken her two-and-a-half-year-old daughter, Ede, to a party given by her neighbour, Mrs Markey, whom she considers 'snippy and common'. Edith has not come to admire the other children; she has eyes only for her little girl:

> 'You're a darling,' she whispered to her child, drawing her suddenly against her knee. 'Do you know you're a darling?'
>
> Ede laughed. 'Bow-wow,' she said suddenly.
>
> 'Bow-wow?' Edith looked around. 'There isn't any bow-wow.'

> 'Bow-wow,' repeated Ede. 'I want a bow-wow.'
>
> Edith followed the small pointing finger.
>
> 'That isn't a bow-wow, dearest, that's a teddy-bear.'
>
> 'Bear?'
>
> 'Yes, that's a teddy-bear, and it belongs to Billy Markey. You don't want Billy Markey's teddy-bear, do you?'
>
> Ede did want it.
>
> She broke away from her mother and approached Billy Markey, who held the toy closely in his arms. Ede stood regarding him with inscrutable eyes, and Billy laughed.

The imaginative moment, surely born out of reverie and recollection, a compelling 'illusion of resemblance', is this realisation of the appalling laughter of very young children, strident, triumphal, assertive, sometimes horridly empty of adult meaning. Ede laughs (we guess) because she sees something she likes; Billy laughs, perhaps because it is his nature – he is described as 'a stout laughing baby' – or perhaps because he knows what little Ede wants and is disinclined to yield it up to her. In less than half a page, this happens:

> There was a sudden wail. Ede had obtained Billy's teddy-bear by pulling it forcibly from his arms, and on Billy's attempt to recover it, she had pushed him casually to the floor.
>
> 'Why, Ede!' cried her mother, repressing an inclination to laugh.

Now it is the mother who laughs – or almost laughs; 'thus' is tending into 'therefore', 'like this' moves towards 'consequently', the game of progression unfolds. In the course of the next half-page, Ede knocks Billy down again, and he bumps his head badly as he falls. His mother is outraged:

> 'Oh, *Billy*,' she cried, 'what a terrible bump! She ought to be spanked.'
>
> Edith, who had rushed immediately to her daughter, heard this remark, and her lips came tightly together.
>
> 'Why, Ede,' she whispered perfunctorily, 'you bad girl!'
>
> Ede put back her little head suddenly and laughed. It was a loud laugh, a triumphant laugh with victory in it and challenge and contempt. Unfortunately it was also an infectious laugh. Before her mother realized the delicacy of the situation, she too had laughed, an audible, distinct laugh not unlike the baby's, and partaking of the same overtones.

Now the laughter of the mother converges with the laughter of the child – and how dense and insistent is the laughter of that last paragraph: 'loud', 'triumphant', 'infectious', 'audible', 'distinct'. The rift between the neighbours is almost complete:

> . . . Mrs Markey lost her temper. 'I don't see anything funny about a child being hurt!' she said in a trembling voice.
>
> Little Ede meanwhile had been looking at her mother curiously. She noted that her own laugh had produced her mother's, and she wondered if the same cause would always produce the same effect. So she chose this moment to throw back her head and laugh again.
>
> To her mother the additional mirth added the final touch of hysteria to the situation. Pressing her handkerchief to her mouth she giggled irrepressibly. It was more than nervousness – she felt that in a peculiar way she was laughing with her child – they were laughing together.
>
> It was in a way defiance – those two against the world.

The game of progression is here complete; 'thus' has happened, and 'therefore' has taken its course. This is the logic of narrative, which is not the logic of the philosophical demonstrator, but a poetic necessity, conceived in reverie. That moment of defiance – 'those two against the world' – is anticipated two pages earlier, with 'Ede laughed'. At that point the laughing seems innocent and insignificant; readers themselves may even laugh, or at least smile, at the childish error that takes a teddy-bear for a bow-wow. But when Billy Markey laughs, we begin a meditation on laughter and antagonism; and presently the laughing is at the symbolic centre of the action. The word 'laugh/ed/ing' becomes a key term; it occurs thirteen times in the two pages of this episode, and every occurrence marks a significant point in the imaginative progression. One can speculate on what might have become of the story had little Ede 'uttered a happy cry' when she saw the 'bow-wow', and if Billy had merely 'chuckled' as he clasped it, while, a little later, Edith had politely 'hidden a grin'. The dream might have lost its creative shape, its progression broken, its marks of prediction lost, its outcome lost.

Stylistic devices – of vocabulary, of grammar, of punctuation and presentation, of textual cohesion – are moves in literary games; but the games are the products of dreaming, of trance, of states of reverie beyond the strict comprehension of the stylistic analyst. Herein lies the real problem, perhaps the absurdity, of the Creative Writing class. It is possible to teach composition, to teach it well and thoroughly, so thoroughly that the apprentice becomes adept in managing the tools and materials of a verbal trade. But can someone teach anyone the happy knack of daydreaming?; instruct them in the craft of reverie? That is something only to be done by Literature itself; it is reading that induces the mind-flooding trance. We are lost, we are absorbed, 'taken out of ourselves'; there is a vocabulary to describe the experience of reading, and it suggests that for the reader as much as for the writer 'I' is 'another'.

At the age of 90, Alice James, invalid sister of the philosopher William and the novelist Henry, wrote in her journal: 'What one reads, or rather all that comes to us is surely only of interest and value in proportion as we find ourselves therein, form given to what was vague, what slumbered stirred to life' (James 1964). The wording of that sentence comprehends the games of literature. In many 'slumbers' – meditations, reveries, daydreams – we are taken out of ourselves; but as we explore the forms in which dreams take substance, the conventions of verse or narrative, the devices of exposition and style, we are astonished and gratified to find ourselves again. The personality in the text is a brother or a sister; the place, a scene from the world we have always known and never known; and the progress of the story is a strange manifest of our own powers of understanding and prophecy. This is the *ludus litterarius*, the schooling or sporting of the imagination; and it is a touchingly serious business, even while it goes on being a game – a wonderful, engrossing game, a game of writing for reading's sake.

NOTES

1 See her poem entitled 'Poetry' (Moore 1951). Of poetry, she says:

not till the poets among us can be
'literalists of
the imagination' – above
insolence and triviality and can present

for inspection, imaginary gardens with real toads in
them, shall we have
it

She is talking of the possible incorporation of raw experience ('real toads') into the artifice ('imaginary gardens') of poetry.

2 The narratorial stance, and its attendant linguistic features, is extensively described in Simpson (1993), particularly in Chapter 3, 'Point of View in Narrative Fiction: a Modal Grammar'. Simpson distinguishes broadly between Category A narratives, 'those which are narrated in the first person by *a participating character* within the story, and Category B narratives, which 'possess a third-person narrative framework and are told by an invisible, disembodied, non-participating narrator'. There are further distinctions within each category, turning on the 'modality' of the narration, i.e. its temporal, spatial and attitudinal perspectives.

3 Some fictions, indeed, employ a diversity of 'character-narrators', proceeding from 'I' to 'I' as the chapters or sections of the book proceed; for instance, Wilkie Collins' *The Woman in White*, or, in a very different style, William Faulkner's *As I Lay Dying*.

4 What linguists call the *theme* is the first informative element in the sentence, e.g. the noun phrase 'The assessors' in 'The assessors have already been told most of this'. Given the normal word-order of the English declarative sentence, informational *theme* and grammatical *subject* frequently coincide. They do not coincide, however, in 'Most of this the assessors have already been told'. In that case, a new theme, represented by 'most of this', has been created by *fronting* a phrase, that is, by moving it out of its 'normal' position and placing it at the head of the sentence. On *theme* and related matters, see Quirk *et al.* (1985) and, more particularly, Halliday (1985).

5 The meaning is quite clear, and easily paraphrased: 'where they have left not a single stone unturned in their determination to get at the rabbit', or 'so determined were they to get at the rabbit', or 'such was their determination . . .', etc. The difficulty lies in identifying the role of *but*. It appears to conflate the meanings of *except*, as in 'Nothing would do but to pull down the wall', and the intensifier *so*, as in 'They left nothing standing, so keen were they to find the treasure'.

6 But it is easy for a modern reader, unconscious or oblivious of the fact that not until 1894 was the Greenwich meridian fixed (by international agreement) as a datum for navigators and cartographers, to misunderstand Gulliver's predicament and Swift's narrative cunning. Captain Gulliver could not give the longitude in terms that his readers might readily grasp. Fixing the longitude was a stubborn problem for navigators and for would-be rulers of the waves; in their edition of *Gulliver's Travels* (Swift 1967), Peter Dixon and John Chalker note that 'from 1714 onwards the British Government offered a series of rewards ranging from £10,000 to £20,000 for any generally practicable method of finding the longitude at sea'. ('The discovery of the *longitude*' is one

of the achievements Captain Gulliver supposes might have been his, if only he had been born a Struldbrugg, with the prospect of living forever – see the Laputa voyage.) For *observation* the mariner had his sextant, and by sighting on the sun at noon could calculate absolutely his 'southing', or latitude; but for longitude he would be dependent on *computation*, or the 'dead reckoning' furnished by compass, log and some kind of timepiece (Gulliver's pocket watch impresses the Lilliputians); and these would only provide him with a rough position in relationship to the last calculated 'easting' or 'westing'. Advances in chronometry, notably the work of William Harrison, contributed most to the solution of the problem; James Cook was able to make reliable charts because he had thoroughly accurate watches – the 'hi-tech' of his time. The story of the search for a reliable navigational chronometer is told by Dava Sobel in her book *Longitude* (Sobel 1996).

Robert Boyle (scientist and founder-member of the Royal Society) had urged mariners, in the cause of science, to provide accurate accounts of their voyages, including detailed descriptions of terrain and, of course, navigational data. Gulliver going north–south is thus the very model of a modern merchantman; Gulliver straying east–west is that plausible parabolist devised by Jonathan Swift.

REFERENCES

ARISTOTLE. *The Poetics*, trans. W. Hamilton Fyfe. London: Loeb Classical Library, 1926, repr. 1947.

BRONTË, EMILY. *Wuthering Heights*. Harmondsworth: Penguin English Library, 1965.

CONRAD, JOSEPH. *The Nigger of the Narcissus*. London: J.M. Dent, repr. 1957.

DICKENS, CHARLES. 'The Signalman', in Christopher Dolley (ed.) *The Penguin Book of English Short Stories*. Harmondsworth: Penguin Books, repr. 1975.

ELIOT, GEORGE. *The Mill on the Floss* London: Collins/Fontana, repr. 1979.

FITZGERALD, F. SCOTT. 'The Baby Party', in *Treasury of Great Short Stories*. London: Octopus Books, 1984.

FOWLES, JOHN. *The French Lieutenant's Woman*. London: Panther Books, repr. 1976.

FROST, ROBERT. 'Mending Wall', in *Robert Frost*, selected by himself and with an introduction by C. Day Lewis. Harmondsworth: Penguin Books, 1955.

HALLIDAY, M.A.K. *An Introduction to Functional Grammar*. London: Arnold, 1985.

JAMES, ALICE. *Diary of Alice James*. Harmondsworth: Penguin Books, 1964.
MOORE, MARIANNE. *Collected Poems*. London: Faber & Faber, 1951.
QUIRK, RANDOLPH *et al. A Comprehensive Grammar of the English Language*. London: Longman, 1985.
SIMPSON, PAUL. *Language, Ideology and Point of View*. London: Routledge, 1993.
SOBEL, DAVA. *Longitude*. London: Fourth Estate, 1996.
SWIFT, JONATHAN. *Gulliver's Travels and Selected Writings in Prose and Verse*, ed. John Hayward for the Nonesuch Press, Bloomsbury. New York: Random House, 1944.
SWIFT, JONATHAN. *Gulliver's Travels*, ed. Peter Dixon and John Chalker, with an Introduction by Michael Foot. Harmondsworth: Penguin English Library, 1967; p. 253 and n.
VIRGIL. *P. Vergili Maronis Opera*, ed. F.A. Hirtzel. Oxford: Clarendon Press, 1900.

Part II

The formation of the text

Four

Punctuating Gulliver

Readers in general have little interest in punctuation, as long as the constructions fall easily into place and make good grammatical sense, without ambiguities and false relationships. Whatever the mark, be it a comma, be it a semi-colon – or even a dash – the gentle reader, immersed in the story or the argument, gently reads on. Authors, by contrast, are anxiously convinced of the creative importance of their points and stops, and grow restive (as long as they are not already dead and beyond restiveness) if editorial critics assume the right to 'correct' their work. When Bacon, in his *Advancement of Learning* (Bacon 1605), spoke of 'the rash diligence' of '*Critiques*' ('rash diligence hath don gret preiudice', he said) he was referring to ignorant changes of wording, but he might just as well have been talking about incautious meddling with punctuation.

The older the author, it sometimes appears, the more the meddling. These old writers, the implication runs, hardly knew what they were doing, and if they were doing it now they would do it differently, so we had better do it for them. Punctuation thus gets 'modernised', along with spelling, with which it is paired, as something mechanical, conventional, peripheral to any matter of real literary concern; and in the course of modernisation something may be lost or distorted – something perhaps as little as a local emphasis, something possibly as large as a page-long rhetorical pattern.

For instance: I open at random a reputable anthology of eighteenth-century writing (the third volume of *The Oxford Anthology of English Literature*), which includes, from *Gulliver's Travels*, the account of the Voyage to the Houyhnhnms (Price 1973). My random impulse soon turns to regular pursuit, Swift carrying me with him in his usual compulsive way, until I come to a point in the narrative at which Gulliver, deep in customary trouble, is treed by a gang of howling Yahoos. The anthology text proceeds:

> In the midst of this distress, I observed them all to run away on a sudden as fast as they could, at which I ventured to leave the tree and pursue the road, wondering what it was that could put them to this fright. But looking on my left hand, I saw a horse walking softly in the field, which, my persecutors having sooner discovered, was the cause of their flight.

This is a sample of tacitly modernised punctuation. The passage is punctuated in almost exactly the same way in the Penguin Classics edition of the *Travels*, except that there is no comma after *which* in 'which, my persecutors having sooner discovered'. The Penguin Classics text is ostensibly based on Motte's edition of 1726 (Swift 1926); but its reading of this passage is not quite the same as that of Motte, or of his (arguably) more reliable successor, Faulkner (1735).[1] Faulkner gives us this:

> In the Midst of this Distress, I observed them all to run away on a sudden as fast as they could; at which I ventured to leave the Tree, and pursue the Road, wondering what it was that could put them into this Fright. But looking on my Left-Hand, I saw a Horse walking softly in the Field; which my Persecutors having sooner discovered, was the Cause of their Flight.

Motte has no semi-colon after *could*, but sets a full colon after *field*.[2] He and Faulkner are agreed on one significant rhetorical point, nullified in modernised versions. Where the modern punctuation reads 'a horse walking in a field, which [,] my persecutors having sooner discovered', the eighteenth-century editors crucially set a colon or a semi-colon, reading 'a horse walking in a field; which my persecutors having sooner discovered . . .'.

That is, it might seem, a trivial difference, but the trivial difference here makes *all* the difference. The pointing of the text after 'walking softly in the field' is particularly important, for the choice of a semi-colon or a comma must determine the antecedent scope of *which*. To what word, in the preceding text, does it refer? The reader will reject the immediate antecedent, 'field', and make a backward scan for the next most likely term. This, if *which* is preceded by a comma, would appear to be 'horse'. But a semi-colon invites a different or somewhat modified reading. Then, arguably, the scope of backward reference widens to 'a horse *walking softly in the field*', with the implication that it is the awareness of the horse's walking, its quiet, deliberate approach, that has precipitated the Yahoos' flight.

We must imagine that they notice the horse *because* of its movement. 'We must imagine', because the semi-colons ask us to imagine; to imagine Swift imagining Gulliver; to put ourselves, perception by perception, in Gulliver's place as he observes, and struggles to interpret, a remarkable train of events or, rather, a *series*, for there appears at first to be little of the connectedness that could be called a 'train'. The sequence, marked out in the narrative by semi-colons, is this: (1) Gulliver sees the Yahoos run away; (2) he gets down from the tree and (still looking at the Yahoos on his right) walks along the road; (3) he looks to the left, and sees – what? – a *horse*? Only a horse walking in a field? An ordinary horse, of the kind that grazes in ordinary fields all over this ordinary earth? We must taste Gulliver's perplexity. It is, of course, no ordinary quadruped, as readers are generally aware, since most know the story from previous reading or at the very least by hearsay; but perhaps our privileged knowledge does us a disservice in preventing us from sharing a moment of necessary surprise and bewilderment.

If we try to read without preconceptions, we have to perceive this episode as something out of the ordinary. In fact it has no precedent in any of Gulliver's earlier adventures. In Lilliput, in Brobdingnag, in Laputa, the mariner's first encounter after being cast ashore is with the principal occupants and governing intelligences of the land, and they are shaped, if not sized, in the image of human beings. Only in this final voyage is Gulliver's first encounter with human beings, or humanoids, who are not the dominant species. On this occasion it is the second encounter that introduces him to a representative of the ascendant race; but the encounter is with a horse, and at that moment he does not recognize it as more than a horse, or perceive its moral and intellectual superiority over the humanoids.

When, presently, it begins to dawn on him that these horses command some peculiar skills, he snatches at a wild conjecture, that they are magicians who have 'metamorphosed themselves upon some design' – that is, that they are humans in disguise, not horses at all.

It is the puzzling condition of being just a horse that is brought into focus, in the texts of 1726 and 1735, by a colon or semi-colon; and it is the progressive puzzlement, or graduated predicament, of the hapless Gulliver that is expressed, step-wise, through a series of *cola* – meaning stretches of text bounded by semi-colons or a full stop. Commas do not work to the same purpose.

This example may allow us to suppose that Swift probably knew what he was about, and that if he wrote a semi-colon, a semi-colon was what he meant, and not a comma. Understanding the punctuation, with a decent respect for the author's intention, is part of the business of decoding the text. But such 'decoding' must often be an intuitive procedure, and in its own way a creative act not incontrovertibly supported by rules and categorical distinctions. Rules are in any case hard to come by in the writings of a secretive author like Swift, who was in the habit of smuggling his text to the publisher and thereafter keeping his distance, with the result that the textual history of *Gulliver's Travels* is obscure and confused.[3] We know that Swift denounced Motte for liberties taken with the text, and gave to Faulkner something as close to approval and consent as might be expected from an author at once so fastidious and so evasive. It seems reasonable, consequently, to accept the Faulkner version, *including the punctuation*, as consistently representing Swift's intention; and that acceptance governs the suppositions made hereafter concerning the punctuational style of the *Travels*.

The 1735 text suggests that Swift combines or conflates two types of punctuation, the one representing current orthographical convention, the other some pattern, or 'strategy' in rhetoric. His general conventions – his house style, as it were – are not desperately unmodern, though some practices might now invite a copy-editor's pencil. For example, he regularly sets a comma between a reporting verb ('say', 'tell', 'object', 'complain', 'protest', 'allege', etc.) and a following *that*-clause; and when the subject of a sentence is a complex noun phrase, he writes a comma between the noun phrase and the following verb, e.g.: 'The Empire of *Blefuscu*, is an Island situated to the North North-East Side of *Lilliput*.'

Some of his punctuations read ambivalently, suggesting that the conventional partitioning of the sentence is accompanied by the registration of an emphasis or a rhetorical gesture. Certain conjunctions and connectives – for instance, *and*, *but*, *although*, *for*, *wherein*, *whereupon*, *which*, *where*, *when* – are preceded either by a comma or, yet more often it seems, by a semi-colon marking the rhetorical status of the following phrase or clause. The example of the horse in the field (see above) brings out a meaningful distinction between *comma + which* and *semi-colon + which* in a particular narrative context. The conjunction *for* is very frequently preceded by a colon or semi-colon (and occasionally followed by a comma), suggesting, in context, the making of an inference or the presentation of an argument. *When* takes a comma as a usual mark of the subordinate temporal clause, but may be coloned, with the emphatic narrative implication of 'all of a sudden' or 'lo and behold':

> I walked a while among the Rocks, the Sky was perfectly clear, and the Sun so hot, that I was forced to turn my face from it: When all on a Sudden it became obscured, as I thought, in a Manner very different from what happens by the Interposition of a Cloud.

This is an example of what might be called the 'marked conjunct' punctuation, of which Gulliver supplies numerous examples. Here the conjunction is further marked by the capital *w* in 'When'.[4]

In such instances there is a merging of the punctuation that marks out the syntax of the sentence and a punctuation for rhetorical effect, the pointing that warns the reader, 'pause!', 'see here!', 'reflect on this'. There is, let us say, a grammatical level and a level of rhetoric or demonstration. Taken at the purely grammatical level, Swift's punctuation may have some technical interest for the student of English orthography. At the rhetorical/demonstrative level the interest broadens considerably. Gulliverian stylistics reflect the classic system that defines units of compositional structure in a hierarchy of *periods* (whole sentences), *cola* (distinct, non-subordinate 'sentential' constituents building up into periods) and *commata* (comma-linked constructions forming periods or cola).[5] Swift adapts this system to the many varieties of composition that occur in *Gulliver's Travels* – which is indeed a book of great stylistic variety, highly sophisticated in its changes of pace and demeanour. It is a cunningly-told tale.

Gulliver, the teller, would have us believe that his account is the work of a plain unvarnished sea-captain and part-time semi-varnished surgeon, setting down the words as well as his awkward honesty knows how, without affectation or pretension. If we take Gulliver's word for it, then we take it that *Gulliver's Travels* is stylistically uniform from start to finish. But of course it is not.

The book is a compendium of stylistic types. There are narrations; there are descriptions and factual reports of various kinds; there are representations of speech; there are passages of exposition and propositional argument, presenting trains of reasoning; there are furiously sardonic tirades; there are apophthegms, maxims and one-liners. Above all, there are parodies. These, in places, follow each other so engagingly that it sometimes seems that Gulliver – or Swift manipulating Gulliver – can never write unparodically.

Gulliver, at the behest of his literary maker, is even obliged to parody himself: his manic enthusiasm for facts and figures (e.g. he measures Brobdingnagian hailstones), his prodigious talent for applied linguistics (e.g. he perceives at once that the Houyhnhnm language is more adaptable than Chinese to alphabetic representation) and his punctilious commendations of fellow mariners, as though they were so many bishops or Deans of Chapters, are among the running jokes of the book. There are parodies of nautical language (for example, the account of the storm-beset manoeuvres at the beginning of the Brobdingnag voyage, a passage almost impossible to reduce to intelligibility); there are parodies of legal language, as in the Lilliputian *Articles of Impeachment against Quinbus Flestrin*; there are parodies of scientists' and mathematicians' prose, a particularly pleasant example being the account, in the Laputa voyage, of the astronomers' observations of Martian satellites:

> They have likewise discovered two lesser stars, or *satellites*, which revolve about Mars, whereof the innermost is distant from the centre of the primary planet exactly three of his diameters, and the outermost five; the former revolves in the space of ten hours, the latter in twenty-one and a half; so that the squares of their periodical times are very near in the same proportion with the cubes of their distance from the centre of Mars, which evidently shows them to be governed by the same law of gravitation, that influences the other heavenly bodies.

'Evidently' (= 'quite obviously') is a wicked touch, the sort of wild invention, founded in sober truth, that makes lesser humorists groan with envy.

The management of these diverse styles is seen in some contrastive punctuational options; in particular, there is a broad distinction, most clearly evident in the Faulkner text, between punctuating by *cola* (colons and semi-colons) and punctuating by *commata* (commas dividing phrases and clauses). In narrative episodes, for example, Swift often marshals the progress of the tale by *cola*, almost abruptly, the punctuation sometimes intruding in unexpected, 'ungrammatical' positions. There is a typical episode of bustling comedy in the second voyage, in which he describes the antics of an inquisitive Brobdingnagian monkey, who finds the box in which the manikin Gulliver is housed. The Faulkner (1735) text reads:

> I retreated to the farther Corner of my Room, or Box; but the Monkey looking in at every Side, put me into such a Fright, that I wanted Presence of Mind to conceal myself under the Bed, as I might easily have done. After some time spent in peeping, grinning and chattering, he at last espyed me; and reaching one of his Paws in at the Door, as a Cat does when she plays with a Mouse, although I often shifted Place to avoid him; he at length seized the Lappet of my Coat (which being made of that Country Silk, was very thick and strong) and dragged me out. He took me up in his right Fore-foot, and held me as a Nurse doth a Child she is going to suckle; just as I have seen the same Sort of Creature do with a Kitten in *Europe*: And when I offered to struggle, he squeezed me so hard, that I thought it more prudent to submit. I have good Reason to believe that he took me for a young one of his own Species, by his often stroaking my Face very gently with his other Paw. In these Diversions he was interrupted by a Noise at the Closet Door, as if some Body were opening it; whereupon he suddenly leaped up to the Window at which he had come in, and thence upon the Leads and Gutters, walking upon three Legs, and holding me in the fourth, till he clambered up to a Roof that was next to ours. I heard *Glumdalclitch* give a Shriek at the Moment he was carrying me out. The poor Girl was almost distracted: That Quarter of the Palace was all in an Uproar; the Servants ran for Ladders; the Monkey was seen by Hundreds in the Court, sitting upon the Ridge of a Building, holding me like a Baby on one side of his Chaps, and patting me when I would not eat; whereat many of the Rabble below could not forbear laughing; neither do I think they justly ought to be blamed; for without Question, the Sight was ridiculous enough to every Body but my self. Some of the People threw up Stones, hoping to drive the Monkey down; but this was strictly forbidden, or else very probably my Brains had been dashed out.

There is a striking contrast between the versions of this passage presented by Faulkner on the one hand, and on the other by Motte and the Penguin Classics editors. In the early part of the extract, Motte and the moderns punctuate by *commata* rather than by *cola*. Their version reads:

I retreated to the farther corner of my room, or box, but the monkey, looking in at every side, put me into such a fright, that I wanted presence of mind to conceal myself under the bed, as I might easily have done. After some time spent in peeping, grinning, and chattering, he at last espied me, and reaching one of his paws in at the door, as a cat does when she plays with a mouse, although I often shifted place to avoid him, he at length seized the lappet of my coat (which being made of that country silk, was very thick and strong) and dragged me out.

To modern eyes, this reads very fluently. It sits tidily on the page, linking the subordinate clauses with commas, keeping up the pace of the narrative, not interrupting it at any awkward or seemingly irrational junction. Faulkner's version, by contrast, seems full of stops and starts from beginning to end, a nervous hopping from moment to moment, act to act. Yet that in itself supports the intuition that Faulkner's version lies nearer to what Swift intended.

The tale of the Brobdingnagian monkey will serve as well as any, in all of the *Travels*, as an instance of Swift's style of narration by *cola*. In the passage quoted, there are eight sentences (crudely definable as grammatically independent units beginning with a capital letter and ending with a full stop). Two are simple constructions not partitioned into *cola*. In the remainder, however, the narration marches from colon to colon, and there are twenty-one *cola* in all. Here as in other narrative passages, the longer *cola* are sectioned into *commata*, coordinated or dependent strings, often of non-finite (participial) clauses. The construction may be delineated thus (the indentations marked > represent phases of dependency):

The Monkey was seen by Hundreds in the Court,
    > sitting upon the Ridge of a Building,
    > holding me like a baby in one of his Fore-paws,
    > and feeding me with the other,
        > by cramming into my mouth some victuals

> he had squeezed out of a Bag on one side of his Chops,
> and patting me when I would not eat

In this way, Swift creates a depth of commentary and amplification, a kind of 'vertical' procedure, within the 'horizontal' progression from stage to stage of the story. The latter is powerfully illustrated by the dramatic climax of the narration, from 'The poor Girl was almost distracted'. Here the colon-governed movement clearly reflects an intention to 'fix' each phase in the telling of a vivid tale, like a film camera moving from 'shot' to 'shot': the nurse's horror; the servants running; the monkey on the roof ridge; the laughing crowd below.

In a somewhat different narrative style, perhaps less common than the patterned progression of *commata* within *cola*, Gulliver punctuates first with the comma and then, by gradations, with the semi-colon. Thus he recalls the practical details of his stranding on the shores of Laputa:

This Island was at a greater Distance than I expected, and I did not reach it in less than five Hours. I encompassed it almost round before I could find a convenient Place to land in, which was a small Creek, about three Times the Wideness of my Canoe. I found the Island to be all rocky, only a little intermingled with Tufts of Grass, and sweet smelling Herbs. I took out my small Provisions, and after having refreshed myself, I secured the Remainder in a Cave, whereof there were great Numbers. I gathered plenty of Eggs upon the Rocks, and got a Quantity of dry Sea-weed, and parched Grass, which I designed to kindle the next Day, and roast my Eggs as well as I could. (For I had about me my Flint, Steel, Match, and Burning-glass.) I lay all night in the Cave where I had lodged my Provisions. My Bed was the same dry Grass and Sea-weed which I intended for Fewel.

That is Gulliver reporting in his downright seamanly way. Each sentence is a little report in itself, and most begin with *I*, (apart from one that begins *my*.) In each, the governing mark of punctuation is the comma. It is very businesslike and objective. But then reflectiveness begins to creep in, with intermittent semi-colons:

I slept very little; for the Disquiets of my Mind prevailed over my Wearyness, and kept me awake. I considered how impossible it was to preserve my Life, in so desolate a Place; and how miserable

> my End must be. Yet I found myself so listless and desponding, that I had not the Heart to rise; and before I could get Spirits enough to creep out of my Cave, the Day was far advanced.

This ruminative slowing of the narrative is bringing us towards the big pause, the juncture at which Gulliver for a moment leaves his incessant 'I' and turns his attention to something else:

> I walked awhile among the Rocks, the Sky was perfectly clear, and the Sun so hot, that I was forced to turn my Face from it: When all on a Sudden it became obscured, as I thought, in a Manner very different from what happens by the Interposition of a Cloud.

'When all on a Sudden' – there it is, the marked conjunct (see p. 69 above), marked by a full colon. We have come to this point via a representation, graded through different styles of punctuation, of various Gulliverian postures: 'what I did', 'what I thought and felt' and finally 'what happened next'.

Long passages of *commata* uncontrolled by intervening semi-colons, or long sequences of simple sentences, are comparatively rare in the *Travels*. They occur now and then in episodes of 'objective' reporting, like the description, quoted above, of Gulliver's first actions and experiences on the island of Laputa; in accounts of structures and practical devices, such as the description of the machine that carries the recumbent Gulliver into Mindendo (Lilliput, Chapter 1); and also in some parodic contexts, such as the 'scientific' description of the Floating Island (in Chapter 3 of the Laputa voyage), which proceeds mainly by comma-connection, like some laboratory report, until the moment comes for a burlesque of the the kind of mathematical demonstration familiar to anyone whose schooldays have embraced the ritual of letting *x* equal *y*. Then once again the semi-colon gravely rules (the text quoted is, as usual, Faulkner's; Motte proceeds by commas):

> To explain the Manner of its Progess, let *A B* represent a Line drawn cross the Dominions of *Balnibarbi*; let the Line *c d* represent the Load-stone, of which let *d* be the repelling End and *c* the attracting End, the Island being over *C*; let the Stone be placed in the Position *c d* with its repelling End downwards; then the Island will be driven obliquely towards *D*.

Such is the style of the Royal Society geometer presenting his propositions and proofs; the *cola* mark out stages of the solemn demonstration.

This mathematical style has a mimetic counterpart in the frequent pastiches of a philosophical style, to which Gulliver resorts when he is expounding an argument or reporting a train of reasoning. Key words *for, but, because, therefore* and *which* are always preceded by a colon or semi-colon. A typical instance of the method is his examination of the Lilliputians' criteria of fitness for public office:

> In chusing Persons for all Employments, they have more Regard to good Morals than to great Abilities: For, since Government is necessary to Mankind, they believe that the common Size of human Understandings, is fitted to some Station or other; and that Providence never intended to make the Management of publick Affairs a Mystery, to be comprehended only by a few Persons of sublime Genius, of which there seldom are three born in an Age: But, they suppose Truth, Justice, Temperance, and the like, to be in every Man's Power; the Practice of which Virtues, assisted by Experience and a good Intention, would qualify any Man for the Service of his Country, except where a Course of Study is required.

There is a parodic impulse here, a straightfaced performance of a scholastic exercise, the expansion of a rhetorical *topos*. The punctuation by *cola* marks the phasing of an exposition which reads as follows:

- *Topic*: they have more regard to good morals than to great abilities:
- *Argument*: For, since Government is necessary to mankind, they believe that the common Size of human Understandings, is fitted to some Station or other;
- *Development*: and that Providence never intended to make the Management of publick affairs a Mystery, . . . , etc.;
- *Topic resumed*: But, they suppose Truth, Justice, Temperance, and the like, to be in every Man's Power;
- *Conclusion*: the Practice of which Virtues . . . would qualify any Man for the Service of his Country, . . . , etc.

Procedures of this kind, in the fashion of the philosophical demonstrator, occur throughout the *Travels*, whenever Gulliver has occasion to expound the practices, beliefs and ideologies of the strangers of whom he is the captive observer.

Here is a more elaborate example from the Lilliput voyage, a disquisition on the rearing of children:

> Their Notions relating to the Duties of Parents and Children differ extremely from ours. For, since the Conjunction of Male and Female is founded upon the great Law of Nature, in order to propagate and continue the Species; the *Lilliputians* will needs have it, that Men and Women are joined together like other Animals, by the Motives of Concupiscence; and that their Tenderness towards their Young, proceedeth from the like natural Principle: For which Reason they will never allow, that a Child is under any Obligation to his Father for begetting him, or to his Mother for bringing him into the World; which, considering the Miseries of human Life, was neither a Benefit in itself, nor intended so by his Parents, whose Thoughts in their Love-encounters were otherwise employed. Upon these, and the like Reasonings, their Opinion is, that Parents are the last of all others to be trusted with the Education of their own Children: And therefore they have in every Town publick Nurseries, where all Parents, except Cottagers and Labourers, are obliged to send their Infants of both Sexes to be reared and educated when they come to the Age of twenty Moons; at which Time they are supposed to have some Rudiments of Docility.

In such passages, the *cola* presenting reasons or inferences will often begin with a capital letter: so here, 'For which Reason', 'And therefore they have in every Town'. There is in this example a fairly long sentence, or *period*, beginning 'For, since the Conjunction of Male and Female' and ending 'were otherwise employed'. This is a stretch of some 115 words, but it reads quite easily because the organisation by *cola* represents the structuring of point-by-point argument, thus:

'For,'	*introduces*
'since . . . Species;'	*premise*
'the *Lilliputians* . . . Concupiscence;'	*inference*
'and . . . natural Principle:'	*linked inference*
'For which Reason . . . World;'	*major conclusion*
'which . . . employed'	*coda*

The Penguin text, following Motte, prints a comma rather than an apparently ungrammatical (or asyntactic) semi-colon after 'species'; but to do this is to misunderstand Swift's miming of a scholastic procedure. The semi-colon is necessary because it marks a stage in the methodical representation of an argument, the completed statement of its premise.[6]

Gulliver's presentation of long speeches also goes, as a rule, by *cola*. In the *Travels* generally, there are few examples of direct speech. Mostly, speeches are indirect (in the form 'he observed that . . .' or rather 'he observed, that . . .'), and after the first clause following the reporting verb, the *that*-clauses are separated by colons, semicolons or even by full stops when the report goes on across sentence boundaries. A typical example is this reporting of one of the speakers in the Lilliputian Council, when Gulliver's alleged treason is debated:

> *Bolgolam*, the Admiral, could not preserve his Temper; but rising up in Fury, said, he wondered how the Secretary durst presume to give his Opinion for preserving the Life of a Traytour: That the Services you had performed, were, by all true Reasons of State, the great Aggravation of your Crimes; that you, who were able to extinguish the Fire, by discharge of Urine in her Majesty's Apartment (which he mentioned with Horror) might, at another Time, raise an Inundation by the same Means, to drown the whole Palace; and the same Strength which enabled you to bring over the Enemy's Fleet, might serve, upon the first Discontent, to carry it back: That he had good Reasons to think you were a *Big-Endian* in your Heart; and as Treason begins in the Heart before it begins in Overt-Acts; so he accused you as a Traytour on that Account, and therefore insisted you should be put to Death.

The semi-colons and colons are equivalent to marks of enumeration: 'He said, (1), (2), (3), etc.' Only in one instance is a colon-mark used in another way, and that is at the end of the passage, in the *as . . . so* construction 'as Treason begins in the Heart . . . ; so he accused you as a Traytour . . . etc.'. There, Swift's punctuation apparently requires a pause, a more or less emphatic balancing or 'hefting' of the two halves of the construction, after the manner of an orator. (But here again Faulkner differs from Motte, who separates the two halves of the proposition with a comma).

One of the most engaging speakers in the *Travels* is the King of Brobdingnag – a personage who might well qualify for the title of hero, if there were such a thing in Gulliver's philosophy – and he figures more than once in direct speech. There is, for example, this truly majestic dismissal of Western civilization in all its pretensions. Gulliver is crouching in the King's hand, like a pet mouse:

> Then turning to his first Minister, who waited behind him with a white Staff, near as tall as the Mainmast of the *Royal Sovereign*, he observed how contemptible a thing was Grandeur, which could be mimicked by such diminutive Insects as I: And yet, said he, I dare engage, those Creatures have their Titles and Distinctions of Honour; they contrive little Nests and Burrows, that they call Houses and Cities; they make a Figure in Dress and Equipage; they love, they fight, they dispute, they cheat, they betray. And thus he continued on, while my Colour came and went several Times, with Indignation to hear our noble Country, the Mistress of Arts and Arms, the Scourge of *France*, the Arbitress of *Europe*, the Seat of Virtue, Piety, Honour and Truth, the Pride and Envy of the World, so contemptuously treated.

The colons pace out the King's remarks in a kind of *andante nobile*, until the speech comes to a cadence in the *commata* of 'they love, they fight, they dispute, they cheat, they betray'.

Gulliver's response to this stately pronouncement is not spoken aloud, but nevertheless conveys the illusion of vehement speech, in its angry listing of 'our noble Country, the Mistress of Arts and Arms, the Scourge of *France*', etc. The contrast of styles, between the measured *cola* of the King's talk and the tumbling *commata* of Gulliver's reaction, suggests that the punctuation has value here almost as a means of characterisation: the King self-possessed, dignified, ironic; Gulliver indignant, earnest, ruffled. And indeed, Gulliver resorts to the asyndetic list, or comma-controlled tirade, whenever feelings – his own, or those of another character – get the better of calm objectivity. When the King of Brobdingnag learns something of the history of England in the seventeenth century, he is so scandalised as to lose, temporarily, his wonted self-possession:

> He was perfectly astonished with the historical Account I gave him of our Affairs during the last Century; protesting that it was only an Heap of Conspiracies, Rebellions, Banishments; the very worst Effects that Avarice, Faction, Hypocrisy, Perfidiousness, Cruelty, Rage, Madness, Hatred, Envy, Lust, Malice, and Ambition could produce.

Gulliver expresses to another monarch, the King of Laputa, his own judgement on the natives of *Tribnia* and *Langden* (anagrammatically, 'Britain' and 'England'):

> I told him, that in the Kingdom of *Tribnia*, by the Natives called *Langden*, where I had long sojourned, the Bulk of the People consisted wholly of Discoverers, Witnesses, Informers, Accusers, Prosecutors, Evidencers, Swearers; together with their several subservient and subaltern Instruments; all under the Colours, the Conduct, and pay of Ministers and their Deputies.

The impulse to splenetic diatribe is most marked in the account of the Houyhnhnm voyage, and in the concluding pages of the *Travels*, where Gulliver, in crackpot despair of humanity, breaks into bitterly ironic tirades. He is, he tells us towards the close, almost reconciled to the Yahoo race, except on one point:

> I am not in the least provoked at the Sight of a Lawyer, a Pickpocket, a Colonel, a Fool, a Lord, a Gamester, a Politician, a Whoremunger, a Physician, an Evidence, a Suborner, an Attorney, a Traytor, or the like: This is all according to the due Course of Things: But when I behold a lump of Deformity, and Diseases both in Body and Mind, smitten with *Pride*, it immediately breaks all the measures of my Patience; neither shall I be ever able to comprehend how such an Animal and such a Vice could tally together.

'Tallying together' – or not tallying together – is one of the interesting stylistic features of the first *colon* in this period. We might expect an asyndetic series – a list – to be a gradation of similar or related items; but here a lawyer jostles by a pickpocket, a whoremonger by a physician, an attorney by a traitor, bad and good, respectable and culpable, indifferently and ironically mixed, as though Gulliver/Swift were set on rejecting all human society in one undifferentiated lump.

The cascading energy of these outbursts represents exactly what the rhetorician Demetrius called the **deinos charakter**, the 'forceful style' (Demetrius 1965: 303). As Demetrius describes it, the **deinos** is the counterpart of the **megaloprepes**, the dignified periodic style. Gulliver in his furious irony manages to combine both. The most impressively sustained piece of tirading in the *Travels*, in the tenth chapter of the Houyhnhnms adventure, amasses tirade upon tirade, list upon list, within a framework of carefully measured *cola*. Gulliver proclaims his happiness among the horses in terms that damn all humans:

> I wanted no Fence against Fraud or Oppression: Here was neither Physician to destroy my Body, nor Lawyer to ruin my Fortune: No Informer to watch my Words and Actions, or forge Accusations against me for Hire: Here were no Gibers, Censurers, Backbiters, Pick-pockets, Highwaymen, House-breakers, Attorneys, Bawds, Buffoons, Gamesters, Politicians, Wits, Spleneticks, tedious Talkers, Controversists, Ravishers, Murderers, Robbers, Virtuoso's; no Leaders or Followers of Party and Faction; no Encouragers to Vice, by Seducement or Examples: No Dungeon, Axes, Gibbets, Whipping posts, or Pillories; No cheating Shop-keepers or Mechanicks; No Pride, Vanity or Affectation; No Fops, Bullies, Drunkards, strolling Whores, or Poxes: No ranting, lewd, expensive Wives: No stupid, proud Pedants: No importunate, over-bearing, quarrelsome, noisy, roaring, empty, conceited, swearing Companions: No Scoundrels raised from the Dust upon the Merit of their Vices; or Nobility thrown into it on account of their Virtues: No Lords, Fidlers, Judges or Dancing-Masters.

That is arguably the climax of the *Travels*, the destination to which all Gulliver's traipsings have been leading. He is at last pleased with what he finds; and his pleasure is expressed in a torrent of negatives. His greatest happiness is not in where he is, so much as in where he is not: not in England, not in vicious London, here catalogued with all its blemishes, bores, buffoons and bounders.

The voice of Gulliver at this point mingles with that of Jonathan Swift, the Swift of the polemic essays, the Swift who had some reason to fear informers, the known eccentric who was morosely capable of ranking tedious talkers alongside ravishers and murderers. There are two personalities in the *Travels*, Lemuel and Jonathan, and the reader may have some difficulty at times in knowing them apart, especially when Gulliver sails home to make his uneasy, sardonic peace with sinful, smelly humanity. Lemuel's conclusion seems to coincide with Jonathan's. But we are entitled to question 'seems'; to ask ourselves whether, after all, Gulliver's easy melancholy, his graceless rejection of human love and friendship, his belief that there is better company in the stable than in the street, are indeed the true tenets of his shrewd, humorous, philanthropic, pious creator – for on a good day Jonathan Swift could be all of those things, and we have the *Journal to Stella* to prove it.

Lemuel Gulliver is at the end an embittered and charmless man, but the writer who conceived him and sent him on his travels is full of fun, of creative zest, of discernible, palpable *relish* for the engrossing pantomime of writing. Creating Gulliver allows Swift to play so many roles: navigator, constructor, lawyer, improviser, philosopher, scientist, reporter, orator, victim – and for each of these there is a style to imitate or invent, to the undoubted enjoyment of the inventor. The punctuation is so often the clue to this stylistic variation; perhaps not important in itself, but important for what it reveals. To follow a modern impulse, rejecting or smoothing away what look like obstacles to fluent reading, is to suppress, or at least to disguise, the amazing verve of this classic text.

Is 'verve' too careless, too carefree a word for an author as serious as Swift? No one needs to be reminded that Gulliver's travels obliquely record Swift's travails, his disgust with the inescapable flesh, his disappointment with a race that, given the chance to behave well, will commonly choose to behave badly. But perhaps we can make too much of the philosopher's pessimism, turning our eyes and minds away from the happiness of the writer, which lasts as long as the writing lasts, a happiness in the turn of a phrase, a cadence, the balance of a sentence, seeing it come right on the page, getting it in due form and order, down to the last full stop. Though everything that follows may be a burden and a disappointment, there is always that moment of joy.

NOTES

1 In their note on the complicated history of Swift's text (Swift 1967), Peter Dixon and John Chalker claim that their punctuation 'follows, as closely as is practicable, that of 1726' (i.e. of Motte's edition). What is meant by 'practicable' is not made clear; possibly we are to infer 'reconcilable with modern practice'. Dixon and Chalker are of the opinion that 'Swift would not have concerned himself with small details of style and presentation', and attribute to Faulkner a concern to 'impose upon the whole work a degree of formality and consistency which Swift's manuscript is unlikely to have possessed'. 'Unlikely' in some respects, perhaps; but in punctuation I am convinced that Swift is quite consistent, and I do not believe that Faulkner imposed this consistency on him.

2 Whatever the intentions of authors may have been, it is not always possible to say with confidence how *printers* in the seventeenth and eighteenth century interpreted the difference between colon and semi-colon, or to what extent the insertion of one mark or another depended on the availability of type in the setter's tray. It might be argued that from the printer's point of view the colon and the semi-colon were more or less equivalent, as demarcations of the author's *cola*.

3 The confusions are admirably described in Harold Williams' introduction to his facsimile of the 1726 edition (Swift 1926). Williams' account leads me to place more reliance on Faulkner than on Motte; but I acknowledge that there will always be room for doubt and speculation. Perhaps my notions of Gulliverian style are derived from the daily practice of some fastidious Irish typesetter. My access to Faulkner's text is through John Hayward's *Swift; Gulliver's Travels and Selected Writings in Prose and Verse* (Swift 1944). Hayward, coming out strongly for Faulkner, says: 'It is now known that Swift, though originally antagonistic to Faulkner's proposal (to print the *Travels*) eventually submitted to it and was persuaded to look over the sheets of the first four volumes.' Further: 'While it is true that the text of the first edition has a sentimental interest as the original version given to the world, it is obvious that Faulkner's revision follows more closely Swift's MS.'

4 Conjuncts, in the words of Quirk *et al.* (1985), 'have the function of conjoining independent units rather than one of contributing another facet of information to a single integrated unit'. The word *when* in the sentence 'I bought it when I went to America' is not a conjunct; it is a *conjunction*, 'contributing another facet of information to a single integrated unit'. But in 'I listened with heart fit to break. When glided in Porphyria' (Browning), it becomes a conjunct, 'conjoining independent units'. So also in Gulliver's description, 'I was forced to turn my face from it; When all on a Sudden, etc.'. The conjunct there is 'marked', or 'emphasised', in part by the capital letter, and in part by the phrase 'all on a Sudden'.

5 See, for example, the discussion of 'period', 'colon' and 'comma' in the *Rhetorica ad Herennium* (Caplan 1954). In terms of classical rhetoric, the English sentence 'London, with all its wealth and magnificence, lay before Juan's gaze; looking at it, he found it inspiring; then he was set upon by a gang of robbers', is a *period* consisting of three *cola* (marked by the semi-colons), the first and second of which are divided into *commata* (indicated by the commas).

6 Perhaps here, and possibly elsewhere, I am merely rationalising the working practices of my 'fastidious Irish typesetter' (see note 4 above); but if that were so, he would have to be a typesetter with some training in the principles of classical rhetoric. On the whole, it seems more likely that Swift supplied the punctuation that displays the *taxis* of his arguments.

REFERENCES

BACON, FRANCIS. *The Two Bookes of FRANCIS BACON. Of the proficience and aduancement of Learning, diuine and humane.* London, 1605; II, 68–9.

CAPLAN, H. (ed. and transl.). *Rhetorica ad Herennium.* London: Loeb Classical Library, 1954; IV.ix.

DEMETRIUS [of Phalerum]. *On Style*, ed. and transl. W. Rhys Roberts. London: Loeb Classical Library, repr. 1965.

PRICE, MARTIN (ed.). *The Restoration and the Eighteenth Century*, in Frank Kermode and John Hollander (general eds), *The Oxford Anthology of English Literature*, 6 vols, paperback. New York: Oxford University Press, 1973.

QUIRK, RANDOLPH *et al. A Comprehensive Grammar of the English Language.* London: Longman, 1985; ch. 8.134.

SWIFT, JONATHAN. *Gulliver's Travels*, ed. Peter Dixon and John Chalker, with an Introduction by Michael Foot. Harmondsworth: Penguin English Library, 1967; p. 255 and n.

SWIFT, JONATHAN. *Gulliver's Travels and Selected Writings in Prose and Verse.* ed. John Hayward, for the Nonesuch Press, Bloomsbury. New York: Random House, 1944.

SWIFT, JONATHAN. *Gulliver's Travels*, ed. Harold Williams, facsimile of 1726 (Motte's) edn. London: OUP, First Edition Club, 1926.

Five

Gray's grammar: or the intricacy of simple music

I sit at the piano, doing my wretchedly inadequate best to urge eight fingers and two thumbs through the fourth counterpoint in J.S. Bach's *Die Kunst der Fuge*. An ordinarily competent, well-coordinated keyboard player would have no difficulty in realising the eloquent restlessness of this music, making its phrases sound out in seamless progressions, but I cannot get through half a dozen bars at a time without stumbling. I am simply not equal to saying what Bach tells me to say. Yet even in my incompetence I appreciate the design of the music, and can see how its repeated combinations and permutations of notes rehearse a message that appeals to the heart as well to the head. This, evidently, is what musicians mean when they talk about the 'vocabulary' or even the 'syntax' of a musical composition. There is a basic grammar out of which the intricate discursive pattern of the whole fugue is generated.

I have no training in the strict terms of musical analysis, but in the general, impressionistic, way of an amateur I think I can identify the elements or constituents of Bach's fugal grammar. This intricate music has simple foundations. Firstly, I perceive a kind of thematic sentence, the 'first subject' of the fugue, a variant of the theme that opens each of the fifteen fugues of *Die Kunst*. Then there comes a little hovering figure, a motif of four quavers half-circling upon itself in repetitive, irresolute impulses. This short motif is followed by an even briefer phrase, a sequence of two notes, a crotchet followed by a minim, in an interval of a falling third. That two-note utterance almost inevitably suggests to the listener/player the notion of 'calling' or 'appealing', and it is this repeated quasi-vocal mannerism, together with the restless movement of the quaver-figure, that colours the whole piece with a feeling of distraction and anxiety.

These are the quite simple means that provide for an evolving compositional structure – the evolution that soon grows too tricky for my Sunday-afternoon fingers. The composition is 138 bars long, but its basic material, in the shape of the ground theme or first subject, the hovering figure and the calling figure, is stated within the first twenty bars. For the 118 or so bars that remain, Bach displays his customary ingenuity – a passionate ingenuity of technique. The form of the fugue requires four 'voices'; each in turn takes up the primary figures, and each in turn accompanies, counters and mimics the others in the intricate patterns of a period style, a demonstration of contrapuntal skill which, in this particular instance, flowers into a poem of the pensive temperament. This is, typically, the language of the baroque. Simple, compositional material is progressively elaborated into an intensity of expression that some will commend for its warm humanity and others might dismiss as frigid rhetoric. Baroque art has that effect. Few phenomena lend more substance to the cliché that there is no accounting for tastes.

A taste for the baroque, in music, in architecture or in literary art, certainly involves a taste for rhetoric and an understanding of its functions; which implies a taste for style at its most demonstrative, a taste for artifice and performance, which further includes, odd though the expression may sound, an appetite for syntax. All great baroque performances invite the audience to predict the turning of the long sentence, the homing of the sinuous paragraph. We hear this in Bach's counterpoints; in poetry, we see it fixed on the page. I am thinking of an English poem almost contemporary with the music of *Die Kunst der Fuge*: Thomas Gray's *Elegy written in a Country Churchyard*. (The *Elegy* was published, after some years in the making, in 1751; *Die Kunst* in 1752, two years after Bach's death.) Gray's poem is another example of simple music with intricate fingering, and its structure is worth a little study.

In modern assessments of eighteenth-century art, the *Elegy* appears to be a station on the way to the Romantics.[1] It is a well-bred poem, but its heart is rightly in tune with Nature and the Common Man. Its style is quietly impeccable. Critics have praised its 'evenness of tone', its 'placid melancholy', its 'noble and finished transparency'. The general view is of a typical genre-piece (the graveyard genre), night-thoughtful and low-keyed – solace for the solitary and self-communing. And yet that view (if I have described it correctly) is quite at odds with the artifice and style of a poem in the grand epideictic manner,[2] a funeral address that misses no device of oratory, a compendum of rhetoric constructed upon adroit variations of syntax.

The *Elegy*, purportedly murmured by a private man among irrevocably private citizens, has all the apparatus of a speech declaimed in a public assembly, with pauses, with gestures, with variations of loudness and timbre, but above all with the shifts of sentence-structure that keep an audience attentive and guessing. As an oration over the anonymous dead, the *Elegy* begins simply, almost hesitantly; but its complexities follow within a few lines, and as its declamatory passion unwinds, so its language unwinds, paradoxically spinning intricate textures out of elementary stuff. The primary syntax of the *Elegy* is very simple; its development in the progress of the poem may be one of the most complex things in eighteenth-century verse. 'Noble' it may possibly be called; its 'transparency' is an illusion.

It reads very confidently, so confidently that it comes as something of a surprise to learn that Gray had his compositional doubts about it.[3] The title he originally proposed – *Stanza's wrote in a Country Churchyard* – indicates a choice of verse-form. The 'Stanza's' were to be quatrains, a prosodic equivalent, as Gray appears to have seen it, to the elegiac measures of the classical poets. But Latin elegiacs are based on the distich, a two-line unit, self-contained semantically and syntactically; and Gray soon discovered that although some of his stanzas kept their grammar and their meaning comfortably within the palisade of four lines, others did not. The *Elegy* does not keep an unvarying measure. There are passages in which the meaning runs over the boundaries of the quatrain, extending sometimes to two or even three stanzas. It is a stanzaic poem, but it has 'flights' (let us borrow that sense from 'fugue') which resist the chief impediment of the quatrain, the natural terminus of the fourth line.

Even within the stanza there are variations in the relationship between syntactic unit and verse-line. In some quatrains, the four lines are taken up by a single unbroken sentence; in some, each line contains a finite clause; in others, the sense breaks into a balance, two-by-two, at the second line; and so with other permutations. The quatrain, indeed, is a very slippery equivalent of the elegiac distich (if there is any equivalence at all), and the dynamic impulse of Gray's *Elegy* is correspondingly shifty. It is sometimes a poem and sometimes an exhortation to the reader; it keeps slipping out of stanzas and into paragraphs, some of which, with a little suppression of rhyme, might be re-cast as eighteenth-century rhetorical prose. It is clear that from the start the peculiar discursiveness of the *Elegy* presented structural problems. Gray recognized the difficulty of confining the sense to the quatrain, and changed his mind about the division into stanzas. His revised intention was to print the poem without stanza-breaks, and so he did; but later editors have restored the breaks, and in doing so may have helped to disguise the poem's changes of rhetorical pace.

The poem in its present form is an oration on fame and death, expounding a sequence of topics, each of which occupies three or four stanzas, as far as the 23rd of its thirty-two quatrains. At that point – roughly, we must suppose, the point at which Gray began to experience compositional doubts – it turns into a romantic memorial for the orator anticipating his own death. This is the structural scheme:

Stanzas 1–3	Topic: The churchyard at nightfall.
Stanzas 4–7	Topic: The rustic dead; their simple, useful lives.
Stanzas 8–11	Topic: The vanity of ambition and pomp.
Stanzas 12–15	Topic: Hidden talent, buried gifts.
Stanzas 16–20	Topic: The virtue of obscurity.
Stanzas 20–3	Topic: Our need to be remembered.

(The structure changes here.)

Stanzas 24–9	In this sequence of six stanzas, the orator has sentimental premonitions of his own death, in the character of a half-crazed poet and lover, and of what, 'haply', might be said about him.
Stanzas 31–2	Labelled 'The Epitaph', these conclude the theme of 24–9.

This representation of the structure of the *Elegy* implies a view of the poem as a discursive hybrid, two-thirds epideictic oratory ('epideictic' = 'celebrating', 'commemorating') and one-third introvert fantasy. The introspection of the last nine stanzas purportedly reflects themes declaimed in the first twenty-three ('as with these obscure but worthy peasants, so with me, a poor unknown poet'), yet there must be many readers for whom the transition from 'the unhonour'd dead' to 'a youth, to fortune and to fame unknown' is less than convincingly demonstrated. My own estimate is that for twenty-three stanzas Gray deals in honest sentiment, speaking up well and sturdily on behalf of the poor, but when he turns the talk to his own account, in rustic rigout as the village eccentric interred beneath the aged thorn, with an epitaph composed for the benefit of the not wholly analphabetic passer-by, he becomes embarrassingly mawkish, even insincere. These judgements, however, are for individual readers. What is indisputable is that the formal organisation of the poem does change after stanza 23, and that there are concomitant changes of language and style.

To attempt a grammatical analysis of all thirty-two stanzas would be to burden the *Elegy* with more exegetical paraphernalia than any poem deserves, or any reader can be expected to tolerate. But we can at least take soundings; and a good place to begin is at the beginning, with the first three quatrains, the description of the churchyard in the twilight. Nothing could be plainer than the first stanza – as plain as the opening of a Bach fugue, the bars that almost any amateur can play:[4]

The curfew tolls the knell of parting day,
The lowing herd wind slowly o'er the lea,
The ploughman homeward plods his weary way,
And leaves the world to darkness and to me.

Consider the relationship here between the grammatical unit, *clause*, and the prosodic unit, *line*. There are four clauses, and each clause occupies a line exactly; but the third and fourth clauses have a common Subject ('the ploughman') and are linked by a coordinating conjunction ('and'). The *grammetric* procedure (i.e. the patterning of syntactic units onto line-units) is symmetrical, four-square, *a,b,c* and *d*. It could not be much simpler; only the linking of the two final lines makes a little variation on the repeated prosodic structure.

Each of these clauses embodies the elements of **S**ubject and **V**erb; and then either a direct **O**bject, or an **A**dverbial, or **O**bject and **A**dverbial together.[5] So in line 1:

S	**V**	**O**
The curfew	tolls	the knell of parting day

The order of the elements is the commonplace **SVO**, said to characterise the usual, 'unmarked' prose order in English. There are no surprises here, no opening on a rhetorical upbeat, with a 'fronting' of the **O**bject, **OSV**, 'The knell of parting day the curfew tolls'.[6] The clause is end-weighted (again, a normal feature of English structure)[7]; of the phrases that represent each of its component elements, the most elaborate, in informational terms, commonly occurs at the end of the clause. So on to line 2:

S	**V**	**A**	**A**
The lowing herd	wind	slowly	o'er the lea

The structure of the clause resembles that of line 1, but here the elements following the basic **SV** stem are **A**dverbials – i.e. an adverb of manner ('slowly') followed by a prepositional phrase ('o'er the lea') which functions as a place-adverb (like 'there', or 'yonder'). In line 3, there is an **O**bject and an **A**dverbial:

S	**A**	**V**	**O**
The ploughman	homeward	plods	his weary way

The Adverbial ('homeward') is placed between the **S**ubject and the **V**erb, as the metre necessitates, but with a consequent hint of accentuation, a rhetorical inversion ('homeward plods', not 'plods homeward'). Line 4 introduces another variant:

&	**[S]**	**V**	**O**	**A**
And	[the ploughman]	leaves	the world	to darkness and
A				
to me				

A minor complication here is that this final clause shares a **S**ubject with its predecessor. Further, there is some gentle semantic play with the **A**dverbials 'to darkness' and 'to me'. The playfulness is akin to the rhetorical figure of *zeugma* (e.g. 'She left in a fit of rage and a Rolls Royce') in which grammatically concordant but semantically distinct constructions are yoked. Gray's line is not quite a zeugma, yet it does suggest an ambivalent reading of 'leave', in the senses of 'abandon' (*leaves the world to darkness*) and 'bequeath' (*leaves the world to me*).

So the first stanza closes, simple music with hints of more intricate harmonics to come. It gives the reader basic instructions in the rhetorical potential of four clause elements, the Subject (**S**), the Verb (**V**), the direct Object (**O**) and the Adverbial (**A**). The 'potential' at this point is in the combination and ordering of the elements (the four illustrated cases being **SVO**, **SVAA**, **SAVO**, **[S]VAA**), and in their relative weighting, their realisation as simple or more complex phrases. One type of clause constituent, the **C**omplement (**C**) is not represented in this opening stanza and remains a fugitive element, generally absent from the poem, until the closing quatrains, where (as will be noted in due course) it makes a brief but significant appearance.

The first stanza establishes the baroque rhetoric of the *Elegy* as a game played with the syntactic components **SVOA**. But the baroque involutions and convolutions have yet to come; we are as yet in the first bars of the counterpoint, where the reading is easy. The second and third stanzas make more difficult fingering:

> Now fades the glimmering landscape on the sight,
> And all the air a solemn stillness holds,
> Save where the beetle wheels his droning flight,
> And drowsy tinklings lull the distant folds;

(This follows a modern, or post-eighteenth-century punctuation; in the 1751 text there is a colon after 'holds' and a full stop after 'folds' – see p. 18). Notice now that the first two lines of this stanza repeat the grammetric pattern of the last two lines of the preceding quatrain; there are two coordinated clauses, each occupying a line, *a & b*.[8] But the third line of this stanza is grammatically dependent on the second, and the fourth line is grammatically coordinated with the third. The grammetric scheme, then, is *a & b* > *c & d* (the notation & = a coordinator, 'and'; > = a subordinator, 'save where'). Through the links of 'and', 'save where', 'and', the stanza presents a continuous sentence, but one in which the grammatical constituents, the clauses, are still confined within the boundaries of the verse-line.

The line-clause correspondence is dramatically broken in the next quatrain, where a complex subordinate clause is spread over four lines, with no line-end breaks of sense:

> Save that from yonder ivy-mantled tower
> The moping owl does to the moon complain
> Of such as, wandering near her secret bower,
> Molest her ancient solitary reign.

The subordinating expression is 'save that', in parallel with the 'save where' of the preceding stanza, and both of those 'saves' are dependent on 'a solemn stillness holds'. The ensuing complex construction begins with an **A**dverbial, 'from yonder ivy-mantled tower', in the first line; proceeds in the second line to a **S**ubject, 'the moping owl', and a **V**erb, 'does . . . complain' – this verb phrase being interrupted by a second **A**dverbial, 'to the moon'; then in the third and fourth lines the sense of the Verb, 'complain', is completed by a dependent **A**dverbial clause, 'of such as . . . molest her ancient solitary reign'.

That dependent clause is in its turn interrupted by a non-finite (participial) clause 'wandering near her ancient bower'. The initially simple syntactic structures can be seen at this point as yielding to more intricate patterns of expressions boxed into other expressions in ways that indeed suggest a verbal equivalent to the growth of a musical counterpoint. The syntactic/rhetorical/grammetric pattern of the third stanza is rather easier to read than to describe, but still not as easy to read as the pattern of the poem's opening lines; but now the fugue is up and running; the voices are beginning to speak, all at once. And yet those subordinations enfolded in subordinations are still constructed from the simple elements, **SVO** and **SVA**: 'the beetle wheels his droning flight', **SVO**; 'drowsy tinklings lull the distant folds', **SVO**; 'the moping owl does to the moon complain' (**S*v*AV**, where ***v*** = the auxiliary, 'does'); 'such as molest her ancient solitary reign', **SVO**. The primary patterns remain simple; the modes that are becoming sophisticated are those of interconnection and superimposition.

Into succeeding sections of the poem Gray introduces additional grammatical modes: for example, negation ('no more shall rouse them . . . for them no more . . . no children run . . .', stanzas 5–6); interjection ('how jocund did they drive . . .', 'how bowed the woods . . .', stanza 7); imperatives ('let not Ambition', 'nor you, ye proud, impute', stanzas 8, 10); rhetorical questions ('Can storied urn . . . ?', 'Can honour's voice . . . ?', stanza 11). He is an orator rehearsing the resources of rhetoric, creating increasingly complex patterns, matching the complexity to the topic and its attendant emotions. There is a good deal of eloquent recursion – the repetition of a grammatical structure – but these parallels are subtle, never repeating quite the same syntactic pattern or semantic implication.

As to the grammetrics, the match, or 'mapping' of grammatical units, e.g. clauses and sentences, on lines of verse, no two quatrains are managed in quite the same way. In stanza 3, for example, one carefully articulated sentence is distributed across four lines:

Beneath those rugged elms, that yew-tree's shade,
Where heaves the turf in many a mouldering heap,
Each in his narrow cell for ever laid,
The rude forefathers of the hamlet sleep.

The distinguishing rhetorical feature of this is that the sentence's principal clause comes in the last line, the three preceding lines containing the subordinate structures; the sentence is what is sometimes termed a 'left-branching' construction, in which all dependent, contributory material lies to the 'left', textually, of the main, information-clinching statement.[9] Because there is something like a symmetrical correspondence of grammatical units and line units, it is possible, for illustration's sake, to shuffle the structural order, e.g.:

The rude forefathers of the hamlet sleep
Beneath that rugged elm, that yew-tree's shade,
Where heaves the turf in many a mouldering heap,
Each in his narrow cell for ever laid.

Or thus:

The rude forefathers of the hamlet sleep,
Each in his narrow cell for ever laid,
Where heaves the turf in many a mouldering heap,
Beneath that rugged elm, that yew-tree's shade.

These are 'right branching'; the main item comes first, the qualifying matter follows to the 'right' – compare 'Beneath that elm the forefathers sleep' (left branch) and 'The forefathers sleep beneath that elm' (right branch). Right branching, beginning with the main clause, is in general the 'normal' prose order; but all preachers and political orators know the value of the left branch, which keeps an audience waiting for the completion of the message, capturing attention. So here, as Gray embarks upon the second topic in his descriptive programme (his evocation of the dead) the left-branching rhetoric suspends the attention, obliges the reader to follow the closure of the perspective, from '*that* yew tree', to '*many* a mouldering heap', to '*each* in his narrow cell', and so at last to the theme, the 'rude forefathers'.

In that instance, the spread of the grammatical structure over all four lines of the quatrain is obviously related to the unfolding drama of the poem. The verse-sentence says 'Behold!' or 'Pay attention!'. Compare that with what happens in the 9th stanza, where the grammar-line distribution is three-plus-one (three lines containing one sentence, followed by one sentence-containing line):

The boast of heraldry, the pomp of pow'r,
And all that beauty, all that wealth e'er gave,
Await alike th' inevitable hour.
The paths of glory lead but to the grave.[10]

The first three lines are a sentence with the structure **SVAO**. The element **S** is complex. It consists of two apposed phrases, 'the boast of heraldry' and 'the pomp of power', followed by a clause in which one **V**erb ('gave') is under the linked government of two **S**ubjects ('all that beauty e'er gave' + 'all that wealth e'er gave'). The predicate is 'await . . . the inevitable hour', but it is reached only after the complex, left-branching Subject. Once again, the reader must wait to learn what the 'inevitable hour' means. The definitive, 'explanatory' pronouncement comes in the fourth line, as an independent sentence, 'The paths of glory lead but to the grave'. Because of the way it is introduced, that line is rhetorically enhanced; it is played, as it were, *marcato*. The asymmetrical division of the quatrain, three-and-one, draws attention to the message it proclaims.

Some stanzas divide smoothly into two-and-two, for instance number 14:

Full many a gem of purest ray serene
The dark unfathomed caves of ocean bear:
Full many a flower is born to blush unseen
And waste its sweetness on the desert air.

This is a cunningly recursive structure. Because of their thematic positioning at the beginning of lines, the phrases 'full many a gem' and 'full many a flower' seem to be exactly parallel. In fact, it is a semantic parallel with a syntactic difference, since 'full many a gem, &c' is **O**, the **O**bject of the sentence in the first two lines, whereas 'Full many a flower' is **S**, the **S**ubject of the next sentence. There is a gently asymmetrical symmetry, a change of grammatical step that makes the verse *reiterative* but not mechanically *repetitive*.

In stanzas 16–18, the limits of the quatrain are overrun, and Gray writes a verse-paragraph in which he plays rhetorical games of recursion and inversion, sustaining a topic through twelve brilliant lines. Nowhere in the *Elegy* is the stance of the public orator more apparent than here:

> The applause of list'ning senates to command,
> The threats of pain and ruin to despise,
> To scatter plenty o'er a smiling land,
> And read their history in a nation's eyes,
>
> Their lot forbade; nor circumscribed alone
> Their growing virtues, but their crimes confined;
> Forbade to wade thro' slaughter to a throne,
> And shut the gates of mercy on mankind,
>
> The struggling pangs of conscious truth to hide,
> To quench the blushes of ingenuous shame,
> Or heap the shrine of Luxury and Pride
> With incense kindled at the Muse's flame.

The obvious rhetorical/grammatical core of this is the infinitive clause ('to command . . . to despise . . . to scatter . . . to wade . . . to hide . . . to quench . . .'). Indeed, all the **V**erbs in this passage are infinitives, with the important exceptions of 'forbade', 'circumscribed' and 'confined' at the beginning of the second quatrain. There, the line and a half of text between (semi-) colons marks a rhetorical turnabout, separating the procession of infinitive clauses homing *onto* the main **V**erb, 'forbade', from the sequence of infinitive clauses branching *out from* a repetition of the same **V**erb: thus, 'to command . . . to despise . . . [their lot] forbade'**:** then '[their lot] forbade . . . to wade . . . to shut . . .'.

Within the infinitive clauses (the 'to'-clauses), the pattern of elements alternates between the sequence of **V + O** (etc.) and the inversion **O** (etc.) **+ V**, e.g.:

Th' applause of list'ning senates / to command	**O + V**
To scatter / plenty / o'er a smiling land	**V + O + A**
The struggling pangs of conscious truth / to hide	**O + V**
To quench / the blushes of ingenuous shame	**V + O**

The alternations facilitate shifts of 'angle' throughout the three quatrains, enabling the orator to throw emphasis on this phrase or that, and negotiate the shaping of the text. (At the end of stanza 18, for example, which is the close of the verse 'paragraph', the order **V + O + A** fits a cadence in which each element is longer, or 'weightier', than its predecessor: **V** ['heap'], **O** ['the shrine of Luxury and Pride'], **A** ['with incense kindled at the Muse's flame']).

Even those lines in which finite **V**erbs intrude upon the sequence of non-finite clauses ('nor circumscribed alone/ Their growing virtues, but their crimes confined') follow the principle of rhetorical alternation. 'Nor circumscribed alone their growing virtues' has the order **V . . . O**; 'but their crimes confined' reads **O + V**. This is by no means the only place in the text where Gray inverts the order of grammatical elements from line to line, or within a line. This particular inversion, however, occurs in a passage that makes a lively, meaningful exploration of inversion as a stylistic principle. It is the heart of the *Elegy*, a feat of stylistic virtuosity, a demonstration of how to raise syntax into sensibility. It may be artifice, but it is warm artifice; it has power to move, as, in a different context, with another reference, the Gettysburg Address has great and continued power to move. Lincoln celebrates 'these honoured dead' – as Gray propitiates 'the unhonoured dead'; and Gray, like Lincoln, does so in a style that projects the spontaneity of feeling through a pattern of studied phrases, an elegant set of syntactic variations.

Of the *Elegy*, Dr Johnson declared (in his *Lives of the Poets*), 'had Gray written often thus, it had been vain to blame, and useless to praise him'. In private he spoke rather less generously of Gray, especially the Gray of the Pindaric odes, attributing his success to a capacity for finding new ways of being dull; however, echoing his commendation in the *Life*, he allowed the *Elegy* to be 'a happy selection of images', and in conversation with Boswell and Mrs Thrale observed, in what is perhaps a back-handed compliment, that 'there are but two good stanzas in Gray's poetry, which are in his *Elegy in a Country Church-yard*'. Boswell tells us, 'He then repeated the stanza, "For who to dumb forgetfulness a prey", &c. mistaking one word; for instead of *precincts* he said *confines*. He added, "The other stanza I forget".'[11]

Johnson's phrase, 'a happy *selection* of images' (my italics) consciously or unconsciously reveals something important about the style and construction – the *lexis* and *taxis*, the rhetorical sum – of the *Elegy*. Any well-annotated edition of the poem will show how images from literary sources have been recollected and adapted to a new context; the original adaptation of a conventional resource is in the very nature of the ancient *heuresis*, which the Romans called *inventio* and our eighteenth-century critics called 'invention'. There is a further 'happy selection' of themes and sentiments, or *topoi*, or 'topics', most clearly evident in stanzas 1–23. (See the scheme suggested on p. 87 above.) Up to this point in the poem, at least, Gray is not saying anything 'original', in the modern understanding of that word. The pictures have been seen before, the sentiments have been heard before, the argument has been presented before. The 'originality' lies in the selection, the modification, the arrangement, the creation of a satisfying structure, a verbal scaffolding, which, however, is a more than mechanical thing; it is an apparatus for a certain kind of intellect and sensibility.

Through twenty-three quatrains the *Elegy*, in its style and construction, develops the harmonious 'horizontal' proportions of a Georgian house, its sequence of topics forming a façade of numerically proportionate stanza-groups: 3, 4, 4, 4, 4, 4. Then, from stanza 24 onwards, the building becomes 'vertical', Gothic; the level, classical demeanour is lost, proportion disappears, 'that yew tree's shade' (spreading outwards) gives place to 'yonder nodding beech that wreathes its old fantastic roots so high' (writhing upwards). There is a change of *persona*, of the poem's central, implicit 'I'; 'I' the nobly eloquent orator, a calm, commanding presence, a personage of oracular confidence, gives place to 'he' – the eccentric, the drop-out, the distraught failure in life and art, the *youth to fortune and to fame unknown*. And with that change come interesting modifications of style.

Gray's first intention, as a study of the manuscript drafts will suggest, was to end the piece on a note of stoic acceptance, with the churchyard obituarist exhorting himself to 'give anxious cares and endless wishes room', and 'through the cool sequestered vale of life' to 'pursue the silent tenor of thy doom'. The orator was, in short, to identify himself with the human objects of his oration; peasant or poet, the same destiny awaited all. In the event, this gave place to something rather less restrained and self-effacing, less 'Augustan', an assertion of the strangeness, the wild otherness of the modern poet. Poets, as Gray fancies them, do not spend their lives stumbling behind the plough or felling timber; they go mad with melancholy, felled by an excess of sensibility. The speaker addresses himself, saying (in paraphrase), 'and what about you, speculating on the lives of the peasantry – suppose someone like yourself were to come along and enquire about *your* life and death?'

This cues the introduction of a second speaker, the 'hoary-headed swain', who respectfully describes (in a most literary, non-hoary, un-swainlike idiom) the brief, useless career, the feverish, pathetic end, and the burial of the poetic obituarist.[12] It is an act of 'double distancing': the poem begins with a supposed speaker in a supposed location musing on supposed lives, and ends with supposed speaker number two in supposed location number two, describing the fate of supposed speaker number one. Roger Lonsdale comments editorially on this re-casting of roles and places: 'The figure of the Poet is no longer the urbane, wordly, rational Augustan man among men, with his own place in society; what G[ray] dramatises is the poet as outsider, with an uneasy consciousness of a sensibility and imagination at once unique and burdensome'. What Gray dramatises, one might further add, is that nightmare of the romantic conscience so sternly summarised by Goethe (who lived to a ripe old age): *Ein unnütz Leben ist ein früher Tod*, 'A useless life is an early death'.

The scene-setting at the beginning of the poem is purportedly realistic, even though there is scarcely a detail or an image that does not have its literary analogue. The verbs assert the factuality of the scene: the ploughman *plods*, the landscape *fades* (and fades *now*), the owl *complains*, the turf *heaves*. This is here, the words say; this lies before us, this is real. But the closing stanzas of the poem no longer deal in what *is*. They tell of what *might* be, 'if chance' and 'haply'. Verbs are modalised to meet the conditions of 'perhaps': 'if chance . . . some lonely spirit *shall* enquire', 'haply some hoary-headed swain *may* say', 'his listless length *would* he stretch', 'muttering his wayward fancies *would* he rove'. These modal expressions are not conspicuous elsewhere in the *Elegy*. Of the peasantry it is asserted 'Their furrow oft the stubborn glebe *has* broke', and 'How jocund *did* they drive their team afield'. (Not *would break, would they drive.*) But 'may' and 'would' mark a step from fact – at least, quasi-fact – to fantasy.

The fantasy takes shape in a passage of reported speech, the imputed monologue of 'some hoary-headed swain'. The text here blossoms into the quotation marks of the poetical speaker inventing a poetical speech. And then inventing a piece of poetical writing (the Epitaph); for lest we should think that the last three stanzas are also spoken by the hoary-headed swain, Gray is at some pains to insist that the Epitaph is to be *read* (not, like the rest of the poem, 'heard' or 'overheard') and, what is more, read by someone with claims to literary sensitivity somewhat above those of the peasantry (the point, surely, of the parenthetical *for thou canst read* – the text here has greater pretensions than 'their name, their years, spelt by the unlettered muse'). The reader, finally, is invited into the poem, to consider the poet's written *apologia* for a poetical career; meanwhile, the rude forefathers of the hamlet sleep on in their simple, unreadable graves.

The shift from 'consider these' to 'look at me' is accented in the grammatical 'fingering' of the penultimate stanza:

Large was his bounty and his soul sincere,
Heaven did a recompense as largely send:
He gave to Misery all he had, a tear,
He gained from Heaven ('twas all he wished) a friend.

The first line of this quatrain introduces an element hitherto unexploited in the grammar of the principal declarative clause, the Subject Complement.[13] It occurs in two linked and artfully inverted clauses:

C	**V**	**S**	**&**	**S**	**[V]**	**C**
Large	was	his bounty	and	his soul	[was]	sincere

'Artful', rather than 'artistic', seems to be the right word for this quatrain, and perhaps for the other stanzas in the Epitaph, where a sort of nodding antithesis or smooth automatic turnaround is the evident principle of structure.

It is remarkable that commentators seem not to have questioned much the meaning of the stanza beginning 'Large was his bounty'. The claim that his 'bounty', meaning his charitable giving, was 'large', in accordance with the eighteenth-century virtue of *benevolence*, amounts, it seems, to no more than the gift of a tear; in recompense for which largesse, this man of 'sincere' sentiment is allotted 'a friend'. This is mere nonsense, or repellent cant, or perhaps an ironic commentary on the poetic state of having nothing to offer but your sententiousness; most of all, though, it looks like making verses to thoughtless order, through the practised assembly of rhetorical-syntactic formulae. Much as I admire the *Elegy* as a performance, a polished demonstration of the skills of language – language that takes impetus from the emotions, and in turn quickens the pulse of feeling – I can only regard the last nine quatrains of the poem, in the form that has come down to us, as superior specimens of what practitioners of word-processing call *boilerplate.*

But my thoughts return to Bach, and *Die Kunst der Fuge*, and I find myself thinking the unthinkable, that maybe the master musician might have 'boilerplated' a counterpoint now and then. I put that thought from me, unexamined, for there is no composition in the whole awesome set that does not touch me with its emotional bounty and its intellectual rigour, all the way through to that almost unbearable moment in the fifteenth fugue, when the letters of his name, B A C H, worked into the score, 'the place of fame and elegy supply'. Less than a page later the music stops in mid-sentence. It is the last of Bach; he will write no more; *hic jacet*; no longer seek his merits to disclose.

Yet I know that what so grieves me is an artifice of my own mind's contriving; reason quietly tells me that Bach did not know he was so close to death, had no sense that his music was foretelling his demise. All that his music did was to work out the possibilities, until all the possibilities spoke of what is complete and perfect. Bach's music pursues the passionate logic of his material, the grammar of his rhythms and sounds and note-values. It drives the mind inexorably, allows no escape from its discursive compulsion. Poetry can never be quite like that, for all that it may show a comparable patterning, a comparable intricacy. Poetry is tainted by the human will to explain, comment, excuse, to make cases, even tell lies – and perhaps, finally, that is what has to be said about *Elegy in a Country Churchyard*. I do not wish to abandon my intuition that there is a grammar of the baroque in poetry which may be compared with the syntax of baroque music; but in the end, I perceive, the musical design has a sovereignty, an autonomy, an *inevitability* not granted to the poet's textual procedures.

NOTES

1 See George Sherburn in Baugh (1950: 1014): 'in its placid melancholy and its rustic setting it is perhaps slightly romantic'. Then see also Price (1973: 661), where the *Elegy* is described as 'restrained and classical in spirit'. In his prefatory remarks to the text, Lonsdale (1969) quotes comparable appraisals of the 'tone' of this poem: its character as oratory, rising at points to heights of *pathos* in the grand style, is seldom considered.

2 In classical terms, 'epideictic' or 'deliberative' rhetoric was a style appropriate, to debate, to ceremonial, to commemorative occasions. Lincoln's *Gettysburg Address* is a modern (relatively!) instance of the epideictic stance.

3 Gray's compositional problems are described in the Introduction to *Thomas Gray, An Elegy wrote in a Country Church Yard*, the Eton Manuscript and the First Edition, 1751 (Gray 1975). See my Chapter 1, p. 17. See also Roger Lonsdale's introduction to the poem in Lonsdale (1969).

4 Although the text of the 1751 edition (see note 1 above) gives better support to some points in my general argument, for purposes of quotation I have used the Longman Annotated English Poets text (Lonsdale 1969), as perhaps more concordant with the modern reader's notion of *the look of the page*. (There is a good deal to be said, however, in favour of rehabilitating the 1751 text.) The text of the *Elegy* in its entirety is reproduced here in Appendix I.

5 I take it that these basic grammatical terms will be generally familiar; but if some reminder of distant things is needed, the reader may like to refer to Quirk *et al.* (1985), chapter 10, 'The simple sentence', esp. 10.6–10.9. My grammatical analyses here are in no way 'deep', my purpose being only to trace shifts in the surface organisation of the text. A fuller examination of the stylistic procedures of the poem might have been achieved by complementing a study of its grammatical structures with a view of its *thematic* procedures – that is, of various ways in which the focus and 'topic-shift' of information are managed from line to line, clause to clause, stanza to stanza; further, perhaps, by some account of so-called 'transitivity patterns', reflecting various processes of action, thought, event, relationship. On *theme*, see Halliday (1985). On transitivity, see Halliday, and also, for a brief and lucid account, Berry (1975). It would doubtless have been a happily heuristic exercise to examine the text – however cursorily – at these three complementary linguistic levels of structure, theme and transitivity; but it would have resulted in a chapter three times as long, with some consequent burdening of the reader.

6 On 'fronting', see Chapter 3, note 5.

7 On the principle of 'end-weighting', see Quirk *et al.* (1985).

8 Although commentators have discerned ambiguities elsewhere in the *Elegy* (see in particular note 10 below), it seems to have passed generally without notice that the second line (and clause) in this quatrain is grammatically ambiguous. 'And all the air a solemn stillness holds', may be read as **SOV** (signifying 'All the air holds a solemn stillness'), or as **OSV** (meaning 'A solemn stillness holds all the air'). The instance illustrates by the way the importance of word-order in English, in the absence of nominal case. It should be noted that the choice of *grammatical* reading makes a difference to the *lexis* of the verb, 'hold'. 'All the air holds a solemn stillness' implies the meaning 'contain', 'enfold'; 'A solemn stillness holds all the air' suggests 'command', 'control', 'take possession of'. I favour the latter reading because of its relationship to the ensuing subordinate clauses: 'A solemn stillness takes possession of all the air, except where the beetle, etc., and except that the moping owl, etc.' Thus I would read the clause-element pattern of this line as **OSV**.

9 On 'branching', see Quirk *et al.* (1985: ch. 14.38–9).

10 This stanza has given rise to a surprising amount of discussion among interpreters, some of whom would complicate its grammar with the suggestion that the subject of the sentence in the first three lines is 'the inevitable hour'. This entails the reading 'awaits': 'The inevitable hour awaits alike the boast of heraldry, the pomp of power, and all that beauty, all that wealth e'er gave.' Lonsdale (1969) claims: 'G(ray) undoubtedly intended "Awaits", with "hour" as the subject, in spite of the fact that "await" appears in *edd 9–12*, in Dodsley's *Collection* in 1755, and in 1775.' I see no reason for *undoubtedly*. The fact remains that the early editions read 'await', and that the grammar of the quatrain makes straightforward sense with 'the boast of heraldry', etc., as **S**ubject. The nature, or implication, of 'the inevitable hour' is announced in the final line. Gray often elaborates his text with grammatical inversions, but they are as a rule patterned, rhetorical inversions, within the prosodic frame of the text, often pairing antithetically with a companion structure; not such a tortuous turnabout as is necessitated if 'hour' is to be read as **S**ubject. The *theme* of the verse-sentence, furthermore, its 'topic', as opposed to its grammatical 'subject' is clearly 'the boast of heraldry, the pomp of power . . .'.

11 For Johnson on Gray's 'dullness', see Boswell's *Life*, Tuesday, 28 March 1775 (Chapman 1983): 'Next day I dined with him at Mr. Thrale's. He attacked Gray, calling him a "dull fellow". BOSWELL. "I understand he was reserved, and might appear dull in company; but surely he was not dull in poetry." JOHNSON. "Sir, he was dull in company, dull in his closet, dull everywhere. He was dull in a new way, and that made many people think him GREAT. He was a mechanical poet." ' His

remark that 'there are but two good stanza in Gray's poetry' (one of which he could not remember) was made on the same occasion. His commendation of the *Elegy*'s 'happy selection of images' comes in Boswell's report of the conversation at the Mitre on Saturday, 25 June 1763. The *Elegy* is singled out as the best performance in an indifferent collection: 'Sir, I do not think Gray a first-rate poet. He has not a bold imagination, not much command of words. The obscurity in which he has involved himself will not persuade us that he is sublime. His *Elegy in a Country Church-Yard* has a happy selection of images, but I don't like what are called his great things.'

12 Lonsdale (reference below) notes: 'Significantly, G(ray)'s description of the lonely, melancholy poet is riddled with phrases and diction borrowed from Spenser, Shakespeare and Milton.' He adds (rightly, in my view), 'The texture of these stanzas is fanciful, consciously "poetic", archaic in tone.'

13 But there is a kind of 'buried' complementation in some adjectival clauses, e.g. 'Some heart [that was] once *pregnant* with celestial fire' (stanza 12); 'Some Cromwell [who was] *guiltless* of his country's blood' (stanza 15).

REFERENCES

BAUGH, A.C. (ed.). *A Literary History of England*. London: Routledge & Kegan Paul, 1950.

BERRY, MARGARET. *Introduction to Systemic Linguistics, 1: Structures and Systems*. London: Batsford, 1975.

CHAPMAN, R.A. (ed.). James Boswell, *Life of Samuel Johnson*. Oxford: University Press, The World's Classics, repr. 1983.

GRAY, THOMAS. *An ELEGY wrote in a Country Church Yard*. The Eton Manuscript and the First Edition, 1751. Reproduced in facsimile by Alastair Macdonald. London: The Scolar Press, 1975.

HALLIDAY, M.A.K. *An Introduction to Functional Grammar*. London: Arnold, 1985; ch. 3.

LONSDALE, ROGER (ed.). *The Poems of Thomas Gray, William Collins, Oliver Goldsmith*. London: Longman, Annotated English Poets, 1969.

PRICE, MARTIN (ed.). *The Restoration and the Eighteenth Century*, in Frank Kermode and John Hollander (general eds), *The Oxford Anthology of English Literature*, 6 vols, paperback. New York: Oxford University Press, 1973.

QUIRK, RANDOLPH *et al. A Comprehensive Grammar of the English Language*. London: Longman, 1985; chs 18.9, 14.38–9.

Six

Rewording Wordsworth: a passage from 'The Prelude'

The reader who takes courage and resolves to accompany Wordsworth from first to last through the long, arduous ramble of 'The Prelude' is soon rewarded by one of the journey's great visionary moments; it comes a little more than half way through the first book (to be exact, at line 340 of the 1850 version), with this unforgettable declaration of poetic faith:

> Dust as we are, the immortal spirit grows
> Like harmony in music; there is a dark
> Inscrutable workmanship that reconciles
> Discordant elements, makes them cling together
> In one society.

The *dark inscrutable workmanship* is the operation of Nature on the human psyche – on that aggregate of perceiving, feeling, recollecting, associating and reflecting, which people of a literary turn call 'sensibility'. For Wordsworth the process is of more than aesthetic importance. He describes it in the language of the theologian. He talks habitually of 'visitings', and more powerfully of 'interventions'. Nature, like a saviour, a paraclete, will *intervene* in the history of the individual soul, to guide, to discipline, to correct and to create purpose out of formlessness, integrity out of division, harmony out of dissonance and, at length, *poesis* – true creativeness – out of the haphazard of *morphosis* – mere construction.

The 'declaration of poetic faith', as I have called it, precedes a passage of exemplification, the record of one of Nature's interventions in the spiritual life of the young Wordsworth. It describes how he borrowed a boat, without the owner's permission, to go joyriding – which we should perhaps call 'joyrowing'. His plea in mitigation of this act of boyish mischief is that he was even then under the spell of Nature: 'led by her', he asserts in the 1850 version, suppressing the note of caution in the 1805 text, which reads '*surely* I was led by her' (my italics). Here is the story as presented in the 1850 text of 'The Prelude' (Wordsworth 1975):

One summer evening (led by her) I found
A little boat tied to a willow tree
Within a rocky cave, its usual home.
Straight I unloosed her chain, and stepping in
Pushed from the shore. It was an act of stealth
And troubled pleasure, nor without the voice
Of mountain-echoes did my boat move on;
Leaving behing her still, on either side,
Small circles glittering idly in the moon,
Until they melted all into one track
Of sparkling light. But now, like one who rows,
Proud of his skill, to reach a chosen point
With an unswerving line, I fixed my view
Upon the summit of a craggy ridge,
The horizon's utmost boundary, for above
Was nothing but the stars and the grey sky.
She was an elfin pinnace; lustily
I dipped my oars into the silent lake,
And, as I rose upon the stroke, my boat
Went heaving through the water like a swan;
When, from behind that craggy steep till then
The horizon's bound, a huge peak, black and huge,
As if with voluntary power instinct
Upreared its head. I struck and struck again,
And growing still in stature the grim shape
Towered up between me and the stars, and still,
For so it seemed, with purpose of its own,
And measured motion like a living thing,
Strode after me. With trembling oars I turned,
And through the silent water stole my way
Back to the covert of the willow-tree;

There in her mooring-place I left my bark –
And through the meadows homeward went, in grave
And serious mood; but after I had seen
That spectacle, for many days, my brain
Worked with a dim and undetermined sense
Of unknown modes of being; o'er my thoughts
There hung a darkness, call it solitude
Or blank desertion. No familiar shapes
Remained, no pleasant images of trees,
Of sea or sky, no colours of green fields;
But huge and mighty forms that do not live
Like living men, moved slowly through the mind
By day, and were a trouble to my dreams.

Who can read this passage, one might well ask, without gooseflesh – that empirical test of poetic magic that keeps its authority when all the complicated theories have failed? We are seized by a conviction that for us, as well as for that boyish rower, something tremendous and awesome has been revealed. There is more here, much more, than the common tale of a country lad 'borrowing' a boat and then feeling guilty about it. Wordsworth's poem transcends autobiography. Its intention throughout is *parabolic*, in the sense that every event, even the most trivial, is presented as a parable of spiritual experience, which by and by, through a kind of osmosis, becomes the reader's experience as well as the poet's. The growth and literary form of such parables must be of great interest, and it is fortunate indeed that we are able to study the progress of a poet's myth-making by comparing two versions of 'The Prelude'. The comparison enables us in many places to follow the poetic drift from autobiography to parable, from reminiscence to transcendence. This story of the boat is one such place.

The 1850 text of this passage revises the earlier (1805) version in two ways. (See the parallel texts in Appendix II.) There are differences of wording, perhaps not numerous, but none the less significant; and there are cancellations, most notably of a passage of some eleven lines occurring at the beginning of the 1805 narrative. This is a crucial act of poetic reconception. The discarded lines read:

One evening (surely I was led by her)
I went alone into a shepherd's boat,

A skiff that to a willow tree was tied
Within a rocky cave, its usual home.
'Twas by the shores of Patterdale, a vale
Wherein I was a stranger, thither come
A schoolboy traveller, at the holidays.
Forth rambled from the village inn alone,
No sooner had I sight of this small skiff,
Discovered thus by unexpected chance,
Than I unloosed her tether and embarked.

Now what is this? Is *this* the immortal spirit growing as harmony in music? Or some less ethereal growth? There are times when Wordsworth speaks with majestic authority, and there are other times when he embarrasses his most devoted admirers with fits of what is sometimes call 'wittering on'. As J.K. Stephen put it, in a cruel parody, 'Two voices are there, one is of the deep . . . And one is of an old half-witted sheep . . . And, Wordsworth, both are thine.'[1]

The lines quoted from the 1805 text may not deserve the epithet 'half-witted', but there is certainly a sheepishness, or a disconcerting woolliness, about them. 'Forth rambled from the village inn alone' is a pronouncement worthy of some eighteenth-century pastoralist like Dyer, or a rural chronicler like Crabbe. Yet it is a testimony to Wordsworth's sense of poetic theatre that he finally cancelled this garrulous passage; and its flat infelicities of style cannot have been his single motivation for discarding it. He must have perceived that this dull, gossiping preamble has no function other than that of unwanted metacommentary, an announcement of forthcoming purpose; it explicates, it orientates, it overviews, it tediously delineates the attendant circumstances and puts us preposterously in the picture, so that we may feel fully equipped to read on. We are invited to understand how the boy Wordsworth – a stranger who – just happening to be here on holiday, living at the local inn – goes for a walk at night and by chance comes upon a boat – well, not even a boat, more of a little skiff, a shepherd's skiff – then purely on impulse decides to take a row in the moonlight. We are now ready for what follows. But what follows is a tale of enchantment, and tales of enchantment are not enhanced by spasms of prefatory explanation. The strangeness of myth is subverted. To be told ''Twas by the shores of Patterdale' can only unsettle our growing conviction that these events unfold by the Strand of Elsewhere, by the Waters of

Wonderment. In such cases, names on the real map tell us more than we need or want to know about the poetic territory.

In short, the 1805 version 'tethers' the fable – to use a word our poet rather oddly uses of the moored 'skiff' – whereas the 1850 version, in discarding eleven introductory lines, cuts the tether and turns the myth loose, to operate as it will. This liberation of the text opens the way for various changes of wording, expressing a revised, enlarged view of the recollected event. Little revisions, barely noticeable until one begins to make close, line-by-line comparisons, show Wordsworth gradually expanding the perspective of his narrative scene, with intimations of greater height, breadth and distance. For example, in line 398 of the 1805 text we read, 'upon the *top* of that same craggy ridge' (my italics); but at the corresponding place in 1850, 'upon the *summit* of a craggy ridge'. Line 399 of the 1805 version speaks of 'the *bound* of the horizon'; in 1850 this becomes 'the horizon's *utmost boundary*'. In the earlier text, at line 399–400, we read 'for *behind* was nothing'; but in 1850, 'for *above* was nothing', as though this craggy ridge, having acquired a *summit* when previously it had only a *top*, had added to its stature, obliging the observer to look upwards and higher. Each of these changes will seem trivial in itself, the slightest alteration in the look of the page; collectively, though, they amount to a revised staging, or, in filmic terms, a new set of instructions to the camera.

This expansion of the scene is accompanied by changes of wording that intensify the affective power of the poet's imagery, enhancing descriptive statement with an associative colouring. In some instances, a word is replaced by a figuratively stronger synonym; in at least one, the syntax of a line is adjusted to allow for the insertion of an additional, highly significant expression. That instance comes at line 378 of the 1850 text, where the original reading, *The bound of the horizon, a huge cliff* (1805, line 407) is changed to *The horizon's bound, a huge peak, black and huge*. How lucky for the poet that the grammatical resources of English include two ways of managing the genitive, i.e. *the x of the y* and *the y's x*. The altered form of the noun phrase, from 'the bound of the horizon' to 'the horizon's bound' leaves room, prosodically, for the introduction of *black* and the emphatic repetition of *huge*. 'Black' is an especially important little word to have brought into the narrative at this point. It represents one side of that familiar romantic device, the *chiaroscuro*, the stark, bedazzling-and-benighting counterpoint of sheen and shade. Here in the first half of the passage, the light glitters lustily upon the water; in the second half, darkness rears up, a huge darkness that pervades the mind, expunging all impressions of shape and colour. Changing the syntax in line 378 is a most important revision. It coincides, furthermore, with a lexical change; the erstwhile *cliff* grows into a *peak*, just as the 'top' of the craggy ridge became a 'summit'.

In line 381 of the 1850 version, the original 'huge cliff' turns into a *grim shape*, and in line 382 we are told how the grim shape *towered up*, in contrast to the simpler 'rose up' in the 1805 version. There is something theatrical, almost melodramatic, about this insidious refurbishing of the text with expressions of increasingly powerful import. Cliffs become 'peaks'; peaks assume 'grim shapes'; cliffs only rise, but grim shapes 'tower'. A feeling of immensity and overarching darkness is impressed upon us. The descriptive dictionary is transformed into the lexicon of fantasy; resemblance merges with transcendence. The landscape is revised, with a change of responsive emotion, from delight to something near terror. Nature turns Gothic, as though in one of those tremendous scenes painted by Caspar David Friedrich.[2] Something fabulous, in the strict sense of that word – something from the world of fable – is created.

The 1805 text presents, in its vocabulary, some evidence of the change of poetic stance that occurs when an author recalls the past in the light of the present. Consider, for example, the series of terms denoting the 'skiff'. From being a 'skiff' (1805, lines 374 and 380), it becomes first a 'boat' (line 390), then a 'pinnace' (line 401) and finally a 'bark' (line 415). 'Skiff' does not occur in the 1850 version, but the other words remain: 'boat' at line 363, 'pinnace' at line 373 (in a line that will invite further consideration) and 'bark' in line 388. What are we to make of these readings? Are we to regard them simply as examples of stylistic variation – poetic synonymy – or do they have a deeper significance? Do they, for example, represent ways of looking at the facts: the merely descriptive, the subjective, the ironically recollective? A 'skiff' in the first instance is only a species of small boat; but to a young boy, out on a moonlit jaunt, it is a pinnace, an elfin pinnace; and to a man in his maturity, ruefully shaking his head, saying to himself 'Yes, that was how I saw it *then*', it becomes, in benign irony, a 'bark'.

One such re-wording, implying a progressive shift of stance, occurs in the 1850 text alone. In 1805, the boat's mooring place is called first a 'cave' (1805, line 375), then a 'cavern' (line 414). The change from 'cave' to 'cavern' in itself suggests a shift from the ordinary to the poetic. In the 1850 version, however, the shift is greater – almost a shift into another semantic domain. As in the 1805 version, the boat is found in 'a rocky cave', but in the 1850 text it is returned to a *covert*, 'the covert of the willow tree' (1850, line 387). 'Covert' introduces a new sense, that of a hiding place, and hence, it may be said, of something furtive. Not that the boat is furtively concealed by its owner, the shepherd; but it is furtively taken by the boy, in 'an act of stealth'. 'Covert', like 'bark', intimates a retrospective judgement made by the poet wryly pronouncing on himself and on the ambiguity of his boyish motives and feelings.

Variants and alterations of this kind are part of a programme of semantic adjustments, aimed at modifying and revising our view, not only of the scene, but also of the actor. Some changes from the earlier version to the later clearly imply a shift of individual reference, from the autobiographical person, the real William Wordsworth, to a fictional or poetic *persona*, the universal 'I' of the fabulist, the 'I' that appeals to 'you, reader', and ultimately embraces 'we'. This appears most obviously from a comparison of lines 396–7 in 1805, and 367–8 in 1850. The earlier text reads:

> And now, as suited one who proudly rowed
> With his best skill . . .

Note there the past tense, *rowed*; the past historic it may be truly called, for its subject here is an historic person, the actual boy who actually borrowed an actual boat; furthermore, the pronoun *one* must here be personal, with reference to a particular individual – him, the boy, that rower and no one else. But in the revised text we find:

> But now, like one who rows
> Proud of his skill . . .

Rows; that present tense changes the aspect of the comparison. The reference is no longer to a particular person, the young Wordsworth; it applies to any rower, to rowers now as then, here as there; *one* is impersonal, meaning *someone*; *like* signals a general resemblance, broader than *as* or *as suited*. Without 'depersonalising' the lines, these revisions nevertheless modify the perception of personality. 'I' becomes 'I among others', 'I as a representative human being'.

The same tendency is apparent in smaller revisions. Line 412 of the 1805 version reads 'With trembling *hands* I turned', but at the corresponding place in the 1850 text (line 385) the poet has seen fit to substitute the instrument for the human agency: 'With trembling *oars* I turned.' Why introduce this apparently trivial change, with its curious half-hint of a synecdoche (the instrument expressing the agent), if not to make the actor at once less specific and more representative in identity – a rower, a generalised human character, rather than the boy, the particular actor? A similar question is raised by lines at the end of the extract, where the changes from 1805 to 1850 are, it would seem, casual switchabouts of articles and pronouns. Thus, in 1805:

> . . . huge and mighty forms, that do not live
> Like living men, moved slowly through **my** mind
> By day, and were **the** trouble **of** my dreams.

but the 1850 reading changes **three** small words:

> . . . huge and mighty forms, that do not live
> Like living men, moved slowly through **the** mind
> By day, and were **a** trouble **to** my dreams.

The changes are from '*my* mind' to '*the* mind', and from '*the* trouble *of*' to '*a* trouble *to*'. The differences between the two readings in these closing lines of the extract are so very small that the first and most natural explanation might be that they are simply scribal lapses, copyist's errors into which anyone might fall in transcribing a text. A second possibility is that they represent a common kind of unreasoned, unprogrammed revision, the kind we make when we feel that a certain expression 'sounds better this way'. Often we have no idea why it sounds better that way; and sometimes, at a later reading, we feel that it sounded better as we had it in the first place; but these things are symptoms of the fallible humanity of composition.

So Wordsworth, fallible and human, may have decided that 'moved slowly through *the* mind' sounded better, on the whole, than 'moved slowly through *my* mind'. Yet I am inclined to put my faith in a third possibility: that the lines are neither mistranscribed, nor changed on an impulse, but purposefully recast. In the shape they take in the 1850 text, they follow the general programme of revision, which is always to transform the autobiographical figure of the boy into a more generalised shape, an abstraction signifying experience at large.

The shift from '*my* mind' to '*the* mind' mobilises a common rule of English semantics, exemplified by the sentences 'Confession is good for my soul' and 'Confession is good for the soul'; one of these statements applies to a particular person, but its companion is a pronouncement on the life of any human being. Accordingly, 'my mind' records the intimate experience of one man, but 'the mind', with an effect of greater distance and breadth, relates the experience of one to the potential experience of all.

There is one feature of the wording of this intricate piece of verse that does not vary from 1805 to 1850; a most interesting one because it appears to be central to the semantic structure of a passage in which the narrator's point of view shifts elusively between the perspective from 'as I see it now' and the involvement of 'as I knew it then'. The shifts of stance are demonstrably related to occurrences of the *BE+Complement* construction, that is, a syntactic structure consisting of one of the forms of the verb *to be*, followed by the so-called *Subject Complement*, in the shape of an adjective, a noun, or a noun phrase qualifying or identifying the preceding Subject. (As in 'Mary is beautiful', 'Beethoven was a composer', 'This measure was one of the Government's worst mistakes'.)

In the telling of this Wordsworthian tale, there are three significantly placed instances – the only three in the whole passage – of the *Be+Complement* structure. They are:

> It was an act of stealth/ And troubled pleasure (361–2)
> She was an elfin pinnace (373)
> huge and mighty forms . . . were a trouble to my dreams (388–400)

(The line-references are to the 1850 text.) The significance of these assertions, as signposts in the narrative (at its onset, its development and its conclusion), is that they mark moments of *evaluation*. In our common talk we make frequent use of the *Be+Complement* structure, either in strictly factual description, the business of *naming* ('It's a large car, it's a Mercedes'), or in expressions of opinion and judgement ('He's an idler, he's a great disappointment').

Here, however, we are not concerned with common talk; we are engaged in the reading of a poetic text and of language selected and wrought by the poet's imagination. In two of the three instances under scrutiny, the language is manifestly that of affective evaluation, not of simple description. When Wordsworth declares, of the boat, 'She was an elfin pinnace', we are hardly expected to take him at his literal, descriptive word. A boat is only a boat, and this one, so the 1805 text informs us, is nothing grander than a shepherd's skiff. But here she becomes a pinnace, and an elfin pinnace at that. And she is a pinnace because that is how the boy-rower sees her. The standpoint is not that of the man looking back over the years; it is the position of one who returns, who lives it again, who feels what was felt *at that moment.*

Close reading of the text suggests that with this line, *She was an elfin pinnace*, the 'magic' or 'supernatural' or 'transcendental' sense of the narrative begins to displace the literal sense. It is the height of enchantment, this wonderful evocation of rowing, in the moonlight, on the glittering water among the fells; but, from that moment on, the gods alarmingly intervene. Light (as we have noted) is swallowed in darkness; mountains move, humans are chastened in their trivial presumptions, humbled by revelations of 'unknown modes of being'. The message to the rower is not 'Now put that boat back where you found it, William', but rather 'Boy, the world of Nature is no fairy-tale or playground, it is more mysterious, darker, greater, than you can ever imagine'. When the hills rear up their heads, the hands that pulled so lustily, with such a conceit of cleverness, tremble at the oars.

Until that moment, all is descriptive – beautifully, lyrically descriptive – *except* for one important pronouncement: 'It was an act of stealth and troubled pleasure.' In the 1850 text, after the deletion of the talkative lines about the inn and the holiday visit and the after-dinner walk, the statement, *It was an act of stealth*, comes very near to the beginning of the narrated episode. It is the first act of evaluation, as it were, assessing the protagonist's state of mind at the outset. It is also curiously ambivalent. Is the poet making a reminiscent judgement, speaking about an act as he sees it *now*, looking *back*? Or is he representing – no, re-presenting – the immediate feelings of *then*, in a form similar to what stylisticians call Free Indirect Thought? Is it a case of 'That was wrong, I now tell the reader', or 'This is wrong, I then told myself'? The conjoined clause, 'nor without the voice of mountain echoes did my boat move on', tends to support the feeling of something re-presented, an emotion recollected. This is how it was at that moment: the boy feeling misgivings, and seeming to hear the mountains sympathetically echoing his doubts. It is the eternal present of poetry, no less present for being presented in the past.

Yet it is not possible to dismiss the companion sense of recalling the act from afar, and pronouncing considered judgement upon it. The ambiguity of *it was* remains in the text. The reader may choose between 'It was, I then felt' and 'It was, I now judge'. That ambiguity of stance shadows this mysterious, haunting passage, in which the poet keeps shifting creative position, moving between the standpoint of the retrospective commentator and that of the participant whose emotional presence is at its strongest in that lyrical outburst 'She was an elfin pinnace'.

The third instance of the *BE+Complement* structure comes at the end of the passage, completing the narrative route from 'It was an act of stealth and troubled pleasure', through 'She was an elfin pinnace', to 'huge and mighty forms . . . were a trouble to my dreams'. It is not as clearly highlighted as the other two, which are simple clauses; here the *BE+Complement* construction stretches across a more complex grammatical and prosodic sequence, actually spanning two coordinated clauses. What it expresses, furthermore, is not an ambivalent judgement (as in 'it was an act of stealth'), or the immediacy of a feeling (as in 'she was an elfin pinnace'), but the sober recollection of something quite factual, as though the narrator were describing the symptoms of an illness. At the end we come through misgivings and fancies and down to reality, albeit the reality of spiritual terror. And it is not wholly a matter of coincidence, we might think, that the opening of the story is here connected with its close through the word *trouble*: the 'troubled pleasure' leads at length to the 'trouble' of admonitory dreams.

All this was a long time ago. Long, long indeed since the boy stole the boat on a moonlit summer's night in the eighteenth century, by the shores of Patterdale. Almost as long since the poet, brooding and puzzling over his text, made the little changes and corrections over which we, in our turn, are invited to puzzle and speculate so earnestly. Does it really matter to us now? Can the ancient page warrant all this manoeuvring with mere words? Yes, it does matter, and yes, it can. The moonlit boat-ride, such a little happening in such a long life, is ages gone; and yet we have with us still the living presence of poetry, those lines so carefully, so studiously wrought and rewrought, that touch us mystically with that inexplicable, inexpressible, ghostly laying-on-of-hands that Matthew Arnold was to call 'Wordsworth's healing power'.

What Arnold meant by that was certainly something deeper than the capacity to speak soothing words on sundry occasions. Wordsworth's healing is sometimes of the kind that can open old wounds. His work, furthermore, is repeatedly and doggedly a process of self-healing, of reliving the past until past and present harmonise. It is no doubt a lucky circumstance that Wordsworth lived before the age of institutionalised psychiatry; a modern professional therapist would have cured the growing boy beyond hope of recovery, and we would perhaps have lost much of the creative legacy that comes from a productive imbalance, from the commerce of rational and irrational, from discoveries made and extended in the remembrance of things past.

From Wordsworth perhaps more than from any other poet, we have inherited, as a powerful commonplace, the assumption that poetry is a reorganisation of memory. Or say, rather, a revision of visions, recalling how things were; and then, perhaps, how we would like them to have been; and then – ah, then – taking the conclusive, committed step, how it is *necessary* for them to have been, if we are to reconcile past and present and read the complex music of our own lives. An examination of this passage from 'The Prelude' evokes many of those powerful Wordsworthian phrases that testify to his poetic belief in memory as *heuresis*: 'the child is father to the man'; 'emotion recollected in tranquillity'; 'the soul remembering, not *what* it felt, but *how* it felt'; and most poignantly and powerfully, those lines from 'Tintern Abbey' in which he says of himself:

For I have learned
To look on nature, not as in the hour
Of thoughtless youth; but hearing oftentimes
The still, sad music of humanity,
Nor harsh, nor grating, though of ample power
To chasten and subdue.

These are the declarations of one given to revision in the most ample and profound sense of the word: revision allowing *re-vision*. Poetic revising, in Wordsworthian practice, means *revisiting*, perhaps revisiting an actual location (as he does in 'Tintern Abbey'), but more than that, an emotional revisiting, the recovery of a state of mind.[3] Such revisiting demands *revisualising* – seeing, hearing, feeling, knowing, living it all once more. The process is arduous, and raises doubts. What is it that is remembered? What paths of saying will lead us back to the truths of these matters? And so, inevitably, revisualising calls for *reverbalising*, a rewording of experience in terms that will not subvert or betray the original vision, but will enlarge it, endow it with a heightened significance.

Some such heightening, a raising into greater generality, appears to be the object of many of the changes made after 1805 and ultimately realised in the 1850 text of 'The Prelude'. The earlier text has its advocates, and not everyone regards the mutations of the later version as changes made for the better. Yet nearly always, and even in the smallest instances, they can be interpreted as an effort to grow and understand in recollection, a struggle for a self-knowledge that becomes, at length, the common knowledge of human souls. Dust as we are, the poet so memorably tells us, the immortal spirit grows, like harmony in music. (And even those great lines, let it be said, are a new growth of the spirit, a revision of something said earlier and not said so cogently, with such exhilarating conviction, with such an appearance of divine spontaneity.)

NOTES

1 More fully, Stephen's satire reads:

> Two voices are there: one is of the deep;
> It learns the storm cloud's thunderous melody,
> Now roars, now murmurs with the changing sea,
> Now birdlike pipes, now closes soft in sleep:
> And one is of an old half-witted sheep
> Which bleats articulate monotony,
> And indicates that two and one are three,
> That grass is green, lakes damp, and mountains steep:
> And, Wordsworth, both are thine . . .

Robert Graves, in his course of Clark Lectures entitled *The Crowning Privilege* (Graves 1955: 110) remarks that 'Wordsworth so often parodied himself so unmercifully that J.K. Stephen's lines are supererogatory, if just.'

2 German romantic painter, a contemporary (1774–1840) of Wordsworth. His paintings powerfully suggest the immanence, in the natural world, of spiritual and transcendental powers.

3 On the Wordsworthian recovery of the past, see Basil Willey's illuminating essay ' "Nature" in Wordsworth', chapter XII of his book *The Eighteenth Century Background* (Willey 1946). Willey observes: 'At the time when he is writing *The Prelude* he appears already as the historian, rather than the present possessor, of the visionary power. The regular action of the world has already had its effect, and he is turning for stimulus to the past'. Willey's general point in these pages is that Wordsworth's reconstitution of things past is a turn from primitive feeling to a feeling *about* the feeling: from 'I cannot tell what then I was' to 'I have learned to look on Nature, &c'. The merging of 'what I felt' with 'what I feel about what I felt' is evident in the 'boat' passage, in both versions. Further, if in the 1805 version Wordsworth is 'already the historian', in the 1850 version he is the historian of a history – the custodian of recollection at (his own) second hand.

4 The 1805 version (lines 351–5) reads:

> The mind of man is framed even like the breath
> And harmony of music; there is a dark
> Invisible workmanship that reconciles
> Discordant elements, and makes them move
> In one society.

That the subsequent change makes a great, memorable line ('Dust as we are . . . &c') out of something less arresting, few, I think, would dispute. The substitution of 'inscrutable' for 'invisible' is a powerful inspiration; visibility is a property of things (which are either seen or unseen), but *scrutinizing* is a human activity; we try to scrutinise – but cannot – the workings of the creative mind.

REFERENCES

GRAVES, ROBERT. *The Crowning Privilege*, The Clark Lectures, 1954–55. London: Cassell & Co., 1955.

WILLEY, BASIL. *The Eighteenth Century Background*. London: Chatto & Windus, 2nd impr. 1946; pp. 272–81.

WORDSWORTH, WILLIAM. *The Prelude. A Parallel Text*, ed. J.C. Maxwell. Harmondsworth: Penguin Books, 1971, repr. 1975.

Seven

Remodelling models: Tennyson, and 'the old "Morte"'

One day towards the end of May in the year 1835, Alfred Tennyson and Edward Fitzgerald, on holiday at Ambleside, took a boat and rowed out onto Lake Windermere; and there, while they rested on their oars and looked down into the calm water ('quite unruffled and clear', according to Fitzgerald) Tennyson quoted some lines from a poem he had lately composed, lines alluding to a 'lonely maiden of the Lake', and to her handiwork, the sword Excalibur:

> Nine years she wrought it, sitting in the deeps
> Upon the hidden bases of the hills.

These were eloquent words, spoken in an appropriate setting (Windermere being then a remote place, untroubled by tourists, outboard engines and water skiers). Tennyson certainly liked them, approving his own lines with a characteristically gruff comment: 'Not bad that Fitz, is it?' Of which Hallam Tennyson observes: 'This kind of remark he would make when reading his own or others' poetry when he came to lines that he particularly admired, from no vanity but from a pure feeling of aesthetic pleasure.'

Tennyson was then 26 years old, a young man with more than his share of troubles. His undergraduate days at Cambridge had come to an abrupt end with the death of his father, a frustrated man who took refuge from bitterness in the 'illness' of intemperate drinking: he had struggled with the burdens of a family in straitened circumstances, a family of melancholiacs and epileptics, one of whom had taken to opium, while at least one other was mentally ill[1]; he had published, in 1832, a volume of poems which had been savagely attacked by Croker in the *Quarterly Review*; he had mourned (and would go on mourning) the untimely death of a friend, Arthur Hallam, who had seemed to him to be the most marvellously gifted of God's creatures. And at length he had retreated into the pride and silence and dedication of what might be called, without much exaggeration, a heroic decade, his own years of labour in the deeps – years that were to bring forth the poems constituting one of the most remarkable volumes in the literary history of England in the nineteenth century, the collection simply entitled *Poems, 1842*.

He was not easily drawn out of his wounded seclusion, but early in 1835 he was persuaded to accept an invitation, from his college friend James Spedding, to spend some weeks at Bassenthwaite. Fitzgerald also went; and at the end of what was to be quite a long visit, he and Tennyson, their friendship now firmly established, continued their holiday together, spending a week at Ambleside. This period of relaxation among sympathetic friends was a respite that Tennyson greatly needed, though the visit was not from the outset an unqualified social success. Tennyson's depression was too stubborn to budge at the first shift, and old Mr Spedding, his host's father, had a fairly poor opinion of poets in general and his son's friends in particular.

Nevertheless, those weeks at Mirehouses (Spedding's home) may have saved something for English literature by contributing to the recovery of a poetic self-esteem; they brought Tennyson into the company of friends who saw him as a man of genius, and who were confident of the future of his poetry. After the visit Spedding wrote: 'I think Alfred took more pleasure and inspiration than anyone would have supposed who did not know his almost personal dislike of the present, whatever it may be.' Some of his pleasure, at least, consisted in sharing his work with his friends. Throughout his life, as Hallam Tennyson's *Memoir* abundantly testifies, the poet enjoyed reading his work to an audience. In later years, his wife was usually the auditor of newly composed works, but in the early days of his craft it was Fitzgerald and Spedding who had the privilege of hearing him read, from his MS book, some of the poems that were to make up the second 1842 volume. Among the works thus brought into society was the 'Morte d'Arthur' – 'the old "Morte"', as a nostalgic Fitzgerald was later to call it.[2] It was from this poem that Tennyson quoted on that calm Windermere day, watching the water make its tableau in the amphitheatre of the hills.

Many readers (but especially the elderly, with glum recollections of having to memorise and recite in class) know 'Morte d'Arthur' as a poem in its own right, unsupported by any introductory or explanatory composition. It retells Malory's tale of events after the Round Table's last battle, when Sir Bedivere throws the sword Excalibur into the enchanted lake and the three queens come in their ship to take the mortally wounded Arthur to the isle of Avalon. It is a recital complete in itself. Once a poem, one might think, always a poem. Yet Tennyson published the 'Morte' twice, setting it in different contexts, allowing different interpretations. His serial poem, *Idylls of the King*, comes to a fitting epic-theatrical close with the 'Morte' skilfully incorporated into the idyll called 'The Passing of Arthur'. But that is the second, possibly the more ambitious and less immediately personal, of the poem's two settings. In the context of its first publication, the 'Morte' – Fitzgerald's 'old "Morte"' – presents a less monumental aspect. The lighting, so to speak, is different; the lines are played in a different theatre.

A number of the poems in the second part of the 1842 collection are of a genre to which Tennyson gave the name 'English Idyl' – with one *l*, as distinct from the Arthurian Idylls (with two *l*'s) of later decades. The English Idyls present the chronicles and crises of provincial and country life, scenes which Tennyson was well equipped to rehearse and to inform with poetic feeling. They are couched in a style which is sometimes deceptively flat and conversational, with all the sepia serenity of some old photograph album, but which repeatedly flourishes and quickens into brilliantly coloured images and vignettes. Theocritus provided a general model for the poems, but his precedent detracts nothing from their originality. They are an example of the kind of discovery a creative mind can make sometimes, when a crisis has been outlived; Sir Charles Tennyson assigns the development of the English Idyls to the period after the beginning of 1835, when Tennyson was 'able to look at the world with greater serenity and detachment.'[3]

Now, in the 1842 volume, the 'Morte' is presented as a poem within a poem, the outer frame being a brief narrative rendered in a subdued, prosy style with very few touches of rhetoric or ornament. These lines were composed some three or four years after the 'Morte', at a time when Tennyson was developing the blank verse technique that appears to splendid effect in English Idyls such as 'The Gardener's Daughter', 'Audley Court' and 'Walking to the Mail'. Whoever reads a poem like 'Audley Court' will certainly be struck by the mingling of a relaxed conversational manner with images of intensified sensation,[4] and by the apparent ease with which the poet negotiates transitions from diffusion to concentration, from the casual to the formal, from things *spoken* to things *declaimed*. The framing lines called 'The Epic' supply one of the counterpoises in just such a stylistic balance. They are designedly commonplace, creating an 'illusion of resemblance' (see p. 3); until their conversational banality yields to the oratory and ritual splendour of the 'Morte', a Tennysonian 'illusion of transcendence'.

This scene-setting is important to a reading of 'the old "Morte"'. At the very least, it explains why a poem should begin out of nothing, with the word 'So'. What is the 'thus' that leads on to this 'so'? The frame poem tells us. A small group of men at a Christmas Eve gathering (men, we note – not a woman in the company) sit talking regretfully of the decay of customs and manners; one of them, a poet, is persuaded by his host (much as Spedding might have persuaded Tennyson) to read aloud a surviving fragment of the text of a largely destroyed Arthurian epic; after this recital, the observer–narrator of these events retires to sleep, dreams of the coming of a modern Arthur, and is at length woken by the sound of the bells pealing for Christmas Day. Prologue and epilogue together take up only 82 lines (51 before the 'Morte', 31 after), and this very compactness, together with their undemonstrative style, may well account for Fitzgerald's dismissive comment:

> The 'Morte d'Arthur' when read to us from a manuscript in 1835 had no introduction or epilogue; which was added to anticipate or excuse the 'faint Homeric echoes', etc. (as in the 'Day Dream') to give a reason for telling an old-world tale.[5]

The assumption that these lines merely furnish a sort of introduction, leading to the sonorous recital of the 'Morte', is not the whole story, however. Fitzgerald's allusion to the poem (or suite of poems) called 'The Day Dream' is especially misleading. There, the lines that create a setting for the work do that and only that; they do not present the reader with such stylistic contrasts that distinguish the 'Morte' from its frame or promote a reading of the poem as a morally impassioned personal statement – a programme for a poet in trouble and out of sympathy with his own time. The prologue and epilogue of 'The Epic' make up one of the panels in a diptych of confronting styles and ethical stances, the modern/banal versus the ancient/heroic. Without the 'Morte' the framing lines are, of course, pointless, whereas the heroic lines can be read without reference to their 'banal' frame. Yet if this reference is ignored, something is taken from the 'Morte d'Arthur'. It remains as an imaginative poetic interpretation of some vivid pages in Malory, but it loses a dimension – of despair, of hope, of moral exhortation. The framing lines have a more than casual value, and deserve rather more than casual study.[6]

The seasonal setting of 'The Epic' is one of its most significant features: Christmas time, the remembrance of things past, the 'almost personal dislike of the present, whatever it may be', the longing, accentuated by the season's religious significance, for the restoration of some indefinable vanished power:

> At Frances Allen's on the Christmas-eve –
> The game of forfeits done – the girls all kiss'd
> Beneath the sacred bush and past away –
> The parson Holmes, the poet Everard Hall,
> The host, and I sat round the wassail-bowl,
> Then half-way ebb'd: and there we held a talk,
> How all the old honour had from Christmas gone,
> Or gone, or dwindled down to some odd games
> In some odd nooks like this;[7]

These opening lines reflect Tennyson's attachment to domestic and social rituals, particularly those of Christmas, a festival which symbolised for him (as indeed it has done for countless others) the continuity of human experience, of suffering redeemed by hope, from generation to generation. For him, the season had great power to evoke the 'passion of the past' which informs so much of his work. The association of Christmas with the memory of times and persons departed is recorded in 'In Memoriam', LXXVIII, with its mention of 'ancient games', and in CV, which alludes to the 'bowl of wassail', and which asks, with reference to the pastimes and ceremonies of Christmas:

> For who would keep an ancient form
> Through which the spirit breathes no more?

Those lines express in directly personal terms the view expressed in 'The Epic' of 'how the old honour had from Christmas gone'. In the 'In Memoriam' verses the personal concern, the biographical interest, is explicit, whereas the opening of 'The Epic' has a studied air of anecdote; nevertheless, the casual tone of 'it just so happened', in which the gathering at Francis Allen's is presented, cloaks a commitment to the feelings and longings of a season that has not wholly lost its spiritual significance.

In his description of the assembled company, Tennyson allots the explicit role of poet to an *alter ego*, a character called Everard Hall, and relegates himself, as 'I', to the position of a privileged observer, half-drowsing, half-attentive, recording an event and being caught up willy-nilly in its implicatory power. It is the familiar literary device of using a narrative *persona*, an overseeing 'I', to suggest, on the one hand, a benevolent detachment from what goes on and, on the other, a deep sympathetic involvement in whatever significances and consequences the events may have. The characters grouped around this narrator figure are such as Tennyson could readily furnish from his own social experience – the host, a country gentleman in a small way; the parson, whose views and subjects of conversation might be familiar, or at least easily conceivable, to one brought up in a provincial rectory; and the man of letters, at once self-deprecating and authoritative, with more than a hint of Tennyson himself. It is, one might say, a party of fictitious people with known personalities.

Of these characters, Hall eventually dominates the prologue-lines, after a meandering start that leads, with careful casualness, to the theme of poetry, its style, and its use in the modern world. The punctuation of this opening is worth noting. The first full stop in the text occurs in the middle of the 21st line (i.e. just under half way through the entire prologue). Before that point, segments, or 'snippets' of narrative information are bounded by dashes, colons and semicolons. Thus lines 1–6 set the scene with a few impressionistic strokes:

At Francis Allen's on the Christmas-eve –
The game of forfeits done – the girls all kiss'd
Beneath the sacred bush and past away –
The parson Holmes, the poet Everard Hall,
The host, and I sat round the wassail-bowl,
Then half-way ebb'd:

The dashes breaking up the main clause give this the air of something loosely recollected. The same casually retrospective sense is suggested by the quasi-demonstrative use of the definite article in 'the Christmas-eve' – as though the poet were saying 'on *that* Christmas eve', and, indeed, as though we readers had just tuned in to the narrator's reminiscent chat. The next segment bringing us up to the semi-colon in line 9, touches briefly, and with studied informality of language, on the 'ancient form through which the spirit breathes no more':

> and there we held a talk
> How all the old honour had from Christmas gone,
> Or gone, or dwindled down to some odd games
> In some odd nooks like this;

The talkative, off-handed style becomes almost a mannerism in the repetition of *odd* and the choice of a homely word like *nook*. But 'odd' and 'nook' (and 'dwindled'), besides suggesting commonplace talk, also have a belittling import, reducing the significance of things modern by contrast with the heroic dimensions of other times.

The characterisation of unheroic modernity continues in the next segment, which deftly establishes the character of the narrator:

> till I, tired out
> With cutting eights that day upon the pond,
> Where, three times slipping from the outer edge,
> I bump'd the ice into three several stars,
> Fell in a doze;

There is a touch of humorous self-projection in this. Hallam Tennyson, describing his father's days at Beech Hill House, near Epping (where almost certainly the prologue-lines of 'The Epic' were composed), records that 'There was a pond in the park on which in winter my father might be seen skating, sailing about on the ice in his long blue cloak.' The 'pond' upon which the skater slips 'three times', bumping the ice into 'three several stars', suggests an absurd Lilliputian prefiguring of that 'wild water' which is the scene of Bedivere's thrice-enacted trial of loyalty, and where the great brand Excalibur makes 'lightnings in the splendour of the moon'. This narrator is no Bedivere, no duty-burdened warrior at the last pitch of fealty, his senses rioting, his mind in a tumble of apprehensions. He is a dullish chap who goes skating, becomes drowsy with the effect of good food, good drink and a warm fire, and nods into sleep. His somnolence is convenient, since it precludes the technical necessity of detailing every turn in the conversation, and brings us to the character of the parson, Holmes, and to a full stop – at last! – in the twenty-first line:

and half-awake I heard
The parson taking wide and wider sweeps,
Now harping on the church-commissioners,
Now hawking at Geology and schism;
Until I woke, and found him settled down
Upon the general decay of faith
Right thro' the world – 'at home was little left,
And none abroad: there was no anchor, none,
To hold by'.

The detail is realistic and topical. An Ecclesiastical Commission had been established in 1835 to look into the efficiency of the established Church and the distribution of its revenues. This body presented its report in 1836, so that when 'The Epic' was composed it was very topical and was indeed just such a matter that might put Parson Holmes out of humour. As for 'Geology and schism', we know that in 1837 Tennyson was reading Charles Lyell's *The Principles of Geology*, and we may at least guess (Holmes' angry reference to 'abroad' seems to confirm it) that he would have heard something of contemporary German theologians and the challenge to the historicity of Biblical myth.[8]

The things that disgruntle Holmes are, in short, the topical bugbears of a conservative cleric in the 1830s. They also represent, at a masqueraded remove, Tennyson's own bugbears, his 'dislike of the present, whatever it may be'. Through another of his *personae*, Edward Hall, he is about to present images of human action in which the test of value in life is the mystical bond between a sovereign and his followers, and not some well-paragraphed code of bureaucratic efficiency; in which the hope always exists that humanity may arise and re-make its destinies, unfettered by the bitter determinism of scientific law; in which 'myth' is powerful, and in a sense historically true, because of what it begets in terms of human faith and because of its action as a carrier and disseminator of what is essential in our experience.

The worthy and crotchety Holmes would hardly express himself in these terms, but the fact is surely that Tennyson exhibits, in his portrayal of Holmes' professional discontent, one symptom among many of a general sickness of heart. In one respect, these lines concerning Holmes are the most important part of the prologue, for the 'Morte d'Arthur' is an answer to the allegation of 'the general decay of faith/ Right thro' the world'. Of course it is hardly to be anticipated, at this point in the reading, that the answer to that charge will come in the form of a recital of chivalric myth; though hindsight may later suggest that when Tennyson describes Holmes as 'harping' and 'hawking' – not in the epic-chivalric sense of those words, but only in shabby modern transference – he is having an ironic joke at the parson's expense.

The first 21 lines of 'The Epic' thus set an ostensibly casual scene with more than casual implications, and in rapid execution furnish what is literally a 'pre-text' for the heroic narrative of the 'Morte'. But the narrative has yet to be introduced, and with it a spokesman fit to declaim its sonorous lines – a role for which the sleepy skater, the 'I' of the prologue, is manifestly unqualified. So Everard Hall makes his entry. The shift of focus from Holmes to Hall is managed by an amiable interposition of the host-figure, Frances Allen, picking up Holmes' expression 'hold by':

'. . . there was no anchor, none,
To hold by.' Francis, laughing, clapt his hand
On Everard's shoulder, with 'I hold by him.'
'And I', quoth Everard, 'by the wassail-bowl.'
'Why yes,' I said, 'we knew your gift that way
At college: but another which you had,
I mean of verse (for so we held it then),
What came of that?'

With a little banter and a bracketed by-the-by, an all-important theme comes in: the poet and the social relevance of poetic styles. The transition from assertive parson to modest poet is deft, even a little sly. A characteristic feature is the note of nostalgic retrospect; Hall is presented as one who *was once* respected for his verses, but who now merely 'holds by the wassail-bowl'. His confidence in the reality of a poetic vocation has gone, and despair at the apparent irreconcilability of poetic spirit and pragmatic substance has led him to a nihilistic gesture, the destruction of his own work:

'You know,' said Frank, 'he burnt
His epic, his King Arthur, some twelve books' –
And then to me demanding why? 'Oh, sir,

He thought that nothing new was said, or else
Something so said 'twas nothing – that a truth
Looks freshest in the fashion of the day:
God knows: he has a mint of reasons: ask.
It pleased *me* well enough.' 'Nay, nay,' said Hall,
'Why take the style of those heroic times?
For nature brings not back the Mastodon,
Nor we those times: and why should any man
Remodel models? these twelve books of mine
Were faint Homeric echoes, nothing-worth,
Were chaff and draff, much better burnt.'

From the 'mint of reasons' (is it simply coincidental that Allen, the sound modern man, turns a commercial phrase?) one significant plea emerges: it is useless for a poet to attempt the heroic style, for it is dead, as the Mastodon is dead. Indeed, the very tradition of poetry, which in fact requires the continual 'remodelling of models' may be dead. The allusion to the Mastodon recalls the earlier side-glance at 'Geology', and suggests a feeling of hopelessness in the face of the deterministic and evolutionary doctrines of contemporary science. If the development of sentient life on earth, from one phase of collective being to another, is governed by natural and impersonal laws, what place is there for the heroic spirit of self-determination?; and if heroic action is irrelevant, then the heroic imagination, the heroic style, poetic myth and poetry itself, are alike irrelevant – so why not burn one's epic books and take to the wassail-bowl? Thus interpreted, Hall's reluctance to accept the responsibilities of poetry is not a projection of Tennysonian mock-modesty; it is a symptom of perplexity and despair.

Tennyson, however, allows his character an escape from poetic annihilation through the prudent intervention of Allen, who has rescued from the flames one book – the eleventh – of the doomed and discarded epic, and can now propose for it a modest use, in that it offers the pleasant possibility of sweetening Parson Homes's sour temper. To this extent at least, poetry is still relevant:

'But I,'
Said Francis, 'pick'd the eleventh from this hearth
And have it: keep a thing, its use will come.
I hoard it as a sugar-plum for Holmes.'

The supper-table image ('sugar plum') and the penny-wise proverbial phrasing ('keep a thing, its use will come') seem deliberately unheroic, a calculated reduction of style to the most matter-of-fact and mundane level. The guise in which the prologue's narrator then presents himself is even more remote from the world of heroic action:

He laugh'd, and I, tho' sleepy, like a horse
That hears the corn-bin open, prick'd my ears.

Thus the unheroic scene is prepared for the poet's transforming words, and all that remains is to bid him read them; which he does, with a delivery that recalls tributes paid by Fitzgerald and others to Tennyson's own reading. Fitzgerald described Tennyson's voice as 'like the sound of a far sea or of a pinewood'; Carlyle thought it 'musical, metallic, fit for loud laughter and piercing wail, and all that may lie between'; Thomas Wilson recalled how Tennyson would 'read aloud in the evening, in a deep sustained sonorous voice'.[9] It is in such a fashion that Everard Hall begins his recital:

then at my request
He brought it; and the poet little urged,
But with some prelude of disparagement,
Read, mouthing out his hollow oes and aes,
Deep-chested music, and to this result.

The 'Morte' follows, with the 'deep-chested oes and aes', and the 'Homeric echoes' of the very first line; with the onset of a pronounced metrical beat, solemn as a funeral march, unresting, unhasting, at stark variance with the sporadic conversational rhythms of the prologue; and with the description, abruptly initiated by a conjunct adverb, 'So', of a drastic world of battle and death, of honour at risk, of the loss of a world of order in a wide and comfortless waste. There could be no more obtrusive contrast with the 'odd nook' of Francis Allen's house, the 'odd games' of the Christmas Eve party, and the apparently aimless talk of men half-befuddled with warmth and wine and sweetmeats.

Yet this prologue, it must be insisted, is not 'aimless'. Its careful design aims to present contemporary humanity in its more-or-less good-natured, well-fed littleness; to raise the question of whether, given such a 'dwindled' world, the heroic habit of thought and style can ever again be fitting or relevant to the present, whatever it may be; and to introduce, in the person of Everard Hall, the type of a poet who has the gift to find great words for a little age, though for a moment conviction has faltered within him. Hall is not necessarily, or wholly, Tennyson; however, there is indeed much of Tennyson in Hall – *here lies another* – and the prologue as a whole conveys a sense of so much that we think of as 'Tennysonian', i.e. a yearning for the heroic, an attachment to memories of the past, a love of domesticity and custom and a shy vulnerability combined with a strong sense of personal worth.

From the muted and irresolute rhythms of its introduction, the text now breaks away – 'So' – into the sonority and prosodic formality of the 'Morte'. The wintry mountains invade the warm parlour, the skater's pond is lost in the wild water of an enchanted mere, the mumble of desultory conversation drowns in the surges of battle; domesticity – fire-flickering, bounded, secure – fades into the epic prospect of an indeterminate, cheerless and hostile landscape, lit by a baleful moon and swept by a bitter wind. The transmutation is significant and obvious, yet its significance can be lost if the reader regards the prologue-lines of 'The Epic' simply as a piece of inoffensive versifying to whisk us – hey presto! – from Victorian England to the world of Malory (or a made-over Malory).

Though it has long been recognised as a classic text, the 'Morte' has not altogether escaped adverse comment, which in some instances appears to be the result of a refusal to accept the poem on Tennyson's conditions. The critic's task in this instance should be to explore the relationship between a well-known piece of verse, the content of which is derived from a late medieval prose classic, and a verse-context or 'setting' which is not so well known, and which, indeed, is often omitted from anthology reprints. We should not judge the aesthetic value of 'the old "Morte" ' entirely by comparison with Malory – strong though the verbal resemblances may be and striking though the departures from Malory may be; we should consider it also in relationship to the unpoetical-poetic frame that Tennyson devised for it. The poem was there before the frame, to be sure; but the act of framing has inevitably modified the perceptions of the viewer, or reader.

Landscape and 'timescape' are of importance in the 'Morte' – are important, indeed, in the disjunction and vagueness that critics have sometimes deplored. Here, at the outset, there is a contrast with Malory, and a striking departure from his brief but clear indications of time and setting. In Malory, Arthur's fatal encounter with Mordred and his army is described as taking place 'uppon a downe besyde Salysbyry and nat farre from the seesyde', on 'Monday aftir Trynyte Sonday'.[10] Tennyson transforms this unremarkable 'downe' into the rough sea-girt mountains of Lyonesse. This is interesting, but even more interesting is the corollary change of seasonal setting. Trinity Sunday is in midsummer; in Tennyson, the 'last battle in the west' is fought in winter 'among the mountains by the winter sea'. This change in the setting of the 'Morte' would eventually be related to the encompassing scheme of the completed *Idylls of the King*, where each poem in the twelve-book cycle corresponds to a time of year and answers to a mood of growth or maturity or decay.

But we must assume that 'the old "Morte"' was composed with little or no anticipation of its integration into a poetic design worked out many years later. In the 1830s Tennyson may have had ambitions to write an Arthurian epic, but he can hardly have foreseen the stages by which his serial poem would grow, and it is unlikely that he would have had in mind, at such an early date, the details of his 'cyclic' imagery of time.[11] His change from Malory's time and place might be explained in the first instance as a deliberate piece of staging, a resetting of the action with a romantic-symbolic decor which heightens the rhetoric of crisis and emphasises the isolation and interdependence of the two actors, Arthur and Bedivere. But when the framing lines of 'The Epic' came to be composed, it would appear that the change proved doubly convenient: an ordinary midwinter gathering introduces an extraordinary midwinter poem. A correspondence of season and hour (the 'Morte' is a night poem as well as a poem of winter) adds effect to the contrast between the Christmas Eve party, with its gossips and grumblers, and the desolation of the icy battlefields, the eerie landscape and the two stricken survivors of the day-long conflict.

The features of the 'eerie landscape' are hardly identifiable from an Ordnance map – though there have been attempts to locate in reality the doomsday topography set forth in lines like these:

> a chapel nigh the field,
> A broken chancel with a broken cross,
> That stood on a dark strait of barren land.
> On one side lay the Ocean, and on one
> Lay a great water . . .

This 'dark strait of barren land' is a wilderness of 'zig-zag paths and juts of pointed rock', of 'icy caves and barren chasms' and 'juts of slippery crag' standing stark and bleak under 'the splendour of the moon'. A vague landscape, indeed; and if we look for precise directions we shall soon be lost in little inconsistencies. (At one point, for example, Bedivere is described as going 'across the ridge', while the next phase of his triple temptation sees him leaping 'down the ridges'.[12]) But it was hardly Tennyson's business to provide the reader with a versified account of the contours of Lyonesse. The vagueness, the avoidance of consistent points of orientation and the shiftiness of the landscape are surely deliberate. The scene is comfortless, unearthly and vast – a fitting background for Bedivere's ordeal and moral confusion. *Here is elsewhere.* We do not require of heroic action that its terrain should be as considerately signposted as a National Park.

The dramatic landscape appears to specify all sorts of topographical and geological features – rocks, ridges, caves, a beach, an inland mere, the ocean, a ruined chapel – yet still it is elusive, indeterminate; and this indeterminacy only serves to give sharper definition to the two characters who emerge from its moon-mistiness into a humanity somewhat larger than life. The change of personal scale is reflected in the imagery of the poem:

> But the other swiftly strode from ridge to ridge,
> Clothed with his breath, and looking, as he walk'd,
> Larger than human on the frozen hills.

The characters are not dwarfed by their huge environment; on the contrary, their isolation makes their natures more largely evident, their very gestures and actions more studied and significant.

Here again, Tennyson has digressed from Malory, who admits into his doomsday narrative some background figures to give a pathetic or paltry scale to an all-too-human event. In Malory, the stricken king is helped from the field not only by Sir Bedivere, but also by Sir Lucan, himself mortally wounded. The task is laborious and distressing:

> And noble kynge Arthure felle in a swough to the
> erthe, and there he sowned oftyntyme, and sir Lucan
> and sir Bedwere offtetyme hove hym up. And so waykly
> betwyxte them they lad hym to a lytyll chapell nat
> farre from the see . . .

From his refuge in the 'lytyll chapell' the king hears sounds of shouting, and sends Sir Lucan to investigate:

> So sir Lucan departed, for he was grevously wounded in many placis; and so as he yode [went] he saw and harkened by the moonelyght how that pyllours [looters] and robbers were com into the fylde to pylle and to robbe many a ful noble knyght of broches and bees [bracelets] and of many a good rynge and many a ryche juell. And who that were nat dede all oute, there they slew them for their harneys and their ryches.

Sir Lucan, having reported back to Arthur, presently dies of his wounds. Malory describes the event with the tough realism (possibly the relish) of one hardened to war and its ludicrous horrors:

> Than sir Lucan toke up the kynge the tone party and sir Bedwere the othir parte, and in the lyfftyng up the kynge sowned [swooned], and in the lyfftynge sir Lucan fell in a sowne, that parte of his guttis felle oute of hys bodye, and therewith the noble knyght hys harte braste. And whan the kynge awoke he behylde sir Lucan, how he lay fomyng at the mowth and parte of his guttes lay at hys fete.

This is the language of someone who knew what a battlefield was like; Malory is expert in the illusions of resemblance. Tennyson rejects such realism and banishes Sir Lucan from the tale, to make way for a designedly theatrical presentation of the death of a warrior-king. The theatricality is most marked in a passage containing one of those 'faint Homeric echoes', the absurd periphrasis 'drops of onset':

> for all his face was white
> And colourless, and like the withered moon
> Smote by the fresh beam of the springing east;
> And all his greaves and cuisses dash'd with drops
> Of onset.

Drops of onset on the greaves are more picturesque and less upsetting than guts on the ground. But it is Arthur's 'passing away' (for once the traditional cliché holds its own) that occupies the Tennysonian stage. Sir Lucan's groaning mortality would be out of place here.

Arthur is made a more commanding figure by Sir Lucan's absence, and Bedivere also becomes a larger personage. Malory shows Bedivere and Lucan supporting the king 'waykely betwixte them', making their way to the chapel by laborious fits and starts, continually having to stop to lift the king when he falls away in a faint. In the 'Morte', Sir Bedivere, in full armour, lifts and carries Arthur almost without effort. (He breathes a little heavily in the raw night air.) His physical prowess is taken for granted, as a proper attribute of a knight of the Round Table; indeed, an illusion of transcendence. And if there are no 'pyllours and robbers' on the Tennysonian field, it is not only because they would break the awful desolation of the moon-bleak wilderness, but also because such tawdry, villainous creatures destroy the myths of chivalry and diminish the stature of heroes.

The importance of Tennyson's design in reducing the scene to a landscape with two figures is above all that attention is focused on the personal and moral relationship of the doomed king and his sole surviving knight. They are all that is left, in the cold wilderness, of human civilisation. Solely through their bond with each other, through the authority of the king and the sore-tried yet enduring loyalty of the knight, does a world of values and aspirations continue to exist. Arthur's charismatic authority, the half-divinity that makes him appear 'like a rising sun', is dying out of him, dying out in the cold and darkness; Bedivere's human instinct to serve his own desires is beginning to shake free from the restraints of a long-held discipline. Yet authority and discipline hold long enough for Arthur to complete his ritual tasks and pass away safely into a realm out of time, from which, into time, he will return again.

For these last rites the god-king desperately needs his human agent; as Bedivere no less desperately needs his king, and cries out, aghast at the prospect of the imminent lapse of order and meaning:

> Ah! my Lord Arthur, whither shall I go?
> Where shall I hide my forehead and my eyes?
> . . .
> . . . now the whole ROUND TABLE is dissolved
> Which was an image of the mighty world;
> And I, the last, go forth companionless,
> And the days darken round me . . .

Arthur's answer to this desperation is given in terms which, in the wider context of 'The Epic', can be read as a counter to the querulous churchman-spirit of a Parson Holmes complaining that 'there was no anchor, none, to hold by':

The old order changeth, yielding place to new,
And God fulfils Himself in many ways,
Lest one good custom should corrupt the world.
Comfort thyself; what comfort is in me?
I have lived my life, and that which I have done
May he within himself make pure! but thou,
If thou shouldst never see my face again,
Pray for my soul. More things are wrought by prayer
Than this world dreams of. Wherefore, let thy voice
Rise like a fountain for me night and day.
For what are men better than sheep or goats
That nourish a blind life within the brain,
If, knowing God, they lift not hands of prayer
Both for themselves and those who call them friend?
For so the whole round earth is every way
Bound by gold chains about the feet of God.

The illuminist sentiments of this passage may well be Tennyson's poetic answer to an orthodox cleric's disgruntled charge of 'the general decay of faith throughout the world'; and furthermore may be the sort of answer that would have provoked renewed complaints of 'schism' from churchmen of the Holmesian cast.[13] Arthur offers a creed that transcends sectarian boundaries. The outward and visible institution, the Round Table, is merely symptomatic of an inward condition, the immanent spiritual unity of humankind, realized through prayer. The individual may 'comfort himself' through prayer; through prayer he may make his life complete and meaningful; through prayer also he may perfect his fellowship with others, so that he does not 'go forth companionless'.[14]

Arthur's long speech is derived from three laconic sentences in Malory, none of which contains a hint of this doctrine of prayer as the language and action of an ideal brotherhood. Without the information supplied by the prologue-lines, this passage might read like a gratuitous intrusion of Victorian piety. But the prologue makes it clear that Tennyson is raising a question: the outward forms of our life appear so trivial, our aspirations and personal relationships so petty – is it possible to live and act in a spirit of heroic fellowship? Arthur's speech contains the answer which the 'Morte' presents in response to this baffled query; for the poem is not only a criticism of the state of modern man, it is also a consolation. And as a consolation it may be read at another, more directly personal level, for it would be remarkable – given the facts of Tennyson's life at this time – if we did not sometimes glimpse behind the masks of Arthur and Bedivere the faces of Arthur Hallam and Tennyson himself. Seen in this light, the poem becomes an elegiac tribute to a personal 'sun-king', an expression of grief at the loss of one whose confidence gave meaning to life, a profession of faith in the consolatory and constructive power of prayer. But whether the poem is read as a public affirmation or a private meditation, or both, its structure and symbolism demand that action shall turn upon two men and two men alone; the individual who embodies charismatic power and the individual who acknowledges and responds to it.

Malory provided Tennyson with a ritualistic pattern to which the presentation of this master–disciple relationship could be admirably accommodated: the recital of Bedivere's threefold essay with the sword Excalibur. Malory's account occupies some 50 lines or more of prose, from the moment when the king, sensing that his time is at hand, sends Bedivere to throw Excalibur into the lake, to the moment when, the task performed and the temptation overcome, Bedivere carries Arthur to the waiting barge. Tennyson expands this to almost 180 lines of verse; it is, in effect, the core episode of the 'Morte'. The expansions make Arthur and Bedivere alike more talkative, more explicit about events and motives, than they are in Malory. A good deal of this additional material serves to dramatise Bedivere's ordeal and project his thoughts, either through direct speech or, associatively, through imagery which is powerfully evocative, not least in its phonaesthetic appeal.

Malory recounts Bedivere's two lapses from fealty in straightforward style, noting, at the first failure, how Bedivere is tempted by the 'precious stonys' in the hilt of the sword, and reporting the words he says to himself – 'If I throw thys ryche swerde in the water, thereof shall never com good, but harme and losse'; and for the second occasion merely stating that 'hym thought synne and shame to throw away that noble swerde'. Tennyson is more artful (that adjective, though double-edged, is not inappropriate), taking up hints from Malory in order to create a portrait of temptation in its various degrees. In his representation of the first trial, Malory's statement that 'the pomell and the hauffte was all precious stonys' is expanded into an image of coruscating beauty – which, however, is no mere essay in poetic elaboration; it projects Bedivere's own bedazzled astonishment, and explains his abrupt yielding to a moment's impulse. In describing the second temptation, Tennyson takes his cue from Malory's 'thereof shall never com good, but harme and losse', and from this brief formula creates for Bedivere a piece of special pleading, of devious rationalising, that leaves him 'clouded with his own conceit.'[15] The treachery of the distracted senses is followed by the treachery of the perverted reason; and thus Tennyson uses the structual repetitions of the fable to stage the progressions of a moral analysis, implicit in Malory's narrative but not overtly presented there.

Tennyson is also unlike Malory in the dramatisation of his characters' emotions and sensations. There is an obvious example in one of the best-known episodes in the 'Morte', the passage describing how Bedivere carries Arthur down to the lake:

But the other swiftly strode from ridge to ridge,
Clothed with his breath, and looking, as he walk'd,
Larger than human on the frozen hills.
He heard the deep behind him, and a cry
Before. His own thought drove him like a goad.
Dry clash'd his harness in the icy caves
And barren chasms, and all to left and right
The bare black cliff clang'd round him, as he based
His feet on juts of slippery crag that rang
Sharp-smitten with the dint of armed heels –
And on a sudden, lo! the level lake
And the long glories of the winter moon.

Bedivere's haunted grandeur here may be contrasted with the inglorious fatigue of the narrator, the 'I' of the prologue:

tired out
With cutting eights that day upon the pond,
Where, three times slipping from the outer edge,
I bump'd the ice into three several stars.

But the lines in the 'Morte' are something more than a demonstration of the heroic style, or a *locus classicus* of sound-symbolism. They turn on the laconic statement, 'His own thought drove him like a goad'; the strident, discontinuous phonetic character of the lines which follow, with their agglomerations of plosive ('stop') and fricative consonants – the bumpings and scrapings – project this goaded anxiety until, in the last two lines, there is a resolution into the calm, mellow continuity of the lateral approximant consonants (the *l* sounds) and the sonority of back vowels (e.g. 'l*o*ng', 'gl*o*ries', 'm*oo*n'), suggesting the relief with which the character brings his burden safely to the appointed place. Landscape – the unreal, unrecognisable, untopographical landscape of the shivering senses – acquires a value as the projection of psychological states, in the transition from anxiety to calm. There is a further instance of this in the expansion of Malory's account of the mysterious ladies to whom Bedivere brings the dying Arthur. Malory says of them that 'they wepte and shryked when they saw kynge Arthur'. Tennyson's version is:

and from them rose
A cry that shiver'd to the tingling stars,
And, as it were one voice, an agony
Of lamentation, like a wind, that shrills
All night in a waste land, where no one comes,
Or hath come, since the making of the world.

Ostensibly a description of the ladies' pitiful cry, this is in effect yet another evocation of the harsh, eerily untenanted landscape. Isolation and desolation are projected in the synaesthesia that makes a cry 'shiver' or stars 'tingle', in the metonymy that equates a voice with an 'agony', in the personifying metaphor that makes the wind, the invisible, unpersoned wind, 'shrill all night'. The lines are one more reminder that we are not sitting comfortably before the parlour fire with our sugar plums and wine; we are under a cold moon, on a rocky shore, at tether's end.

All this amounts, frankly, to stagecraft; and though it might be more positive, and possibly more just, to dwell on the poet's lyrical powers, it will do Tennyson no great harm to admit that he is often incorrigibly and unashamedly theatrical. (Those who dislike him might say 'stagey' or even 'hammy'.) Everything in the language of the 'Morte' – the crowding effects of sound-symbolism, the incantatory, near-hypnotic repetitions, the sensory images, the frequent similes, the archaisms and 'Homeric echoes', the rephrasings of Malory (which do not always appear as changes for the better) – can be related to the wish to devise a moral enactment, theatrical in its oratory, its scenic grandeur, its symbolic implications, its symmetry of design, its presentation of human psychology. The satisfying completeness of the 'Morte', with its stark delineation of human strength and weakness, and its promise of a redemptory power in spiritual experience, speaks against the diffidences, deprecations and half-commitments of the characters who are represented as listening to it, and even reciting it, for Everard Holmes is reproached by his own creation. The poet who has chosen silence or, at best, wassail-bowl jocosity stands condemned by the words of his dying and deathless king, aspiration's symbol, whose command is:

> Wherefore let they voice
> Rise like a fountain for me night and day.

The 'old "Morte"' ends with the lines:

> long stood Sir Bedivere
> Revolving many memories, till the hull
> Look'd one black dot against the verge of dawn
> And on the mere the wailing died away.

Years later, when the poem was incorporated with 'The Passing of Arthur', Tennyson was obliged to extend the narrative with a coda running to a further 29 lines and describing the disappearance of Arthur's funeral ship into a distance of echoic light. These lines are written with such assurance that readers, even those well acquainted with the 1842 setting, may forget how adeptly the imagery at the end of 'the old "Morte"' is keyed into that of the end-frame or epilogue. With the dying of human voices and the growing of the first light of dawn, the 'Morte' ends; and the epilogue begins:

> Here ended Hall, and our last light that long
> Had wink'd and threaten'd darkness, flared and fell:
> At which the parson, sent to sleep with sound,
> And waked with silence, grunted 'Good!' but we
> Sat rapt:

In the heroic world of the old story there is a promise of light, but a bemused and sleepy darkness besets Hall's auditors; and the one person to whom the recital should have had most to offer – the parson, with his complaints of 'the decay of faith' – has fallen asleep, neglectful of Francis Allen's proffered 'sugar plum'.

The friends sit in silent appreciation of Hall's recital, and yet their pleasure misses the poet's mark, and is attributed to qualities incidental to the serious purport of the poem:

it was the tone in which he read –
Perhaps some modern touches here and there
Redeemed it from the charge of nothingness –
Or else we loved the man and prized his work;
I know not;

The silence is broken by the crowing of the cock – but not to herald the coming of the light that would match in reality the conclusion of the poetic fable. It is a mild irony that the bird is a false harbinger:

but we sitting, as I said,
The cock crew loud; as at that time of year
The lusty bird takes every hour for dawn;[16]

Yet the spell of the recital is at last broken, and the resumption of commonplace activity is heavy-limbed, grudging, almost ill-tempered:

Then Francis, muttering, like a man ill-used,
'There now – that's nothing!' drew a little back,
And drove his heel into the smoulder'd log,
That sent a blast of sparkles up the flue;

The last sparks of fellowship fly brusquely away; the night's entertainment breaks under a heavy heel – 'There now – that's nothing!' His words refer to the state of the crumbled log, yet it is almost as though he were describing a response to the poetic experience; Francis Allen, having rescued the eleventh book of the epic 'from this hearth', now seems almost to be returning it whence it came.

But of Hall's listeners, one at least is haunted by his recital: the narrator, the 'I', the drowsy skater. In his dreams he has a vision of Arthur returning to his secular realm:

like a modern gentleman
Of stateliest port; and all the people cried
'Arthur is come again: he cannot die'.
Then those that stood upon the hills behind
Repeated – 'Come again, and thrice as fair'.

The dreamer's vision ends with the pealing of the bells ringing in Christmas Day. His dream of Arthur, the redemptory figure reborn in the time of the Redeemer, reads like a promise for humankind – if redeemers can exchange greaves and cuisses for frock coats and sideburns. It also reads wistfully, as an attempt at personal consolation, an affirmation by Tennyson that his dead friend will come again, in some form or other, in new hopes and new enterprises.

One of the most significant changes made in adapting 'the old "Morte"' to its new setting in 'The Passing of Arthur' was to make the promissory light at the end of the poem the sunrise of New Year's Day – a fitting end for a cycle of poems governed by the symbolism of changing seasons. But in the context of 'The Epic' it is Christmas morning that dawns with a new hope – and for Tennyson, as the relevant sections of 'In Memoriam' testify, Christmas was a season of personal and poignant significance:

Our voices took a higher range:
  Once more we sang: 'They do not die
  Nor lose their mortal sympathy,
Nor change to us, although they change;

'Rapt from the fickle and the frail
  With gathered power, yet the same
  Pierces the keen seraphic flame
From orb to orb, from veil to veil.'

Rise, happy morn, rise, holy morn,
  Draw forth the cheerful day from night:
  O Father, touch the east, and light
The light that shone when Hope was born.

('In Memoriam', XXX)

The closing lines of 'The Epic' present a striking parallel with another 'In Memoriam' passage. 'Come again, and thrice as fair' is the cry heard by the dreamer, and in that instance 'come' is, of course, a participle ('he has come'), not an imperative; yet the line is shadowed by ambiguity, as though it concealed a call to the departed, as Tennyson calls to Hallam in 'In Memoriam', XCI:

Come, wear the form by which I know
  Thy spirit in time among thy peers;

Come; not in watches of the night,
  But where the sunbeam broodeth warm,
  Come, beauteous in thine after form
And like a finer light in light.

It is in 'watches of the night' that King Arthur acts out the last scenes of his authority, but it is towards the 'verge of dawn' that his funeral ship takes him, and it is in a dawn-dream that he comes again, 'beauteous' in his 'after-form'.

To study 'The Epic' closely is to realise that its poem-within-a-poem, the 'Morte d'Arthur' is a deeply personal testament. It can be read as an encoded tribute to Arthur Hallam, but that is, perhaps, no more than an option for the receptive reader. The obligatory reading is one that sees the 'Morte' as a resounding poetic answer to the fretful puzzlings of modern man. How do we get along nowadays? Are we decadent? Have we lost touch with the true nature and meaning of experience? Are our customs trivial, our institutions corrupt? Is it best, after all, to drink up and let the world go by? We are uncertain; but poetry survives and is constant, a way of acting and knowing. The conviction of art outspeaks the unfaith of living – that above all is the sense in which 'the old "Morte"' is a personal declaration.

If we read it in that sense, it is because the frame-poem, the carefully devised *setting*, encourages such a reading. In its later context, at the close of 'The Passing of Arthur', the last of the *Idylls of the King*, the 'Morte' sheds its personal meaning and takes its place as the concluding episode in a cycle of works devoted to the deeds of the Round Table and the great King who comes, mysteriously, out of the sea and at last returns to the sea ('from the great deep to the great deep he goes'). This is – to repeat a phrase used earlier – a different theatre, though the script may read the same, word for word.

The question of setting and resetting, or 'remodelling models' is one that must at some time occupy any creative artist. Musicians have been known to use the same piece more than once in different contexts of form and intention; painters paraphrase their own work, and find repeated use for the studies recorded in their sketchbooks; and writers are ready enough to relocate a serviceable text, pointing yesterday's words in today's direction. Is this no more than a species of professional economy, a saving of creative labour? Sometimes, no doubt; but it can be seen in another way. If a text is the product of a dream – the creative trance described on p. 2 of this book – the resetting of the text arguably demands that the dream be dreamed again, a new illusion be recovered by a new imaginative effort, the Gate of Horn be revisited. Only TV cooks and craftpersons can say 'Here's one I made earlier'. For poets there is no ready-made language; there is, at most, language to be re-experienced in the creative trance and redirected to new ends.

NOTES

1 In 1832 Tennyson's brother Edward was committed to a home for the insane, in York, and stayed there until his death in 1890. Charles Tennyson (who later changed his name to Turner) was the opium addict, having become 'a hopeless victim of the drug' by 1834. Arthur Tennyson became 'so hopelessly addicted to alcohol that in 1842 he had to go to a mental hospital in Scotland, unsuccessfully taking the cure'. Septimus, who described himself as 'the most morbid of the Tennysons' suffered from depression. For an instructive account of this unhappy band of kinsmen, see chapter 9 of Robert Bernard Martin's *Tennyson, The Unquiet Heart* (Martin 1980).

2 Hallam Tennyson, *Memoir*, Vol. I, p. 153. Fitzgerald wrote to Tennyson in praise of 'Gareth and Lynette': 'I don't think it is mere perversity that makes me like it better than all its predecessors, save and except (of course) the old "Morte".' The 'predecessors' were the existent Arthurian *Idylls*. Fitzgerald disliked on the whole the first volume of *Idylls*, and welcomed a poem on the 'masculine' theme of endurance and attainment.

3 See Sir Charles Tennyson (1950: 178). The 'serenity' and 'detachment' must be relative terms. Tennyson's father had died in 1831; his brother Edward had been committed to an asylum in 1832; his first volume of poems had been savaged by the critics in 1833; in the same year his best friend had died unexpectedly; his own security, material and psychological, was in the balance.

4 This poem ('Audley Court') contains a short passage (lines 22–5) that might qualify as the most richly sensuous description of a game pie ever to figure in a serious poem; it is worth comparing with the description of Excalibur in 'Morte d'Arthur' (lines 56–8).

5 For Fitzgerald's comment, see Hallam Tennyson, *Memoir*, Vol. I, p. 194. The 'faint Homeric echoes' are defined by Christopher Ricks, *The Poems of Tennyson* (Ricks 1969): 'set epithets, and set lines introducing and closing speeches; the words of one speaker being quoted by another; repetitions of words and lines; and soliloquies'.

6 For an excellent short study of 'The Epic' in relation to the 'Morte', see Lawry (1959: 400–3).

7 The edition used in this essay is that of Ricks (1969).

8 Tennyson's reading of Lyell is mentioned in Hallam Tennyson, *Memoir*, Vol. I, p. 162. His interest in theology, particularly in reformist theology, is noted in the *Memoir*, I, p. 186. Hallam Tennyson's comment on the theological *Zeitgeist* is worth recording for its relevance to the spirit of 'Morte d'Arthur': 'Meanwhile Maurice, Kingsley and the Cambridge men were striving to make thought more tolerant, and to impress all men with a sense of brotherhood.' As for developments 'abroad', D.F. Strauss's *Leben Jesu*, which denied the historicity of all supernatural elements in the Gospels, had been published in 1835–6. There is no evidence that Tennyson knew it, or knew of it, at the time when 'The Epic' was composed, but he may have heard something of it; he certainly came to know it. Benjamin Jowett, writing in 1893, records: 'More than thirty years ago I remember his making what appeared at the time to be a very striking remark, namely that "the true origin of modern Biblical Criticism was to be ascribed not to Strauss, but to Niebuhr, who lived a generation earlier"'. See Hallam Tennyson (1897: II, 463).

9 On the quality of Tennyson's voice and his manner of reading aloud, see Hallam Tennyson (1897: I, 187, 194, 512).

10 The text of Malory used by Tennyson at the time of composition of 'Morte d'Arthur' was that of Walker and Edwards (1816). In my quotations I have used the text most conveniently available, i.e. that of Eugene Vinaver (1967).

11 On Tennyson's plans for an Arthurian epic, and on the serial evolution of the *Idylls*, see Tillotson (1965: 80–109) and Gray (1980).

12 This is one of a number of adverse critical points raised in Baum (1948: 89).

13 On the mysticism and eclecticism of Tennyson's religious views, see Jowett's 'Recollections' in Hallam Tennyson (1897), in particular Vol. II, pp. 464–5; see also Vol. I, p. 324.

14 'Prayer is, to take a mundane simile, like opening a sluice between the great ocean and our little channels when the great sea gathers itself together and flows in at full tide.' Quoted by Hallam Tennyson (1897: I, 324).

15 The passages referred to here are 'Morte', lines 52–65 and lines 88–112.

16 The line 'The lusty bird takes every hour for dawn' is surely an 'unconscious reminiscence', if not a deliberate borrowing from *Hamlet*, I.i.158–60: 'Some say that ever 'gainst that season comes/ Wherein our Saviour's birth is celebrated/ This bird of dawning singeth all night long.'

REFERENCES

BAUM, P.F. *Tennyson Sixty Years After.* Chapel Hill, North Carolina: University of North Carolina Press, 1948.

GRAY, J.M. *Thro' the Vision of the Night.* A Study of Sources, Evolution and Structure in Tennyson's *Idylls of the King.* Edinburgh: University Press, 1980.

LAWRY, J.S. 'Tennyson's "The Epic": A Gesture of Recovered Faith.' *Modern Language Notes,* Vol. LXXIV, May 1959.

MARTIN, R.B. *Tennyson, The Unquiet Heart.* Oxford: Clarendon Press, and London: Faber & Faber, 1980.

RICKS, CHRISTOPHER (ed.). *The Poems of Tennyson.* London: Longman, 1969.

TENNYSON, SIR CHARLES. *Alfred Tennyson.* London: Macmillan, 1950.

TENNYSON, HALLAM LORD. *Alfred Lord Tennyson: A Memoir,* Vols I and II. London: Macmillan, 1897.

TILLOTSON, KATHLEEN 'Tennyson's Serial Poem', in *Mid-Victorian Studies* (with Geoffrey Tillotson). London: Athlone Press, 1965.

VINAVER, EUGENE (ed.). *The Works of Thomas Malory,* 3 vols. Oxford: Clarendon Press, 1967; Vol. 3, 'The Most Piteous Tale of the Morte Arthur Saunz Guerdon'.

Eight

Form and feeling: Browning's 'Porphyria'

On a windswept, rainy night, a man sits in a dark, cheerless cottage, listening distractedly to the noise of a storm that echoes and taunts his despair. Presently a visitor intrudes upon his pathetic inertia: a woman, who sets about making the house warm and comfortable. She is beautiful, it seems, and desirable – but of a higher social rank than he. This is not her cottage; she is a visitor from some much grander residence. Her very name – Porphyria – suggests 'one born to the purple', the colour of the aristocracy. That name is in itself enough to accentuate a social difference. This is no Daisy or Dorothy or commonplace Debbie-next-door; she is the lady from the Great House. When she visits him, she comes down in the world, and that presents an intractable problem, he being what modern vulgarity might call 'her bit of rough'. She is physically drawn to him – oh indeed, the sexual attraction is powerful – but *live* with him?, *marry* him? Well, hear the tale as Robert Browning tells it:

> The rain set early in tonight,
>   The sullen wind was soon awake,
> It tore the elm-tops down for spite
>   And did its worst to vex the lake:
>   I listened with heart fit to break.
> When glided in Porphyria; straight
>   She shut the cold out and the storm,
> And kneeled and made the cheerless grate
>   Blaze up, and all the cottage warm;
>   Which done, she rose, and from her form

Withdrew the dripping cloak and shawl,
  And laid her soiled gloves by, untied
Her hat and let the damp hair fall,
  And, last, she sat down by my side
  And called me. When no voice replied,
She put my arm about her waist,
  And made her smooth white shoulder bare,
And all her yellow hair displaced,
  And, stooping, made my cheek lie there,
  And spread, o'er all, her yellow hair,
Murmuring how she loved me – she,
  Too weak, for all her heart's endeavour
To set its struggling passions free
  From pride, and vainer ties dissever,
  And give herself to me for ever.
But passion sometimes would prevail,
  Nor could to-night's gay feast restrain
A sudden thought of one so pale
  For love of her, and all in vain:
  So, she was come through wind and rain.
Be sure I looked up at her eyes
  Happy and proud; at last I knew
Porphyria worshipped me; surprise
  Made my heart swell, and still it grew
  While I debated what to do.
That moment she was mine, mine, fair,
  Perfectly pure and good; I found
A thing to do, and all her hair
  In one long yellow string I wound
  Three times her little throat around,
And strangled her. No pain felt she;
  I am quite sure she felt no pain.
As a shut bud that holds a bee,
  I warily oped her lids: again
  Laughed the blue eyes without a stain,
And I untightened next the tress
  About her neck; her cheek once more
Blushed bright beneath my burning kiss:
  I propped her head up as before,
  Only, this time my shoulder bore

Her head, which droops upon it still;
  The smiling, rosy little head,
So glad it has its utmost will,
  That all it scorned at once is fled,
  And I, its love, am gained instead!
Porphyria's love: she guessed not how
  Her darling one wish would be heard.
And thus we sit together now,
  And all night long we have not stirred,
  And yet God has not said a word!

'Porphyria's Lover' is a concert piece, an anthology piece, a classic of English nineteenth-century literature. Any devotee of Browning, anyone who reads poetry and stores up its rhythms and turns of phrase, as resources for a lifetime, knows this poem. And yet there is a sense in which it is not so easy to *know*; to know in its technical depth and virtuosity, to know how its peculiar, everlasting excitement has been created. It is the product of a strange craft: at once so lucid and so fugitive.

The story it tells is of a kind familiar enough to modern readers. One can imagine the tabloid headlines trumpeting the fate of a latterday Porphyria – 'Socialite strangled in love-nest drama', 'Dead-beat throttles debutante', 'Hair-do horror – I choked for love, madman confesses'. One can picture – having seen so many – the film episodes in which the eerie psychopath, such a softie in word and demeanour, makes his glassy-eyed assault on his love-victim. One can recall – having read so many – those passages of popular fiction, 'thriller' fiction, describing the murderous trance of the mind-warped lover. We are all too well acquainted with such things. They feed our appetite for the sensational and the shocking, and have been doing it for long enough, in these days of mass and multiple communications, to have become clichés of the sensibility. But in the 1830s, when 'Porphyria's Lover' was written, they were not clichés, and Browning's sensationalism, if one may use that word of his power to jolt his readers into a state of startled recognition, is of a different order from the sensationalism of *The News of the World* or the airport blockbuster. It involves an almost clinical knowledge of the heart and its reasons; it is an essay in dramatic psychology, so accurately composed as to convince a reader, even now, after so many decades of publicised murders and madmen, that this is exactly how a driven man, a man at the end of his tether, would think and speak.

This illusion, for that is what it is, is established by a considerable effort of the imagination, resulting in a triumphantly original exercise in poetics. What are the principles of the exercise? How is the illusion worked? To begin to answer that question is to enter into procedures that lovers of poetry generally detest because, apparently, any analysis undoes the magic of the poem and demeans its status as a sacred act. Nevertheless, how does Browning create the illusion of the nameless man killing the oddly-named woman?

In a broad sense he does it quite simply, by offsetting the apparently free drift of speech against the regularity, the imposed necessity, of a strict poetic form. Herein lies the source of the poem's peculiar excitement and tension. The speaker in the poem has gone patently mad, with an aberration that shows in the very structure and pulse of his utterances; but those wayward sentences are boxed into a strictly formal prosodic pattern.

In its primary shape, the piece is symmetrical. It contains 60 lines in all, and the lover's recital comes to a division at line 30, 'So, she was come through wind and rain'. The text up to that point is the story of 'my state of mind'; the remaining 30 lines, from 'Be sure I looked up at her eyes' to the end of the poem, tell the tale of 'what I did about it'. (It will be convenient from here on to refer to lines 1–30 as *Part I* and lines 31–60 as *Part II*.)

That is the general plot of the poetic structure, readily discernible with reference to the poem's content, and even to its wording. (The rain and wind of lines 1–2 recur as the wind and rain of line 30.) However, because the poem is printed as continuous text, with no indication, to the eye, of anything like a division into stanzas, its interior organisation is at least partly disguised from the reader, or hearer, or reader-as-hearer, who is left to discover – possibly through transiently noting its haunting recurrences of rhyme – that the text consists of twelve *stanza-like* structures, each of five lines (call them, perhaps, *quintains*) each with the rhyme-scheme *ababb*. But that regular, quasi-stanzaic rhyme-pattern is ambivalent, its symmetry ministering to the poem's essential illusion of something asymmetrical, the push and pause of speech; the *b* rhyme at the end of the quintain is in some cases a mark of closure (as in lines 5, 25, 30) completing and isolating a foregoing sense-group, and in other instances – the majority

– a token of continuity, as the sense runs on, or a new sense group begins (e.g. 10, 15, 20).

Closure and continuity, perhaps not obvious to the ear, become apparent to the inspecting eye: it is easy to see how the quintains are regularly grouped. The 'groupings' of *Part I* (lines 1–30) are as follows: 1–5, *closure*; 6–25, *continuity*; 26–30, *closure*. (Thus, six 'quintains' running *ababb / ababb, ababb, ababb, ababb / ababb*. *Part II* of the poem (lines 31–60) matches exactly this prosodic plan, thus: 31–5, *closure*; 36–55, *continuity*; 56–60, *closure*. (Again, *ababb / ababb, ababb, ababb, ababb / ababb*.) The insistent, almost manic, regularity of the scheme may help to explain the unusual punctuation and syntax of 5–6, where a full stop is followed by a sentence consisting of a detached adverbial clause. (That is, rather than 'I listened with heart fit to break, when glided in Porphyria', the apparently deviant 'I listened with heart fit to break. When glided in Porphyria'. *When*, ordinarily a subordinating conjunction, becomes a 'transitional conjunct' – see Chapter 4, note 4.)

The punctuation of course affects the drama of the poem – its tracing of the speaker's perceptions and reactions, and its marking of the theatrical event – and here, as always, Browning is scrupulous in his punctuational scripting; but in keeping with that, and not conflicting with it, is the insistence on the regularity of a governing form. There has to be a full stop at line 5, the first 'closure' of *Part I*, and correspondingly, a full stop at line 35, the first 'closure' of *Part II*. In this (as indeed in his works generally), Browning is meticulously observant of the punctuational form of the poem.[1]

The poem's punctuation, closely observed, is a guide to its 'grammetrics', the plotting of a sustained utterance, with all its syntactic twists and turns, on a fixed metrical grid; it also conveys to the reader some instructions as to accent and intonation. Its pointing, or 'stopping', works at four levels:

(a) *End stops*, when a syntactic unit (e.g. a sentence) concludes at the end of a line. Marked with a period (.), or a colon (:) or a semi-colon (;). Typically, 4–5:

> And did its worst to vex the lake:
> I listened with heart fit to break.

(b) *Mid-stops*, when the syntactic unit concludes in mid-line, or within the line. Marked, like the end stops, with a period (.) or a colon (:) or a semi-colon (;). Typically, 14–15:

And, last, she sat down by my side
And called me.

(c) *End links*, when the end of the line coincides with the end of a clause, but not with the end of a verse-sentence. Marked with a comma (,). Typically, 15–16:

When no voice replied,
She put my arm about her waist,

(d) *Overruns*, when the line ends in the middle of a grammatical unit which is completed in the following line (quite often with a mid-stop). Overruns are not punctuated. Typically, 46–7:

And I untightened next the tress
About her neck.

These terms are useful descriptively, in the process of identifying the poem's dramatic moments and shifts of mood. In the opening, for example:

The rain set early in tonight,
The sullen wind was soon awake,
It tore the elm-tops down for spite,
And did its worst to vex the lake:
I listened with heart fit to break.

Here is a sequence of three end-linked lines, followed by two further lines, one end-stopped with a colon, the other more decisively end-stopped with the period that marks the closure of this opening quintain. Each clause is contained in its own line, with an effect of flat recital in a flat mood, a mood almost of inertia – here is none of the querulous agitation that comes later on. Then read the quintain that closes *Part I* (lines 26–30):

But passion sometimes would prevail,
Nor could to-night's gay feast restrain
A sudden thought of one so pale
For love of her, and all in vain:
So, she was come through wind and rain.

The sequence here is an end-link, followed by an overrun, then a second overrun, then an end-stop (with a colon, as in the corresponding line of the first quintain), and then another end-stop, with a period. Those overruns are symptomatic of what has been happening in the text after the tight control of the first five lines; the increasing impetus of speech has been pushing against the metrical restraint, suggesting an emotion unleashed.

That unleashing, that breaking of formal control, appears in the first quintain of *Part II*:

> Be sure I looked up at her eyes
>   Happy and proud; at last I knew
> Porphyria worshipped me; surprise
>   Made my heart swell, and still it grew
>   While I debated what to do.

In that passage there are four overruns and two mid-stops; a symptom of a vocal coming-to-life, the increasing insistence and emotional emphasis of the speech-patterns. But by the end of *Part II*, with the final closure of lines 56–60, a calm, self-contained, almost self-assured formality returns:

> Porphyria's love: she guessed not how
>   Her darling one wish would be heard.
> And thus we sit together now,
>   And all night long we have not stirred,
>   And yet God has not said a word!

Those last three lines – each line containing one finite clause, end-linked, leading to the final end-stop – make a cadence, the very formality and decorum of which heighten the horridly grotesque power of the extraordinary final statement.

These brief observations on four important passages (the 'closed' quintains, 1–5, 26–30; 31–5, 56–60) may suggest something of the embodying relationship between the poem's prosody and its emotional fluctuations. A closer analysis would be required to demonstrate in detail how the punctuation generally reflects a contrast of feeling, of posture, of *will*, between *Parts I* and *II*. The two parts, matching each other in their outer design (as demonstrated on p. 147 above) are in the details of their interior patterning metrically diverse, in ways that only a tedious process of counting – one of those aridities that allegedly dry the poetry out of poetics – would make wholly accessible. A quite cursory scan brings out some interesting features.

It appears, for example, that there are rather more mid-stops in *Part II* than in *Part I*. To be precise, *I* has two mid-stops, in lines

6 and 15, but *II* has seven, in lines 32, 33, 37, 41, 44, 47 and 56. There is a more even distribution of end-stops: in *I*, the six end-stops of lines 4, 5, 9, 25, 29, 30, and in *II* the seven instances of lines 35, 41, 48, 51, 55, 57 and 60. To judge the significance of this one should, of course, examine each instance of end-stopping, to determine whether the function of the stops is to assert the formal/symmetrical design of the verse, as in lines 4–5 and 29–30, or to suggest a dramatic moment, or a speech-pause, as, for example, in lines 9 and 41. The figures are obviously no more than a handy basis or starting-point for critical assessment. On a raw count, however, it is clear that the combined number of stops (end-stops and mid-stops) in *Part II* is much larger than in *Part I*; fourteen against eight, nearly twice the number.

End-linking, by contrast, is rather more frequent in *I* than in *II*; sixteen occurrences against ten. (In *I*, at lines 1, 2, 3, 7, 11, 13, 15, 16, 17, 18, 19, 20, 21, 22, 24, 26; in *II*, at lines 36, 40, 43, 45, 49, 52, 53, 54, 58, 59.) There is a long sequence in *I*, from line 15 to line 24, where every line but one (the overrun at 23) is end-linked, in a crucial passage that evokes the lover's outpouring of bitterness and despair, and tells, in a confused, half-cryptic way, the cause of his grief (that she will not finally 'give herself to him' because of her 'pride' of birth and social status). There is no such massive design in *II*. It is in the count of overruns that *II* strikingly exceeds *I*: twelve against seven. In a count of overruns plus a count of stops (whether end-stops or mid-stops), *I* totals fifteen and *II* twenty-six. This is the prosodic fact that, above all others, draws critical notice to itself.

What does it signify? Or rather, what does it *express*? To what features in the poet's imagining of a character and an action does it point? The fact that the prosodic surface of *II* is broken more often with those overruns and abrupt mid-stops might suggest, for example, the intention to express a sense of heightened agitation. But the end-linkings of *I*, in lines 15–24, could also qualify for the description 'agitated'. In *Part II* that brooding introspection is turned to active (not to say murderous) intent; the done-by becomes the doer and the roles of love-making are reversed, so that '*this* time *my* shoulder bore *her* head' (an attentive reading will surely accentuate the pronouns). The lover is in control of the beloved (or has convinced himself that his ghastly expedient, his 'thing to do', has put him in charge). He has done something about the woeful impasse of their relationship; he has roused himself to give her the gift he is convinced she would really want; and he is proud of it. He is almost out of breath with it.

Now it may seem implausible or fanciful to make connections between these dramatic impressions and the dry arithmetic of prosodic/punctuational structure. The structures are nonetheless there for the counting, and the count is too striking to be dismissed as an accidental characteristic. There are connections for the interpreter to read. As to whether Browning consciously planned it that way, or whether, more interestingly, he felt it that way, sensed it that way, intuited his way, and, out of his knowledge of the resources of language, *found* the way, is a question to be deferred for the moment.

Rhyme raises a comparable question. Is there a relationship between the acoustic values of rhyme – for instance, in vowel quality – and the affective tone of the poem? Are the rhymes sad or sudden, bleak or bouncy, banal or brilliant? For the reader these are, no doubt, subjective matters; we are all interested in the imagined sound of a poem, but some are more ready than others to make equations of sound and sense, or sentiment. For Browning himself, then, were the sounds of his poem symbols of the subject, conceived as raising the feelings he attributes to the criminally passionate lover, or did they simply drop in by statistical chance, turning up with the words but not colouring the poetic meaning of the words?

On a first consideration, one might not consider the rhymes of 'Porphyria's Lover' as extraordinary, or particularly expressive of its lugubrious content. The rhyming words in the first quintain, for example, are no more than banal: *(to-)night*, *spite*, *awake*, *lake*, *break*. Those monosyllables, in which a vowel – in each case a long vowel or, more correctly, a diphthong – is followed by a single consonant, are of a kind that fills the listings of rhyming dictionaries. Their vocalic elements, represented in phonetic script as /ai/ (in *night*) and /ei/ (in *lake*) are statistically the most frequently recurrent diphthongs in English.[2]

The poem certainly does not begin with any show of virtuosity, or even artfulness, in rhyme. It is worth noting, however, that in *Part I* of the poem the rhyme-vowel (the vowel in the rhyming syllable) /ei/ occurs repeatedly, a remarkable twelve times, across four out of six quintains, in 'aw*a*ke', 'l*a*ke', 'bre*a*k', 'str*ai*ght', 'gr*a*te', 'w*ai*st', 'displ*a*ced', 'prev*ai*l', 'restr*ai*n', 'p*a*le', 'v*ai*n', 'r*ai*n'. The recurrence of /ei/ must chime in the most resistant ear; it is like a sustaining harmonic, a pedal-note in music, or a tonal colour in painting. One must of course have reservations about any notion of phonetic symbolism. It would certainly be naive to conclude that the sound /ei/ symbolises sadness, or dreary self-pity, or the stirring of obsessive resentment, or any such emotion attributable to the poem's central *persona*. And yet, the sound is attestably present in the verse, in some density, and in metrically prominent positions. Once the ear picks it up, it seems to irradiate the verse in this part of the poem, like a home key to which the score constantly returns.

The rhymes in *I* are, with the exception of one crucial passage, uniformly masculine. The passage which stands out against the general monotone is 21–5:

> Murmuring how she loved me – she,
>   Too weak, for all her heart's endeavour,
> To set its struggling passion free
>   From pride, and vainer ties dissever,
>   And give herself to me for ever.

This is powerfully imagined. The rhythm is accelerated with the intrusion of the feminine rhymes that make the second, fourth and fifth lines *hypercatalectic*, having one syllable over the basic metre, the only place in the poem where this happens; more than that, the pace of these lines is subtly affected by the dactylic, 'hurry-up' beat of *murmuring*, the strong accent on *she* at the end of the line, and the thumping spondee (/ /) of *too weak* in line 22.

There are several departures in this quintain from the implied metrical norm of the poem. The reader's assumption is that the poem's normative metre is iambic tetrameter (. / . / . / . /), as displayed in the first four lines, and that the first syllable of each line will as a rule be weak. That assumption holds good for much of the poem, but there are several lines in which the metrical norm is overruled. Line 21 is one of these – it becomes in effect a dactylic/trochaic line (/ . . / . / . /) – and line 22 is an instance of a line in which the first syllable is 'naturally' strong – strong, that is, in accordance with normal English phrasing. In sum, this quintain is a disturbance, a heightening, an oversetting of implied metrical norms, and the reader is left to match this metrical turbulence with a sense of the lover's changing mood, his awakened capacity for bitter resentment.

In *Part II* the rhymes are more diverse and diffuse, less ear-catching. There is, by and large, a different set of rhyme-vowels, including the short vowels of 'still'/'will', 'fled'/'instead', the half-rhyme (also with short vowels) of 'tress'/'kiss', and the approximate quantities of 'she'/'bee' and 'how'/'now'. (Everyday spoken English observes a distinction of length/stress between the *how* of 'I couldn't guess how it happened' [short, 'unmarked'] and 'It happened, I couldn't guess how' [long, 'marked']. Browning's 'how' is short/unmarked by syntax but long/marked by metrical position, and by its rhyme with 'now'.) Altogether, there is less emphasis on the prominence of rhyme and its potential for affective colouring, and much more (in accordance with the frequent overruns) on the handling of metre at line-beginnings. There are rather more instances here than in *Part I* of the line beginning on a strong beat (*happy*, 32; *perfectly*, 37; *laughed*, 45), or on the spondaic double beat of an emphatic phrase (*that moment*, 36; *three times*, 40; *blushed bright*, 48; *her head*, 51; *so glad*, 53).

These phrases characterise a stylistic and prosodic feature recurrent in this part of the poem: the supervening accent that weights whole sequences of syllables, almost eliminating the intervening weak beats, drastically modifying the notion of the metrical foot: as in 'mine, mine, fair, perfectly pure and good' (36–7) or 'all her hair in one long yellow string I wound three times her little throat around' (38–40). In the last example there are (by my count) no fewer than twelve strong pulses in sixteen words. Line 39 ('in one long yellow string I wound') is notionally a tetrameter – a four-beat line, the poem's basic metre – but has five strong beats like a pentameter. There is a kind of breaking of bonds here, a strenuous assertion of the man's active will against his former inertia; the declaration 'I found a thing to do' is reflected in the metre, in the overruns and accented syllables – as well as in the transitive verbs, the verbs of a doer with an object in view, that break into this part of the poem, its murderous and pathetic crisis.

A deranged man speaks in defence of his *crime passionnel* – and we, his audience, understand the working of his sad mind, and understand the circumstances of his deed: this is the illusion that Browning conveys through close imaginative attention to details of form and metre. The achievement is in the details, but detail is something that often invites sceptical comment from the reader who feels that there is something implausible, not to say unpoetic, about an argument over the placing of a comma. Students in literary seminars repeatedly ask, in response to a demonstration of some fact of linguistic organisation in a familiar text, whether the poet could really have had such matters in mind, and how we can be certain that these 'facts' are of any literary significance?

The riddle of what the poet intended is a critical question no less complicated for being, by now, rather less than fresh. Its complications arise most probably from a misreading of the poetic process. The student who asks, in honest doubt, 'but did the poet really intend this?', assumes implicitly two distinct levels of creative process: a level of dreaming or 'musing', and a level of conscious decision at which the forming of a phrase, the arrangement of a line, the turning of a strophe and other particulars are worked out. As the doubting student sees it, the connection between musing and deciding is straightforward, and, so to speak, unidirectional; the text, surfacing from the dream to be realised in the process of deciding, may yield something to subsequent editorial tinkering, but cannot bear reflexively on the musing process. The dreamer is not persuaded, by the telling of his dream, to go back and dream again.

That, however, is what poetic dreamers reportedly and repeatedly do; the interplay of trance and text has been recorded by more than one poet.[3] The illusion begins in that trance of withdrawal so powerfully described in Marvell's *The Garden* (see pp. 1–2). It is prompted by something quite small – a rhythm, a rhyme, a phrase, a metaphor – around which it accrues, bringing with it the possibility of a textual shape. Out of that, the ghost of a text begins to arise, by making its presence so importunately felt that the poet starts to transfer its shape to paper, in the form of a few lines, a distich, a strophe, something distinct enough to suggest a prosodic outline. But this outline of a possible form may raise modifying questions about the dream, sending the poet back into his trance for a session of further consultation with his muse.

The poet can never be wholly sure, at a completely conscious level, what he intends. Henry Austen Dobson put the problem of frustrated intention neatly, if frivolously:

I intended an Ode,
  And it turned to a Sonnet.
It began *à la mode*,

I intended an Ode;
But Rose crossed the road
  In her latest new bonnet;
I intended an Ode
  And it turned to a Sonnet.

The silly-sooth of Dobson's joke is that his poem is neither an ode nor a sonnet, but a *triolet*. Who can be certain from the start the shape a poem will assume? Writings sometimes appear to have a will of their own, and are apt to change their formal intentions, whether because Rose crosses the road or, more seriously, because of what is revealed to the writer, in his cycles of musing, and confirmed in his mind as the text is gradually committed to script or print. 'Intention' is thus both evident and inherent. It lies evidently on the surface of the text, but it also lurks in its psychological depth, so that an intention may exist *in posse* before the poet begins to recognise it, or to feel it as more than a peripheral impulse, vaguely perceived and dimly understood.

Then there is the matter of how readers experience the text and transmit their experiences to others. Until fairly recently the poet was seen as master in his house – the governor, first and last, of the 'meaning' of the poem. Literary theory has of late swung so emphatically against this assumption that critics occasionally appear to believe that the poet has no authority at all over the life of his own work. The current conventional position, however, is not so extreme: its essence is that a poem, at any point in its life after publication, is repeatedly the product of a collaboration between the poet and his readers. We all bring something to the poetic text; each of us shapes it in a slightly different way; each communicates preferred 'shapings' to others, in readings, in seminars, perhaps in something as small as the casual quotation of a phrase or a few lines. We become authors in the margin or, perhaps, like film-makers in the Gallic style, *auteurs*.

In this state we are liable to impose on the text our own marks of 'intention', but what prevents an indulgent mood from running away with us is the necessity of arguing from manifest evidence, which means defining emphases, noting repetitions, pointing to apparent signs of verbal patterning, and in general counting the stylistic currency. We come to the belief that if a reader can show what is regularly countable in text, the count and the regularity have some significance in relationship to the writer's 'intention'. Whatever is convincingly perceived, we might say, is intended, or has been intended at some moment in the passage from the illusional depth of composition to its surface realisation.

Some of Browning's dramatic monologues (for example, 'My Last Duchess') embody the device of the silent listener, one who is placed in the frame of the poem, whose 'body language' is sometimes implied, but who is otherwise a mute attendant. In such recitals, the silent listener-in-the-poem stands in for the external reader-of-the-text; the presence of an attendant figure helps us to read the attitude and purport of the monologist's remarks, to infer, at times, his intonations and emphases.[4] More than that, the inclusion of an observer within the text puts the tale at an objective distance; we are not involved. No such attendant is incorporated into the recital of 'Porphyria's Lover'. We, as readers, listen directly to the madman's confession, whenever we address the poem. It is as though each reading meant entering the cottage, in imagination, and seeing the body on the sofa, clasped in the embrace of that exhilarated lunatic, whose speech has the infantile logic of lunacy: 'it was what she wanted, really'; 'she didn't suffer'; 'if it was wrong, God would have said something'.

Robert Browning imagines our imagination: imagines how one would feel in astonished encounter with a babbling psychotic, who imagines that he can capture love by killing the beloved, who in her turn imagines that she can enjoy her passions without surrendering her social position. It is bemusing. The mirrors of illusion recede from us, reflection upon reflection dwindling, until we are brought again – and again and again – on a dark, rainy, windswept evening, to the door of a cottage wherein sits a murderer on whose shoulder lolls a beautiful corpse. This is the carefully wrought purpose of the prosodies, the punctuations, the formal patterns; though, perhaps, only those with an addict's interest in techniques may care to enquire exactly how the purpose is accomplished.

NOTES

1 See, for example, his short lyric 'Meeting at Night', a poem remarkable (a) for having no main clause and (b) for the symmetry of line-end punctuation in its two stanzas.

2 My authority for this is Gimson (1962: 143). The sounds of British Received Pronunciation, as described by Gimson, may well be rather

different, as to details, from the phonetic state of the language well over a hundred years earlier; I have no reason to believe, however, that the relative *frequency* of vowel sounds can have changed greatly.

3 For example, by Day Lewis (1947: 68–70), and again by Graves (1955: 82).

4 A familiar example is the reading of the first line of 'My Last Duchess'. In alluding to the title of the poem, many (possibly most) people stress the noun: 'My Last *Duchess*' In the poem's opening line, however, the stress must come on *last*: 'That's my *last* Duchess painted on the wall.' We know this, because the words are spoken in the presence of the envoy who has come to negotiate the dowry of the speaker's *next* Duchess. For another example from the same poem, see the overrun 'Nay, we'll go/ Together down, Sir!', as the poem draws to a close. It is not metrical position alone that suggests emphatic stress on *together.* The envoy has, by inference, politely given precedence to the Duke, his social superior, as they go to descend the staircase; but the latter, for the moment a model of aristocratic urbanity, affects to ignore distinctions of protocol and insists that they walk *together.* Nothing is said directly about the envoy's movement; we are led to infer it.

REFERENCES

BROWNING, ROBERT. *Browning. A Selection by W.E. Williams.* Harmondsworth: Penguin Books, 1954.

DAY LEWIS, C. *The Poetic Image,* Clark Lectures 1946. London: Jonathan Cape, 1947.

GIMSON, A.C. *An Introduction to the Pronunciation of English.* London: Arnold, 1962.

GRAVES, ROBERT. *The Crowning Privilege,* Clark Lectures 1954–55. London: Cassell, 1955.

Part III

Modes of Composition

Nine

Translation: the 'Englishing' of a Horatian ode

It used to be told in Cambridge how that severest of scholars, Professor A.E. Housman, would lecture on the lyrical poetry of Horace, expounding each text in uncompromising earnest until he reached the seventh ode of the fourth book, *Diffugere nives*. There, it seemed, commentary was powerless and pointless; he would simply read the text aloud and move on to the next poem. Ah, how touching, one might think, what a sensitive gesture, what a decent avowal of a perfection that leaves nothing more to be said. But Housman did in fact say something about *Diffugere nives* – had said it, indeed, when the poet in him pre-empted the professor: he translated it into English verse, and in doing so produced a text that in its beauties or its blunders (as perceived by diverse readers) strikingly exemplifies a phenomenon, not exactly translation and not purely creative invention, called by our literary ancestors 'Englishing'.

Here is the text of *Diffugere nives*, as printed in a Penguin Classics edition of the *Odes* (Michie 1964):

Diffugere nives, redeunt iam gramina campis
    arboribusque comae;
mutat terra vices, et decrescentia ripas
    flumina praetereunt;
Gratia cum Nymphis geminisque sororibus audet
    ducere nuda choros.
immortalia ne speres, monet annus et almum
    quae rapit hora diem;
frigora mitescunt Zephyris, ver proterit aestas
    interitura simul

pomifer Autumnus fruges effuderit, et mox
bruma recurrit iners.
damna tamen celeres reparant caelestia lunae:
nos ubi decidimus
quo pater Aeneas, quo Tullus dives et Ancus,
pulvis et umbra sumus.
quis scit an adiciant hodiernae crastina summae
tempora di superi?
cuncta manus avidas fugient heredis, amico
quae dederis animo.
cum semel occideris et de te splendida Minos
fecerit arbitria,
non, Torquate, genus, non te facundia, non te
restituet pietas;
infernis neque enim tenebris Diana pudicum
liberat Hippolytum;
nec Letheae valet Theseus abrumpere caro
vincula Pirithoo.

Now what does this poem tell us? Apparently, that we only live once, that nothing lasts for ever, that the hours and days and years are rolling inexorably round, that soon we will all be in Hades with yesterday's worthies, and nobody's family connections or talent or good deserts will get them out: so we had better make the most of life while we have it. A commonplace, in short, but a classic commonplace, a canonic sentiment, one that has taken recurrent shape in European poetry for two thousand years or more. Anyone who can read Latin is held by the poem; its hold, however, is in the language, the typical Horatian *speed* (for want of a better word), the eloquent economy of phrase, the loading of the text with allusions and with metaphors overt and covert. Strip the poem of these stylistic distinctions, attempt a deliberately banal, near-literal prose rendering, and we are left with something like this:

> The snows have gone, the grasses come back to the fields, the leaves return to the trees; earth's seasons change, and swollen rivers, subsiding, keep to their banks. The Grace, attended by the Nymphs and her twin sisters, dares to go naked, leading the dance. Expect nothing to last for ever, the year warns us, and the hour which snatches up the kindly day: frosts are thawed by the west winds, summer treads on the heels of spring, to be

overtaken in turn by apple-bearing autumn, pouring out plenty, and soon lifeless winter comes back. Yet moons swiftly make good the losses of the heavens; we, when we go down to join father Aeneas and rich Tullus and Ancus, are dust and shadow. Who knows if the gods above will give us a to-morrow to add to the sum of to-day? Possessions escape the greedy hands of an heir when you give them to your own dear self. Once you are dead, and Minos has passed his majestic judgement on you, Torquatus, neither your lineage nor your eloquent tongue nor your righteousness will bring you back to life – nor, indeed, will Diana free the chaste Hippolytus from the darkness, or Theseus be able to strike off the chains that bind his dear friend Pirithous.

This 'naked' rendering – in which, however, the text's informing metaphors still lurk – presents the substance of the poem, but necessarily obscures its compositional pattern, which is actually strophic. The Latin text of 28 lines, set out above, is divisible into seven quatrains, each quatrain – and each distich within the quatrain – completing a stage in the cumulative tally of meaning. Here, as in the *Odes* generally, Horace favours a method of collage or juxtaposition, letting his audience make the semantic connections between images. In some of the *Odes*, this compositional method has a wayward look, perhaps leaving the modern reader with the suspicion that the poem is structurally flawed.[1] It is not particularly troublesome in *Diffugere nives*; even so, there are throughout the poem points at which a reader needs to take connections on trust, or ventures to read them into the text, because they are not foregrounded or overtly articulated. An example is the apparent gap or semantic skip between the third and fourth distich, i.e. between *audet ducere nuda choros*, 'naked, dares to lead the dance', and *immortalia ne speres*, 'expect nothing to last for ever'. What have naked nymphs to do with mortal expectations? The connection is implied in the verbs *audere*, 'dare', and *sperare*, 'hope', 'look for', 'expect': 'nymphs, being immortal, may *dare* to do their perennial dance, but you, a mere human, must not *hope* that the good days will always come round'.

The economy of phrase and the abrupt transitions of a Horatian ode can generally be traced to the demands of an intricate governing metre. The primary artifice of these poems is prosodic; the metre is an elaborate mechanism that generates – indeed, compels – further elaborations in syntax and in the lexicon. The lyrics represent in themselves a kind of translation – a transmutation of poetic forms and rhythms by a poet who could boast of being *princeps Aeolium carmen ad Italos deduxisse modos*, 'the first to have adapted the Greek lyric style to our native measures'. The *Odes* might thus be called (without detracting from their literary value) an experimental workshop of metres. Alcaeus and Sappho are obvious models, but for some poems Horace turned to more recondite sources, in variants of the so-called Asclepiadean and Archilochian metres.

The pattern of *Diffugere nives* is named First Archilochian, after Archilochos of Paros, a poet who lived, it may be noted, seven centuries before Horace was born and a century before Alcaeus and Sappho. Horace took a long view of excellence; a very rough idea of his aesthetic commitment to the tradition of Greek letters, and some understanding of the initially cool (or possibly baffled) public reception of his Greek-inspired *Odes*,[2] might be gained if we were to try to imagine one of our own Augustans studiously engaged while colleagues relied on the staple measure of the heroic couplet, in the production of poems imitating the intricate court-metres of the Nordic *skald*, such as the *Drottkvaett*, or the *Dunhenda*.[3] The Greek forms and rhythms may not have been quite as boldly exotic as that, but they were exotic nonetheless. The First Archilochean is technically defined as a dactylic hexameter followed by a dactylic trimeter catalectic – meaning that the last foot in the second line (the trimeter) is incomplete and is suspended on a (usually) long syllable, with an effect, in recital, comparable to that of a 'rest' in music.

To reflect the strophic build-up of the poem presents no great difficulty to a translator; what is extremely difficult is to render into English, a stress-timed language, an idea of a metre based on syllabic timings.[4] Here is the metrical model of *Diffugere nives*, as presented in its first two lines:

— — — ∪ ∪ — ∪ ∪ — — — ∪ ∪ — —
Diffu/gere niv/es, rede/unt iam/ gramina/ campis
— ∪∪ — ∪ ∪ —
arbori/busque com/ae

In J.B. Leishman's (1956) translation this opening couplet is rendered as follows:

Snow's all melted away, green grass comes back to the
meadows, tresses again to the trees

The strophe continues:

> earth's transforming herself, and now with diminishing waters
> rivers are hurrying by.

Leishman's skill in adapting the metre is much to be commended; there is great ingenuity, particularly in the adaptation of the English *ing*-forms ('transforming', 'diminishing', 'hurrying') to the dactylic Graeco-Latin rhythms. But for all the craft of Leishman and others who have attempted the re-creation of Classical syllabic metres, an English mimicry of Latin echoing Greek is not easily sustained.

For the translator this is a more than peripheral inconvenience; the problem of necessary losses and possible compensations, a problem attendant on all translations, begins, in the particular case of Horace, with the poem's rhythms. Anyone wanting to render him into modern English must reckon with the possibility of having to abandon or in some way replace the metre; and then, where Horatian Latin steps lightly, so lightly, as to the sound of flutes, in comes English with galumphing hoof, trumpeting rhymes. More than that, the abandonment of syllabic metre means losing the principal stylistic character, the distinctive 'key' of the *Odes*, for it is in metrical subtlety that Horace finds, and recommends to his reader, what Yeats has called 'the fascination of what's difficult'; and it is out of that difficulty that the delicate, devious style of these lyrics uniquely flowers.

Horatian metres both dictate and accommodate Horatian syntax; in every poem there are striking effects of word-order which, on the one hand, may be said to have been contrived, or *willed*, by the poet, but on the other can be seen as arising from metrical necessity. The novice reader, unaccustomed to bearing a word patiently in mind until its partner belatedly arrives, is repeatedly confronted with questions of normality – what is the 'normal word-order' in poems like these? The answer is, that the only norms are normal abnormalities, judged against the usages of prose. If we can talk of 'prose norms' in Latin generally, we will presumably define them as an order of clause-elements according to which, in principal declarative clauses at least, the Subject precedes the Object, which is followed by the Verb. (In linguists' shorthand, Latin is an SOV language; on which, see Coleman 1987). The inflexional system of Latin, however, made it freely possible to subvert these norms, for rhetorical effect, to 'topicalise' or 'focus' (i.e. to bring particular words and phrases into prominence), or to create the metre-governed structures of poetry, in which the turn of the foot determines the turn of phrase.

In all the *Odes* there is scarcely a strophe, perhaps hardly a line, that does not transmute word-*order* into word-*mosaic*, a deliberate fragmentation that creates for the reader the pleasurable tension of wondering how the sense will be resolved, accompanied by the stimulus of casual associations, as one word runs against another. Take an example from *Diffugere nives*, the line which signals a crucial moment of counterpoise in the poem: *damna tamen celeres reparant caelestia lunae*. Taken in order, the words say 'losses however swift restore heavenly moons', meaning 'swift moons, however, restore heavenly losses'. The inflexions tell us what goes grammatically with what. *Damna* 'goes with' *caelestia* (as a noun followed by its modifier), *celeres* with *lunae* (as a modifier followed by its noun), the verb *reparant* sits in mid-line between the adroitly shuffled noun-phrases, and *tamen* – the adverb, 'yet', which marks an emphatic turn in the poem – is slipped into focusing position after the first word of the verse-sentence. (Note, in the line that follows, a companion emphasis in the pre-posing of *nos* – 'whereas we', 'we by contrast'.)

This typically Horatian conundrum begets English readings that agree slightly to disagree: 'Yet the moons are quick to make good their losses in the sky' (a school textbook, Allcroft and Hayes, no date); 'Moons make speed to repair their heavenly losses' (Michie 1964); 'While, though, waning moons can mend their celestial losses' (Leishman 1956); 'Her losses soon the moon supplies' (Dr Johnson 1784); 'But oh, whate'er the sky-led seasons mar,/ Moon upon moon rebuilds it with her beams' (A.E. Housman 1897, 1936); 'These wounds of the wheeling skies are healed by the moons in their flying' (Edward Marsh 1940). If in some of these instances the writer appears to be trying to get more out of a rendering than a rendering will reasonably yield, the reason may be that in Horace's line there is a fortuitous convergence, a hovering ambivalence, of two possible constructions: the central reading, *celeres lunae*, 'swift – i.e. quickly returning – moons', and the contingent *damna caelestia lunae*, 'the celestial losses of the moon', i.e. the moon's waning.

Possibly the most striking thing about these variants, however, is the number of renderings of *reparant* as 'make good', 'repair', 'mend', 'supply', 'rebuild', 'heal'. The word in the text looks quite straightforward, but the word chosen by the translator tugs the meaning this way or that, gently distorting the text into a shape preferred by one of its readers. Do I want the moon to 'supply her losses' like an efficient steward, or would it be better for her to 'heal wounds' like a surgeon? The choice may depend on who I am, and even on when I live; Edward Marsh's version – 'These wounds of the wheeling skies are healed by the moons in their flying' – was published in wartime, in December 1940 (the year of the Battle of Britain).

To tackle the poem's lexicon, for the purposes of translation, is always to be brought up short by what appear to be the simplest words and expressions. There are places in which the poet's idiom, conceivably forced by the metre, is elegantly terse, an invitation to the reader to fill in the descriptive gaps. An example of this is the phrase *mutat terra vices*, literally 'earth changes turns'. Translators in general make uneasy going of this simple assertion: 'the changing year renews the plain' (Johnson); 'Earth shifts her dress' (Gladstone); 'and altered is the fashion of the earth' (Housman); 'Earth's livery's changed' (Marsh); 'earth's transforming herself' (Leishman); 'the earth suffers her Springtime change' (Michie); 'the earth shakes and changes' (Burton Raffel 1983).

The significant fact here is that Horace turns his metrical phrase in three words; of the renderings quoted, only one is as brief (Leishman), the others running from four words (Raffel) to seven words (Housman). These expansions, furthermore, introduce ideas no more than potentially implied in the Horatian phrase: 'renews the plain', 'fashion', 'suffers', 'shakes'. It is as though these translators were each construing the poem by supplying a vocabulary reflecting a personal perception of the poet's intention – or perhaps in some cases caught from other translators. (Gladstone's *dress*, Housman's *fashion* and Marsh's *livery* have no obvious warrant in the Horatian text, but may arise from a common 'poetic' idea of Nature as clothing.)

And indeed, the lexicon of *Diffugere nives* lends itself repeatedly to the construction of immanent linkages in the lexicon, a strain of metaphor not overt (like the obvious figure of *comae*, 'tresses', in the second line) but operating covertly through the potential spread of reference, the semantic leeway, in certain items of vocabulary. *Diffugere*, for example, is generally translated in the figurative sense 'have dissolved', 'have melted' (with reference to snow), or more directly as 'have gone away', 'have departed', even 'have fled'. As to the latter rendering, one of the possible meanings of *diffugio* is 'take flight', 'scatter in all directions', with reference to the rout of an army.[5] Here is a figure less immediately accessible than the apparent metaphor of 'dissolving', 'melting', yet no less consistent with the poet's intentions. It projects a linkage with *audet*, and even with *nuda*, of which a schoolbook commentary (Allcroft and Hayes, undated) solemnly remarks 'the three Graces were represented as naked, and therefore afraid of chill weather'. That is undoubtedly true, yet one suspects that there is more to the matter than seasonal facilities for dancing in the nude. If *diffugere* signals that winter's troops are on the run – the snows have melted – then the Grace may *dare*, at least for a brief time of truce, to resume her peaceful pastimes.

Furthermore, this 'military' implication of *diffugere* is consistent with other words in the poem presenting suggestions of a strife and a violence that relentlessly overbears the gentle conviviality of ordinary joys: with *rapit*, for example, and *proterit*. Each of these words involves notions of brute force, even of warfare, *rapere* allowing the sense of 'plunder', 'pillage', and *proterere* the meanings 'trample', 'tread under foot', 'put to rout'. The reader who returns frequently to the poem, and (in the way of obsessive readers) delights in noticing meanings potentially nestling within meanings, will begin to be persuaded, by and by, that these hints of battle and brutality are not to be ignored; yet they remain no more than hints, shadows of meaning cast by a powerful text.

Other words in the poem are important, vitally important, as terms rooted in Roman-ness, in the customs and values of the patriarchal state: *pater, heres, genus, facundia, pietas*. The poem may be Greek in form, but these words reflect Roman society and politics, and they all elude, to a greater or lesser extent, comprehensive translation. *Heres*, for example (in *manus avidas heredis*, 'the greedy clutches of your heir'), denotes something perhaps rather less cosy and familial than the English word *heir*; in many Latin contexts it suggests nothing more than a legal designate with a contractual, post-obituary option on some hapless benefactor's goods and chattels.[6] *Pietas* is a notoriously difficult word to render, 'piety' being the last recourse of the weary translator; it is a comprehensive righteousness, involving 'integrity', 'probity', 'purity', 'fidelity', 'devotion', 'decency' – a complex of related moral attributes which Romans sought and recognised in the upright man.

This problem-word occurs in context with two other words, only marginally less problematical for the translator, in what is arguably the poem's centrally significant couplet:

non, Torquate, genus, non te facundia, non te
restituet pietas

Note the management of emphasis in the hexameter, through the initial *non* and the final *te*. J.B. Leishman's translation reads:

then, Torquatus, lineage, eloquence, righteousness shall not
serve to restore you to light

What the translation misses here is the distinctive highlighting effect of the repeated *non*, and the focus on *te* at the end of a line: 'NOT lineage, NOT eloquence, NOT righteousness shall restore YOU.' The *you* so pointedly admonished is the addressee of the poem, Torquatus, a representative Roman, fictionally standing in for the reader at large. Who is Torquatus? A virtuous man.[7] What are his qualifications? He is of good family (*genus*), he is articulate, with the command of language necessary for the conduct of affairs in political assemblies and the lawcourts (*facundia*), and he has *pietas*, meaning active virtue, a strenuous and selfless pursuit of what he believes to be right. Yet none of these manly, marmoreal features of Roman citizenship is going to save him, Horace warns, from annihilation.

This message is closely linked to a supporting pattern of allusions. Horace is a highly allusive poet; names of personages real and mythical fill the *Odes*, and nearly always with something more than a merely decorative intent. They either function as addressees, marking the important 'conversational' or 'interpersonal' character of the *Odes*, or they are figures from the world of gods and heroes. Horace may or may not have believed in the divinities and demi-gods he poetically invokes (he often deals whimsically with them, and he describes himself as *parcus deorum cultor et infrequens* – not much of a church-goer) but they were at the very least a cultural property that he held in common with his audience; he could assume that his readers – represented by Torquatus – would take the point if, in developing a theme, he reminded them of a name out of history or legend. In *Diffugere nives* the names thus shadowing the message with which the poem ends are *Aeneas, Tullus, Ancus, Minos, Diana, Hippolytus, Theseus, Pirithöus*.

Aeneas is the *pater*, the ancestor, the proto-Roman[8]; Tullus and Ancus were early kings of Rome. These names represent the theme of *genus*. Hippolytus, son of Theseus, was put to death at the instigation of his stepmother, Phaedra, whose attempts at seduction he had virtuously resisted. For his chastity he was a particular favourite of the goddess Diana, who, however, could not save him from death and the everlasting dark. This legend evokes the theme of *pietas*, the 'piety' of Hippolytus, a dutiful son and a pure soul. The hero Theseus went down into the underworld to support his friend Pirithous in an attempt to carry off Proserpine, Queen of Hades. Theseus was allowed to escape, but his intercession, as the prisoner's special friend, could not rescue Pirithous from the awful judgement, the *splendida arbitria*, that he should be chained for ever in Hades in punishment for his impious enterprise. Thus *facundia* – eloquent pleading in matters of law or politics – is of no consequence when mortals pass beyond the limits of mortality.

The lexicon and the clustering allusions in the second half of the poem confer upon it a gravity, a sadness not wholly predictable from the opening, which seems to herald a piece on the theme of gathering rosebuds, drinking wine, and making the best of the good times before the infernal walls close in. As a lyric celebration of the coming of Spring, *Diffugere nives* very closely resembles an earlier poem, *Solvitur acris hiems*, the fourth ode of the first book; resembles it in theme, in imagery, in turns of phrase, even in prosody, for the two poems are the only two examples of Archilochian metre in the *Odes*. They might be read in tandem as charming examples of Horace in his most fluently cajoling mood. Ulrich von Wilamowitz-Moellendorff, not a man to be seduced by charm alone, thought rather little of *Diffugere nives*, coupling it with another poem, the twelfth ode of the fourth book, and dismissing the pair alike as *unbedeutenden Fruhlingslieder*, 'unremarkable Spring songs', which '*mahnen nur wie der alte Goethe, "und wenn die Zeit verrauschend fliesst, Jahrzeiten kehren wieder"*', 'only remind us, like Goethe of old, "and if time goes swiftly by, the seasons come again"'.

But that judgement is not well-considered. *Diffugere nives* is a darker poem than Wilamowitz will allow it to be. It is death-haunted, and it discernibly mourns the *mores prisci*, the old ways which Horace valued all his life, and to which, again and again, his verse pays retrospective tribute, until at last he all but confesses that the old ways never were and the good place has not yet been. Is Horace, at the close of a poem published only a few years before the end of his own life, talking *at* and *through* 'Torquatus', talking to Rome, to the culture whose imperial destiny was beginning to seem less and less convincing and whose traditional virtues had become a matter of pious rhetoric? The question eludes a convincing answer;

yet the intuition persists that behind its lyric grace and its elegant melancholia, *Diffugere nives* conceals something close to a political statement of disillusion and regret. W.R. Johnson (in his introduction to Raffel 1983) says:

> Horace died thinking that he had spent most of his life watching the death of freedom and the disintegration of a culture and a civilization that he and many of his generation loved as much as their fathers had loved it.

The snows of yesteryear have gone; but look, there are chains we cannot strike off. (The reader may like to ponder the fact that the second word of the poem is *nives*, and its penultimate word *vincula*.)

This is certainly a difficult poem for any translator to attempt, but then there is no Horatian lyric that could be called 'easy'. There are besetting problems concerning: metre and form; word-order; a lexicon in which patent meanings are shadowed by possibilities of other meanings; the importance of allusion; and above all the Horatian craft that mingles these elements interdependently, in patterns that persist or shift from strophe to strophe. How is anyone to re-create this elaborate art? And, after all, what is the *use* of these poems in modern times? Do we need this old Graeco-Roman game – like Eliot's 'Shakespeherian rag', so elegant, so intelligent? Is it relevant to our literary tradition, our aesthetic sense, our social and psychological concerns? How may it speak to us, as it was designed to speak to Torquatus the Roman?

At one time – probably at any time between the sixteenth century and, for a terminal date, the Second World War – those questions might have been rejected by literate folk as quite foolish and empty; because Horace has been, after all, almost an honorary Briton, so pervasive is his cultural presence. Knowing Horace was once one of the marks of a decent literary education. Even the dunce might come away from school with a phrase or two – *carpe diem, odi profanum vulgus* – and the learned have sometimes gone to extraordinary lengths to get him into and out of their systems. Henry Gunning, a Cambridge don in the eighteenth centry, tells of a college fellow who 'had Horace at his fingertips' – quite literally, for he committed the *Odes* to memory by taking the volume to the privy, learning a poem by heart, then tearing out the page for hygienic uses. Others, not so thoroughgoing, have nonetheless in their own way absorbed Horace, in direct citation, in oblique reflection, in sundry topics and themes, and in a *stance* perceived as Horatian, in accordance with the temper of the times. (Each age promotes its own Horace.) Still others have Englished him, following the promptings of their own tastes and aesthetic perceptions.

Here is Dr Johnson's rendering of the first strophe of *Diffugere nives*:

The snow dissolv'd, no more is seen,
The fields and woods, behold! are green,
The changing year renews the plain,
The rivers know their banks again . . .

And here, one hundred and ten years later, is William Ewart Gladstone, at leisure from Prime Ministerial cares and the alternative recreation of tree-felling on his Hawarden estate:

Snows melt away; the fields are flecked with grass,
        And foliage clothes the tree,
Earth shifts her dress, the rivers shrunken pass
        And travel to the sea.

But here again, almost a century on, is an American poet and scholar, Burton Raffel:

Snow is gone, fields grow green,
Trees open with leaves,
The earth shakes and changes, Spring
Rivers shrink, flow still . . .

What has happened to Horace's text in the course of these centennial transformations? It is hardly the same poem; it seems to have meant more than slightly different things to three different people in different ages, if 'meaning' involves something more than strict fidelity to content (and even then the texts wander away from the original). How can this be called 'translation'?

Contemporary theorists have given much detailed attention to the questions of what a translation is, the kinds of translation that may be attempted, the goals a translator may set, and how they may be achieved. A typical theoretical framework is that proposed in the first chapter of Bell (1991), discussing the methodological requirements of translation. Bell, like other assessors of the translation process (Newmark 1988, 1991; Hatim and Mason 1990) allows for some breadth and diversity of purpose in the translator, and consequently for different translating styles appropriate to different levels of communicative function. (Bell's general model is provided by Hallidayan 'functional' linguistics, with its distinctions between the ideational, interpersonal and textual functions of language.[9]) Newmark (1991) proposes two major concepts, of 'semantic' and 'communicative' translation, the one 'author-centred', 'faithful' and 'informative', the other 'reader-centred', 'freer' and 'effective'; the opposition of 'semantic' and 'communicative' appears to correspond to the time-honoured distinction between the 'literal' and the 'free' (or the 'creative', or the 'translation in the spirit of the thing'). About literality and freedom in the rendering of poetic texts, however, the applied linguists are not altogether at ease; Hatim and Mason allude to Roman Jakobson's argument that in a poem 'formal aspects of the linguistic code become part of the meaning, so that translation proper is impossible' – in other words, that the only option may be some form of creative equation in which the resources of the target language are searched for equivalents or compensatory balances.

This comes as no news to anyone who has ever tried to render into English verse so much as a strophe of Horace. His translators over the past two centuries might be divided into literalists, freewheeling creativists and those – the greater number – who have attempted something in the middle way between Newmark's 'semantic' and 'communicative'; those, indeed, who have attempted to 'English' him. 'Englishing' sets store by faithfulness to the content and general structure of the poem; it does not oblige the translator to reproduce the prosody of the original, but does require the choice of something considered to be a metrical equivalent; it allows the translator some licence in supplying figures, metaphors, etc., in compensation for those too deeply rooted for transplantation from the original language; it relates the translation to current notions of poetic language and form (as, for example, Dr Johnson chose to put Horace into rhymed couplets, but C.S. Calverley, a contemporary of Tennyson, considered the *In Memoriam* stanza the most effective equivalent)[10]; it offers, consequently, something to be considered both as a poem from the original *and* as an original poem; and attempts, in the widest sense, to place the adopted poem in the nurturing environment of the adoptive culture.

For writer and reader, 'Englishing' can involve a play of aesthetic, social and purely personal perceptions that put this odd process just a little outside the reach of the translation theorist. Horace is a particular instance of the way poetic translations are taken personally by those who make them and those who read them. Until quite recently, translations from Horace were not designed to serve the simple informative purpose of telling an inquisitive reader what Horace's writing was like, the sort of thing that might be found in his poems, and whether it might be worth learning a little Latin to find out more. Readers already knew their Horace, and writers knew that readers knew. The writer said, in effect, 'Here is *my* Horace', and the reader responded, in effect, 'This is/is not the Horace that *I* know', appraising the performance from the heart as well as the mind, much as a listener might appraise the rendering of a familiar musical work. All this is involved in 'Englishing', and readers can become quite upset about it; they can, in words already used here, take it personally.

That A.E. Housman took *Diffugere nives* personally, we already know from anecdote – and perhaps might infer from the publishing history of his own Englishing of the poem. His translation was first published in a journal called *The Quarto* (Volume III, 1897). This was one year after the publication of his *A Shropshire Lad*, and incidentally a brief three years after the appearance of Gladstone's translation of Horace. Housman then kept his version for the rest of his life, not collecting it in *A Shropshire Lad* or in his *Last Poems* (1922). It was left to his brother Laurence to include it in the posthumous *More Poems* (1936) and subsequently in the *Collected Poems* (1939). The poem is thus curiously 'displaced', a late Victorian work turning up in the crisp 1930s, the Auden decade.

This is the text from *Collected Poems*, where it is simply entitled DIFFUGERE NIVES, *Horace: Odes iv.* 7[11]:

The snows are fled away, leaves on the shaws
  And grasses in the mead renew their birth,
The river to the river-bed withdraws,
  And altered is the fashion of the earth.

The Nymphs and Graces three put off their fear
  And unapparelled in the woodland play.
The swift hour and the brief prime of the year
  Say to the soul, *Thou wast not born for aye.*

Thaw follows frost; hard on the heel of spring
   Treads summer sure to die, for hard on hers
Comes autumn, with his apples scattering;
   Then back to wintertide, when nothing stirs.

But oh, whate'er the sky-led seasons mar,
   Moon upon moon rebuilds it with her beams:
Come *we* where Tullus and where Ancus are,
   And good Aeneas, we are dust and dreams.

Torquatus, if the gods in heaven shall add
   The morrow to the day, what tongue has told?
Feast then thy heart, for what thy heart has had
   The fingers of no heir will ever hold.

When thou descendest once the shades among,
   The stern assize and equal judgment o'er,
Not thy long lineage nor thy golden tongue,
   No, nor thy righteousness, shall friend thee more.

Night holds Hippolytus the pure of stain,
   Diana steads him nothing, he must stay;
And Theseus leaves Pirithous in the chain
   The love of comrades cannot take away.

This poem might best be read in comparison with Gladstone's version published a few years earlier, a conjunction of Victorian styles in which Housman's poem comes off quite well. However, it invites location in a rather different cultural environment, the aesthetic world of *A Shropshire Lad* and the poet's later volumes. Concerning Housman's lyric style, Andrew Motion has very shrewdly observed: 'Housman's poems are built on a series of complex binary structures. His Shropshire is two places – one real, one imaginary – and his poems speak two languages – one archaic . . . one chatty.'[12] The point may be illustrated by this quatrain from the lyric 'The chestnut casts his flambeaux':

The chestnut casts his flambeaux, and the flowers
   Stream from the hawthorn on the wind away,
The doors clap to, the pane is blind with showers.
   Pass me the can, lad; there's an end of May.

'Pass me the can, lad'; this bluff talkative address undercuts, with sardonic, deprecating effect, the studied artifice of phrasing in the opening lines. This is a stylistic device to which Housman quite often and very effectively resorts: make an exquisitely turned phrase, or progression of phrases, wrought with all the patient care of the literary craftsman, then disturb it with some wry interjection from the common tongue. The charm of it hardly ever fails. But the common tongue is almost absent from Housman's version of *Diffugere nives*. No piquant contrast of styles there, no saving sourness, little sense of the colloquial grimace; all is high artifice and archaism, and the result is a confection of English words in the sweetish dialect, the *poesy*, of a poem from Motion's imaginary land, The Other Shropshire.

Experience (of classroom and common room talk) suggests that readers are evenly divided in their judgement of this text. The young seem disposed not to like it; older people, among them classical scholars, think better of it, feeling perhaps a greater reverence for the name and nature of Alfred Edward Housman. But anyone who takes the poem head-on, as though entering upon a piece of hitherto unfamiliar English verse, is bound to be struck by its crazy-paving of little-used or dialect words ('shaws'), of samples from the literary lexicon ('meads', 'unapparelled'), of old-tyme poetryspeak ('thou wast not born for aye'), of dubiously archaic constructions ('friend thee more', 'steads him nothing'), of blended or cross-bred idioms ('pure of stain'), and of literary reminiscences ('dust and dreams' – a most adroit rendering of *pulvis et umbra*, but one that inevitably recalls Shakespeare and 'we are such stuff as dreams are made on'). The style is artificial, which need not be blameworthy; but the question is how far readers, in their generation, are prepared to tolerate unabashed artifice.

There is something to be said at least for Housman's management of form and structure, and for his transposition of the general content of his original. He uses rhymed quatrains in equivalence to the strophic pattern evident in Horace's poem. The original metre is lost, of course, and with it the lovely lilting pauses at mid-line in the hexameter, and the 'rest' at the end of the trimeter; but still the English quatrain scheme answers generally (there is one exception) to the patterning of the Horatian strophe into distich and answering distich. Housman's version reflects, furthermore, some important turns of emphasis or focal points of procedure in the original text. 'But oh' may be a somewhat pallid rendering of *tamen* (in *damna tamen celeres* etc.), yet still it signals the crucial turn in the poem's argument. Similarly the italicised *we* in the third line of the fifth stanza ('Come *we* where Tullus and good Ancus are') obviously matches the marked effect of the pre-posed *nos* in the Horatian verse (*nos ubi decidimus*). Housman pays strict attention to these prosodic and structural emphases, conveying through them the Horatian sense of addressing the imagined bystander. Note his management of emphatic negatives as he translates the couplet *non . . . genus, non te facundia, non te/ restituet pietas*. He contrives an equivalent emphasis by interpolating a 'no' at the beginning of the second line of his couplet: 'Not thy long lineage, nor thy golden tongue/ No, nor thy righteousness shall friend thee more.'

Thus Housman satisfies those provisions for 'Englishing' which demand respect for the original content and the supplying of a prosody which at least conveys the organisation of the source poem and something of its interpersonal *accent*. But his choice of verse-form has condemned him to the weakness which mars all attempts to match the Horatian strophe with the English quatrain – the weakness of expansion. All translators and commentators note, as a principal characteristic of the Horatian style, his 'compactness' or 'compression'. C.S. Calverley calls the Horatian strophe 'a thing compact, *teres atque rotundum*'. Matthew Arnold refers to Horace's 'allusive and compressed manner' (in his essay 'On Translating Homer'; actually with reference to *pulvis et umbra sumus* in *Odes iv.*7). Gladstone mentions 'the necessity of compression' as the particular object of his own translations – which are in places as uncompressed and haplessly spongy as anyone else's.

This peculiar quality of solid, clenched abstraction appears in phrase after phrase – *mutat terra vices*, *immortalia ne speres*, *quae rapit hora diem*, *hodiernae crastina summae tempora*, *cuncta*, *amico quae dederis animo*. Horace's 'compactness' dwells within the 'compression' of Horatian metres; but as soon as a translator attempts to transpose him into English quatrains, things go askew and adrift, because every compression is paid for with an expansion. There is a nice example in Gladstone's rendering of *decrescentia ripas flumina praetereunt*, 'the rivers shrunken pass/ And travel to the sea'. He is able to render *decrescentia flumina* in a 'compact' phrase, 'rivers shrunken', but has to render *ripas praetereunt* expansively, as 'pass . . . and travel to the sea' (much like Old Father Thames in the song), simply because he needs a rhyme for 'tree'.

Housman's style is no less vulnerable to the distortions of the rhymed quatrain. He, too, expands his phrasing to fit the syllable-count or the rhyme. For *redeunt*, 'return', he gives us 'renew their birth'; for *audet*, 'dare', has 'put off their fear' (with a discreet word-play? putting off fear like putting off a garment?); for *annus*, 'the brief prime of the year'; for *bruma recurrit iners*, 'then back to wintertide, when nothing stirs'; for *quis scit*?, 'what tongue has told?'; for the single word (compression indeed) *cuncta*, a clause, 'what thy heart has had'; and for *neque Diana liberat*, 'Diana steads him nothing, he must stay' (rhyming with 'take away'). The necessity of finding a rhyme plays havoc with the necessity for compression. This is nowhere more apparent than in the sixth quatrain:

> When thou descendest once the shades among,
> The stern assize and equal judgment o'er,
> Not thy long lineage nor thy golden tongue,
> No, nor thy righteousness, shall friend thee more.

'Golden tongue' decently translates *facundia*, but is purchased with a lame rhyme in 'the shades among'. (Horace, in any case, says nothing about 'the shades' at this point.) A ludicrous consequence of the inverted word-order is that the syntactic pattern *noun* + *preposition* ('shades among') might seem to be repeated at the end of the following line ('judgment o'er'), so that instead of understanding a participial construction, 'the stern assize and equal judgment *being* over' (Housman's equivalent for the Future Perfect, *fecerit*), a guileless reader might construe 'When once you descend among the shades, over the stern assize and equal judgment'. The archaic 'o'er' leads to yet another problem of rhyming, solved by 'shall friend thee more', a fairly elaborate rendering of the simple *te . . . restituet*.

The English language itself is structurally and hence stylistically less 'taut', less 'close-knit' than literary Latin, and English rhyming quatrains allow for, or *presuppose*, a relatively open stylistic texture. This is what foxes the translators, even when they are great scholars and accomplished minor poets like A.E. Housman. Take one more example from his *Diffugere nives*: the rendering, at the end of the poem, of *abrumpere* as 'take away', making a rhyme with the filler-phrase (mentioned above), 'he must stay'. The word may certainly be translated so, and it may suggest a final note of resignation, the pathos of a dying fall; but is pathos the intended note? The stronger sense of *abrumpere* is 'strike off', 'wrench loose', and this is surely the last in a progression of 'violent' verbs, beginning with *diffugere* ('break ranks') and going on through *rapere* ('grab') and *proterere* ('trample under foot') before coming to *abrumpere* (or rather, *nec . . . abrumpere*) at the poem's despairing close.

What Housman has given us is a poem quite poignantly suggestive of that sense of private and personal loss that runs through so many of his lyrics; a poem which refers us to the places and voices of The Other Shropshire, where the Graces go, and lads lie untimely in the earth. His 'Englishing' perhaps conveys the message 'My Horace, and mine alone', though he has tried to keep faith with the original text. Inevitably, Housman's Horace will not always be the reader's Horace, and some readers will grumble and go in search of more and later Englishings – for it seems we must 'English' this poet again and again if we are to keep up with him where he stands still, at the end of the first century BC. And there will always be a sense of impertinence and a sense of compulsion – that we are driven to do what we probably ought not to attempt. A modern commentator (West 1967) writes, concerning a few hesitantly sketched lines of his own, 'This is one man's Horace and so delicate in the Latin that *it protests at being made explicit*' (my italics). He goes on to say, 'But the risk is worth taking to show how rich and suggestive this poetry is.' That is one view of the matter, the view of 'Englishing' as a tribute and a service to the original work. Another view, possibly *the* other view, sees 'Englishing' as a way of inducing the past to nourish the creativity of the present. In support of one of these views, James Michie writes: 'It is better that Horace should be "done down" into English than that he should be undone by the gradual disappearance of Latin from our culture.' No one would want to deny that. On the other hand, Burton Raffel writes: 'The translator must turn his back on the original . . . in order to be ultimately loyal to it. He must be free, similarly, in order to be faithful. If he respects and loves his original . . . he must liberate it from the boundaries of time, the boundaries of physical change of all sorts, the boundaries of cultural change.' That is also well said; but let us add that, sometimes, in the very depth of his love, he may have to resign himself to reading the text and, knowing what he knows and feeling what he feels, passing on in silence.

NOTES

1 For instance, Wilamowitz-Moellendorff (1913) dismisses the 'Soracte' ode (*Vides ut alta*, *Odes i.9*), as a patchwork poem: 'es ist freilich ein pasticcio . . . vereinigt widersprechende Züge' – 'it is clearly a pastiche . . . it incorporates contradictory strains'. He sums up, 'Hübsche Verse, aber noch kein Gedicht' – 'pretty verses but not yet a poem'. In fact the poem reads consistently enough, with a little help from the sympathetic interpreter.

2 Michie (1964) comments on the reception of the first three books of the *Odes*: 'Unlike Virgil's *Aeneid*, which appeared four years later, the Odes did not win the widespread appreciation that Horace may have expected.' Michie conjectures that this may have been the reason why Horace returned, for a time, to composition in the hexameter form.

3 Modern English poets have imitated, or at least glanced at, the skaldic metres. For an version of the *Dunhenda* (in which the closing syllables of a line are echoed in the opening syllables of the line following) see Louis MacNeice's 'The Sunlight on the Garden': 'The sunlight on the garden/ Hardens and grows cold,/ We cannot cage the minute/ Within its nets of gold.' MacNeice's poem, incidentally, is noticeably Horatian in content.

4 In spoken English, stressed syllables occur at approximately equal intervals – '*dum*-di-*dum*-didi-*dum*'. This is called stress-timing. In languages like French or Greek, each syllable takes up approximately the same amount of time – '*ta-ta-ta-ta-ta*'. This is called syllable-timing.

5 See the note on this in Shorey and Lang (1960).

6 In *In Memoriam*, XC, Tennyson echoes *manus avidas heredis*: 'The hard heir strides about their lands,/ And will not yield them for a day.'

7 And a wholly mythical one; he has nothing to do with the historical Manlius Torquatus, dictator of Rome in 363 BC.

8 It is worth noting that many translations of *Diffugere nives* refer to Aeneas as 'good', reflecting the Virgilian epithet *pius*. (Leishman (1956) in fact uses 'pious'.) But Horace specifically says *pater*, 'father', the father of the nation.

9 In page xiii of his *An Introduction to Functional Grammar* Halliday (1985) defines the functions, or 'metafunctions' of language thus:

> All languages are organized around two main kinds of meaning, the 'ideational' or reflective, and the 'interpersonal', or active. These components . . . are the manifestations in the linguistic system of the two very general purposes which underlie all uses of language: (i) to understand the environment (ideational), and (ii) to act on the others in it (interpersonal). Combined with these is a third metafunctional component, the 'textual', which breathes relevance into the other two.

10 Calverley (1901: 509) writes:

> A stanza of 'In Memoriam' is a thing compact *teres atque rotundum*, as is a stanza in a Horatian ode. Both writers are equally intolerant of any but the right word, and both have the gift of making it fit into its place by happy accident. The condensed phraseology, the abruptness, the *ease* (attained probably *per laborem plurimum*, until art became a second nature) which characterises the odes of Horace, characterises the cantos, so to call them of 'In Memoriam'.

11 Housman does not invent a title, suggesting an interpretation, as do some other translators: Gladstone calls his version 'To Torquatus; the Contrast of Nature and Life'; and Leishman, 'To Torquatus. On the Return of Spring'.

12 See Motion (1992).

REFERENCES

ALLCROFT, A.H. and HAYES, B.J. (eds). *Horace, Odes, Book IV*. London: W.B. Clive, University Tutorial Press (n.d.).

BELL, ROGER T. *Translation and Translating, Theory and Practice*. London: Longman, 1991.

CALVERLEY, C.S. 'Horae Tennysonianae', in Sir Walter Sendall (ed.), *The Complete Works of C.S. Calverley*. London, 1901; pp. 508–14.

COLEMAN, R.C.G. 'Latin and the Italic Languages', in Bernard Comrie (ed.), *The World's Major Languages*, London: Croom Helm, 1987; pp. 108–202.

GUNNING, HENRY. *Reminiscences of Cambridge*, abbr. edn by D.A. Winstanley. Cambridge: University Press, 1932.

HALLIDAY, M.A.K. *An Introduction to Functional Grammar*, London: Arnold, 1985.

HATIM, BASIL and MASON, IAN. *Discourse and the Translator*. London: Longman, 1990.

HOUSMAN, A.E. *Collected Poems*, Jonathan Cape, 1939.

JOHNSON, SAMUEL. 'Horace Lib IV Ode VII translated', in Sir John Hawkins (ed.), *The Works of Samuel Johnson, LL.D*, Vol. IX. London, 1784; p. 372.

LEISHMAN, J.B. *Translating Horace*. Oxford: Bruno Cassirer, 1956.

MARSH, EDWARD (transl.). *The Odes of Horace*. London: Macmillan, 1940.

MICHIE, JAMES (ed. and transl.). *The Odes of Horace*. Harmondsworth: Penguin Classics, 1964.

MOTION, ANDREW. Review of John Bayley, *Housman's Poems*, in *The Observer*, London, 10 May 1992.

NEWMARK, PETER. *A Textbook of Translation.* Hemel Hempstead: Prentice-Hall International (UK) Ltd, 1988.

NEWMARK, PETER. *About Translation.* Clevedon: Multilingual Matters, 1991.

RAFFEL, BURTON. *The Essential Horace; Odes, Epodes, Satires and Epistles.* San Francisco: North Point Press, 1983.

SHOREY, PAUL and LANG, GORDON J. *Horace: Odes and Epodes.* Pittsburgh: University of Pittsburgh Press, 1960.

WEST, DAVID. *Reading Horace.* Edinburgh: Edinburgh University Press, 1967.

WILAMOWITZ-MOELLENDORFF, ULRICH VON. *Sappho und Simonides.* Berlin: Wiedermannsch Buchhandel, 1913.

Ten

Argument: Chesterton's 'The Wind and the Trees'

> *Sir, I have found you an argument, but I am not obliged to find you an understanding.*
> (Dr Johnson)

Plato considered rhetoric a potentially subversive power, a challenge to the right way of reason; and to this day it is a common stereotype to present rhetoric as logic's malign opposite. The customary implication is that rhetoric is the falsifying agent of propaganda and tendentiousness, whereas logic is the strict, incorruptible, guileless servant of truth. But what must strike anyone interested in the processes of argument is that dialectic nearly always requires a rhetorical foundation. Bare reasoning, untouched by persuasive images of experience, is the domain of mathematicians and the practitioners of symbolic logic. To less austere intellects it commonly appears that arguments cannot touch the mind effectively until they are given a stage to act upon.

There is, for example, in Chesterton (1913: 69–74) a fine esssay called 'The Wind and the Trees' (1909). It begins like this:

> I am sitting under tall trees, with a great wind boiling like surf about the tops of them, so that their living load of leaves rocks and roars in something that is at once exultation and agony. I feel, in fact, as if I were actually sitting at the bottom of the sea among anchors and ropes, while over my head and over the green twilight of water sounded the everlasting rush of the waves and the toil and crash of shipwreck of tremendous ships. The wind tugs at the trees as if it might pluck them root and all out of the earth like tufts of grass. Or, to try yet another desperate figure of speech for this unspeakable energy, the trees are straining and tearing and lashing as if they were a tribe of dragons tied by the tail.

As a piece of description, this certainly merits the adjective 'rhetorical'; but let us enumerate some of the significant facts of its rhetoric. First, it posits something manifestly false, a deception that in fact would deceive none but a simpleton. No one supposes that Chesterton actually wrote these words while he was sitting out of doors, in a gale; and certainly no one is so innocent as to believe that the present tense means what it says – that even as his readers begin to read, they are addressed by someone experiencing the situation described. What the writer proposes is a stratagem, a *scheme*, which readers accept, thereby becoming accomplices to falsehood, if falsehood is the right word. But it is not really falsehood. It is the proposed ground of an argument, the poetic setting for a philosophical play. When we say 'let's pretend', we are not lying.

What is ostensibly a declarative clause describing an actual state of affairs, 'I am sitting under tall trees', is to be understood as a directive to the reader: 'Imagine that I am (and therefore that *you are*) sitting under tall trees', 'Let it be posited that we are now sitting under tall trees'. The reader is asked to accept the implications of *as if*, a conjunction that occurs three times in four sentences. *As if* is the proposed 'fact'; 'as-ifness' is adroitly confused with factuality. 'I feel, in fact, as if I were actually sitting at the bottom of the sea.' But Chesterton knows that he is not *actually* sitting at the bottom of the sea; he knows that he is not sitting under any trees; so that whatever it is he feels, he cannot be actually feeling it in a factual situation; yet he writes, 'I feel, in fact'. His assertion can only be rescued from the charge of blatant mendacity by supplying what any sensible reader will instinctively offer, the interpretation of 'I feel, in fact', as 'In such a situation one might very well feel'. To supply such an interpretion is of course an act of complicity. 'One' has only reached the second sentence of the essay, and 'one' is already persuaded; 'one' has assented to the scheme. By the end of the paragraph the assent is so complete that Chesterton can unabashedly refer to his own rhetorical procedures, in the phrase 'a desperate figure of speech'.

'Desperate' here is a double-sided word. Ostensibly it implies that he despairs of finding expressions adequate to describe the fury of the wind in the trees – a descriptive purpose to which the minor rhetoric of the passage is palpably devoted, in the alliterations ('their *l*iving *l*oad of *l*eaves *r*ocks and *r*oars'), the end-chime ('strain*ing* and tear*ing* and lash*ing*'), the chains of nouns ('the toil and crash of shipwreck of tremendous ships'). But the word suggests something else: a determination at all costs to establish a position from which all subsequent representation can be controlled. That position may be roughly paraphrased thus: that invisible causes produce sensational effects, and worldly events are steered by spiritual powers. It is stated quite explicitly later in the essay, but its statement and acceptance at that later point, as a 'dialectic' proposition, depends vitally on its initial acceptance in rhetorical guise. The rhetorician is 'desperate' to make an audience accept his scenario; that done, he can more or less quietly unfold the plot of his argument.

The next stage in Chesterton's argumentative business, after this spectacular opening, is the execution of a well-tried rhetorical move: the appeal to external business, whether in the form of an acknowledged authority, a friend, a face in the audience, or, more generally, the 'common experience' of 'all right-thinking people'. In this case, the necessary outsider is a small boy, recollected from another experience of 'just such torn skies and tossing trees':

> He did not like the wind at all; it blew in his face too much; it made him shut his eyes; and it blew off his hat, of which he was very proud. He was, as far as I remember, about four. After complaining repeatedly of the atmospheric unrest, he said at last to his mother: 'Well, why don't you take away the trees, and then it wouldn't wind?'

This charming utterance represents a point of view that Chesterton is about to rebut; a point of view which, indeed, he despises. The whole point of his essay is to reject the notion that worldly things can affect the motions of the spirit. But he does not begin by propounding his intention in terms such as: 'There are modern philosophers so utterly wrong-headed as to be capable of supposing that the trees make the wind blow.' He will get to the modern philosophers in due course. At the outset, he guilefully attributes the idea to a mere child of four, a nice, amusing little boy, and comments amiably: 'Nothing could be more intelligent or natural than this mistake.' Within two pages he will abandon the tolerant concession of 'intelligent' and 'natural', and will write: 'The man who represents all thought as an accident of environment' (in other words, the man who can suppose that the trees govern the wind) 'is simply smashing and discrediting all his own thoughts – even that one.' The rhetorical value of that little boy, handily playing in the fictional park, lies in his *childishness*, which is a proper ornament to the child but a reproach to the adult. Chesterton writes: 'My small friend was, in fact, very like the principal modern thinkers; only much nicer.' We notice once more a smuggled *in fact*, which invites the reader to accept an underlying proposition or maxim: 'It is a fact that the principal modern thinkers have the mentality of four-year-old children.'

And now, having charmed, tricked, or otherwise tamed his reader, Chesterton proceeds to his thesis with propositions analogous to the demonstrator's *Let x equal . . .* :

> . . . the trees stand for all visible things and the wind for the invisible. The wind is the spirit which bloweth where it listeth; the trees are the material things of the world which are blown where the spirit lists. The wind is philosophy, religion, revolution; the trees are cities, and civilizations.

Here is the explicit foundation upon which various dialectic propositions – or rather, dialectic *illusions* – might be constructed: for example, 'Our philosophies determine the kind of cities we live in', or 'Religious beliefs change the material character of civilization'. Chesterton goes on to suggest one such construct:

> You cannot see a wind; you can only see that there is a wind. So, also, you cannot see a revolution; you can only see that there is a revolution. And there never has been in the history of the world a real revolution, brutally active and decisive, which was not preceded by unrest and new dogma in the region of invisible things. All revolutions began by being abstract. Most revolutions began by being quite pedantically abstract.

The style, we see, is subtly changing, from the descriptive to the propositional. More and more sentences have the form of some generalising assertions: 'All revolutions began by being abstract.' Such assertions have a thrillingly adventitious air, like things that come to the writer in a lucky moment; but we know of this one, at least, that it depends on the fable of the wind and the trees. Chesterton, indeed, keeps reminding his reader of the rhetorical origin of his argument, only to develop the argument into further stages of dialectic:

> The great human dogma, then, is that the wind moves the trees. The great human heresy is that the trees move the wind. When

> people begin to say that the material circumstances have alone created the moral circumstances, then they have prevented all possibility of serious change. For if my circumstances have made me wholly stupid, how can I be certain even that I am right in altering those circumstances?

The grammatical forms of the sentences suggest, now, processes of reasoning rather than of myth-making, though the argument is rooted in the myth: we begin from *the a is b*, and proceed through *when . . . then* to *for if . . . how*? Certain qualifying expressions, furthermore, are carefully placed as links in the chain of assertions: 'material circumstances have *alone* created . . . then they have prevented *all* possibility'; 'if my circumstances have made me *wholly* stupid, how can I be certain *even* that I am right in altering those circumstances?'

This shift into dialectic assertion is even more marked in the paragraph following the one just cited:

> The man who represents all thought as an accident of environment is simply smashing and discrediting all his own thoughts – even that one. To treat the human mind as having an ultimate authority is necessary to any kind of thinking, even free thinking. And nothing will ever be reformed in this age or country unless we realize that the moral fact comes first.

Here are three sentences, two of which have the outline of *sententiae*, or general propositions ('Each/all/every *x* is/are *y*'; '*x* is required by *y*'), while the third proposes conditionally, 'not *x* unless *y*'. The essay has at this point assumed the *linguistic habit*, so to speak, of logic; furthermore, any one of these three sentences might in itself be the basis for extended dialectic.

By this time, however, Chesterton has effectively concluded his demonstration. Although he devotes a further page to the rebuttal of false positions in specific instances of social debate (notably on the problem of drunkenness, as acute in his day as in ours), his assertion that *the moral fact comes first* is the logical terminus of the short discursive journey that begins with the rhetorical position that the trees do not make the wind. The rest is commentary – but Chesterton cannot resist one final dig at his 'modern thinkers':

> I get up from under the trees, for the wind and the slight rain have ceased. The trees stand up like golden pillars in a clear sunlight. The tossing of the trees and the blowing of the wind

have ceased simultaneously. So I suppose there are still modern philosophers who will maintain that the trees make the wind.

Thus he returns to his rhetorical base. The pragmatic four-year-old has disappeared from the scene, having played his part in emphasising the folly of his philosophical elders. 'I get up from under the trees', says Chesterton, meaning 'I am through with my argument', and 'the trees stand up like golden pillars in a clear sunlight' – which sounds a little as though he were congratulating himself on his own lucidity and soundness of structure; or perhaps as though he were saying *quod erat demonstrandum*.

Anyone who reads this essay by Chesterton will immediately feel the force of its arguments. Its logic seems, if not irresistible, at least difficult to subvert. A second reading, however, may bring demurral. Can it never be the case that a physical fact may have a moral consequence? Is it logically indefensible to allege, for example, that insanitary housing will eventually subvert moral values? Or that drug-taking leads to despair and the collapse of the moral being? But Chesterton debars any such attempt at a defence, because he has framed the discourse with his fable of the wind in the trees – *framed* both in the conventional sense of enclosing within a limiting reference, and also in the underworld slang sense of providing evidence which must produce a conviction.[1] The reader is taken in by Chesterton's 'evidence'.

Of course it would be absurd to allege that the trees make the wind. There is a powerful compulsion upon us to reject that absurdity; we must accept the evident order of the universe. But we are by no means compelled to accept whatever follows from an author's analogies of 'wind' and 'spirit', or 'trees' and 'pillars'. Such metaphors do not preclude us from arguing that architecture can affect habits of thought, or that slum conditions can cause civic unrest. The analogous inference, however, is crucial to Chesterton's argument. It is just at the point of accepting it ('the wind is the spirit . . . the trees are the material things of the world . . . the wind is philosophy, religion, revolution . . . the trees are cities and civilizations') that the reader loses his rights in the debate and becomes the essayist's willing dupe. What makes the acceptance difficult to withhold is that it is required after a page of the most beguiling mythopoeia – the turmoil in the air – the little boy who is in danger of losing his hat and his temper, and who says such a charming thing – most of all, that opening paragraph of strenuously emotive language, in which the author is *desperate* to find a figure of speech. We now understand why he is desperate. It is in the first paragraph of the essay that the argument is won or lost, because it is there that rhetoric must establish the conditions in which dialectic may be effectively concluded.

'The Wind and the Trees' is an essay of great charm – Chestertonian charm, a kind of champagne charm – but it appears on sober analysis merely to support Plato's general point that rhetoric is a way of lying, or at any rate a way of bamboozling your audience into a partisan position. Rhetoric does indeed have a great potential power over the mind. It is possible, nevertheless – indeed it is part of the rhetoric of denouncing rhetoric – to overstate that power. In some respects, rhetoric is of no consequence at all, and will deceive no one. No rhetoric in the world will support or subvert a manifest, absolute, unconditional truth, the truth of what philosophers call brute facts. I cannot rhetorically establish that grass is green, nor may I discolour it with rhetoric. No rhetoric in the world can break a logical chain. I cannot rhetorically unsettle the proposition that $(a + b)(a + b) = a^2 + 2ab + b^2$. Rhetoric only begins to come into its own when the 'truths' it deals with are complex and conditional, and require interpretation: in short, when there is a case to be made.

If I want to argue, for example, that state welfare undermines individual morale, I shall be advocating a thesis which some will immediately accept, murmuring 'true!'; which others will as spontaneously reject, crying 'lies!'; and which others again will observe judiciously, 'it all depends'. I shall find myself in a refracted realm which is not truth, and perhaps not even belief, but the country of what I want to believe to be true. As it happens, I do not believe it; but I might begin to make the case on the basis of the possibility of believing it. Now this is the domain of most political, social, moral and aesthetic questions: the domain of making cases. To make my case I have to elaborate a postulate into a scenario which will furnish my argument with its bearings and points of reference. To make the scenario, I may choose to appeal to brute fact (as indeed Chesterton does in 'The Wind and the Trees'), after which I deploy impeccable logic within the terms I have chosen. In doing this, I shall be subordinating to a rhetorical purpose, to the advocacy of a predetermined principle, those elements of observation and reason which many would suppose to be superordinate in the unconditional search for truth. I shall be working within what modern idiom calls a 'set-up'. This is what affronted Plato: not the rhetorician's style, but his conversion of eternal verity into forensic convenience.

It may be worth recapitulating, briefly, the incorporated logic and brute fact of Chesterton's case. His premise is basically this:

(1) If *a* precedes *b*, *b* cannot cause *a*.

His argument, however, begins with the 'brute fact' assertion to which the logical premise will be repeatedly harnessed: the wind blows the trees, the trees do not blow the wind. 'The wind is up above the world before a twig on the tree has moved', he tells us. This is an order-of-the-universe matter; this *a* eternally precedes that *b*. Corollary propositions are:

(2) Causes are known only through effects.

and

(3) Causes produce effects: effects do not produce effects.

We 'see' the wind only through the movement of the trees; we 'see' a powerful idea only in social and historical consequences – this is the purport of (2). As for (3), it would be absurd to say, for example, that poverty is the prime cause of drunkenness, and equally absurd to argue that drunkenness must cause poverty, for both poverty and drunkenness (as Chesterton sees the matter) are effects of some higher, invisible cause. Chesterton's case thus incorporates logical positions that are hardly to be challenged. It also incorporates a simple physical observation that no one over the age of 4 would think of contesting. For all that, it is not, as perhaps he would like us to believe, a process of incontrovertible reasoning from a brute fact. It remains a *case*; the symptoms of a case being (a) that the argument is seen to work in a setting, or (to revert to a word used earlier) a *scenario*; and (b) that the bare symbols and basic propositional formulae are elaborated in devices of language and style that continually urge upon the reader or hearer the immanence of the argument in the scenario, the propriety of the scenario to the argument.

Language serves the controversial essayist so well (and the theologian, and the lawyer, and the politician) because it is inherently figurative and mutable – a shifty creature of many resemblances and shapes. It is multivalent and multiform; its words do not answer the requirement of mathematics or symbolic logic, that one sign shall have only one significance, but acquire plural references; its syntax generates alternative constructions. No writer much accustomed to using English can fail to be aware of dualities deep in the grain of the language, as though its resources were quite regularly keyed to certain contrasting functions. (No doubt the same is true of other languages; but we speak of what we know.) One of the most striking of these dualities is our twin-stranded vocabulary, which has developed over centuries, partly in response to political events (the Scandinavian and Norman invasions of Britain in the early Middle Ages), and partly as a consequence of cultural growth (expansions of trade and diplomacy, the influence of French and Italian literature, the importance of Latin and Greek in the Renaissance, the association of Greek with the evolution of modern scientific discourse).

These somewhat complex accretions of vocabulary, awesomely documented in the massed volumes of the OED, are in common perception reduced to the simple duality of 'ordinary' words and 'posh' words (or 'out of town words' as an American wit once put it). The common perception is not foolish; only a little broad in the customary manner of its expression. The two discernible 'strands' are made up on the one hand of Germanic words plus everyday terms of mainly French origin, and on the other of Greek and Latin words, whether directly adopted into English, or, as is frequently the case, mediated through French. With the 'native' strand we associate the qualities expressed in such terms as 'concrete', 'particular', 'informal', 'non-academic'; the counter-qualities denoted by 'abstract', 'general', 'formal', 'academic', we generally attribute to the other strand, of Graeco-Roman words. Such perceptions are not always reliable, or correspondent to actual usage, but they represent a prevalent notion of the English vocabulary, a notion lodged in any writer's mind.

The effects of this 'stranding' in the English vocabulary are widespread and striking, and have predisposed writers to certain habits and conventions of usage. There is a demonstrable tendency to use the 'native' strand for purposes of concrete description, and to resort to the 'Romance' or 'Latinate' elements to formulate a position or state a general case. This is seen throughout Chesterton's 'The Wind and the Trees'. In the first paragraph, for example, we read:

> . . . their living load of leaves rocks and roars in something that is at once exultation and agony.

'Live', 'load', 'leaf', 'rock' and 'roar' are all Saxon monosyllables, robustly linked, in Germanic fashion, by alliteration. 'Exultation' and 'agony' belong to the counter-strand of Latin and Greek derivatives; but they occur, it will be noticed, in a clause that defines and *summates* the total impression of that 'something' that 'rocks' and 'roars'. The Germanic words specify; the Graeco-Roman words generalise. A little further on in Chesterton's opening paragraph we find:

> The wind tugs at the trees as if it might pluck them root and all out of the earth like tufts of grass.

Simple, Saxon, concrete and particular, this vividly states its example. But the author is not wholly satisfied, and grasps at the possibility of a better illustration:

> Or, to try yet another desperate figure of speech for this unspeakable energy . . .

Words of Classical/Romance origin ('desperate', 'figure', 'energy') occur as the text momentarily retreats from vivid concrete description into reflectiveness. The phrase *unspeakable energy* strikingly sums up the point: Greek 'energy' is deemed to lie beyond the particularising power of Saxon 'speech'.

Later still in the essay, when Chesterton has finished with his rhetorical scene-setting and is more concerned with its philosophical implications, the change in the mode of thinking is clearly reflected in the vocabulary:

> When people begin to say that the material circumstances have alone created the moral circumstances, then they have prevented all possibility of serious change.

> The man who represents all thought as an accident of environment is simply smashing and discrediting all his own thoughts – even that one.

> Surely it is obvious that the thing which among the English proletariat leads to poverty is the same as the thing which leads to drink: the absence of strong civic dignity, the absence of an instinct that resists degradation.

The density of Latinate/Romance words is striking: *material, moral, serious, obvious, civic, create, prevent, represent, discredit, include, resist, circumstance, possibility, change, accident, environment, proletariat, poverty, absence, dignity, instinct, degradation.* There are Saxon intrusions, of course, but they are comparatively rare, and in two instances function either as an aesthetic counterpoise to the 'Latin' vocabulary (as in *smashing and discrediting*), or as a locus of concrete emphasis in an abstract context ('which leads to *drink*' has the impact of blunt speech, by contrast with, say, 'leads to intoxication' or 'leads to alcoholism'). But the Latinity of these extracts outweighs other elements; a phrase such as *the absence of an instinct that resists degradation* typifies, in its vocabulary, a function of summarising, formulating, generalising. (What it formulates is the reason, according to Chesterton, 'why the Englishman is more drunken than the Frenchman'.)

The 'rhetoricity' of English, though so well developed in its lexicon, does not rest on vocabulary alone. It is important in its grammar also, in the alternatives which the construction of sentences quite regularly provides; in the options of simple and complex, coordinating and subordinating; in the choice of sentence-types, for example *declarative* ('Beethoven was a composer') or *existential* ('There was a composer called Beethoven'); in the contrast of 'unmarked' forms with 'marked' forms such as *fronting* and *topicalisation* ('About that I can say nothing', 'Beer, I drink it every day'); in these, and in many other details. What is evident is that the grammatical repertoire of the language has been adapted to functions that fall within the definition of rhetoric as the art of speaking: functions of narration, exposition, persuasion, and interaction with an audience.

Grammar serves these functions in two ways. It provides for those moments in a text when a point or a theme must be given prominence, or when, perhaps, the speaker/writer stands away from the discourse a little to comment on it. These are, as it were, grammatical *pointers*. But along with 'pointing' there is a facility of 'yoking', or 'coupling', of laying out the text in parallel constructions, and it is here that grammar has the most obvious affinity with traditional, figurative rhetoric. Figures like *parison* (parallel syntactic structures) take shape, in particular languages, from the customary patterns of the clause. A so-called SVO language, for example, lends itself to parisonic sequences of Subject–Verb–Object: 'The wind blows the trees; the spirit moves the earth.' And the rhetorical purpose of such sequences is (usually) to fix the argument in the scenario, or relate the action to the staging.

The three-and-a-half pages of Chesterton's essay are full of syntactic/rhetorical parallels. Again and again he resorts, explicitly or implicitly, to the structure of *just as . . . so*, and he does this either by creating sentences that balance at mid-point, or by devising sequences of two sentences parisonically related (that is, so that the second sentence runs in parallel with the first, reference by reference):

> Just as the ragged outline of a tree grows suddenly more ragged and rises into fantastic crests or tattered tails, so the human city rises under the wind of the spirit into toppling temples or sudden spires.
>
> You cannot see a wind; you can only see that there is a wind. So, also, you cannot see a revolution; you can only see that there is a revolution.
>
> The wind is up above the world before a twig on the tree has moved. So there must always be a battle in the sky before there is a battle on earth.
>
> The great human dogma, then, is that the wind moves the trees. The great human heresy is that the trees move the wind.
>
> You can never have a revolution in order to establish a democracy. You must have a democracy in order to have a revolution.

Each of these extracts embodies the arguments 'if *a* precedes *b*, *b* cannot cause *a*', and 'causes are known only through effects'. But there is something notable about this 'embodiment'. The extracts are listed in order of their occurrence in the essay; the first occurs on its second page, the last comes almost at the end – and indeed is the final argumentative statement before the little coda in which the expositor quits his supposed station under the trees. What is worth noting is that these passages, picked out in a cursory scanning of the piece, are from first to last decreasingly figurative and increasingly formulaic. In the first, the element of 'scenario', the invention of a plausible imagery to support the argument, is almost obtrusive. In the last, there is no scenic support; the background imagery is expunged – even the 'wind', which turns up faithfully in all the other extracts, is absent from this one; only the statement of a proposition remains, with 'democracy' for its *a* and 'revolution' for its *b*.

Syntactic parallelism is a major rhetorical device in this essay. There are other devices of grammar, 'pointing' devices (to use the term suggested above) that indicate the occurrence or recurrence of a certain kind of message. One of these is the use of the existential clause pattern. (A construction on the model of *There* + *be* + *noun phrase*.) One might expect an essay like 'The Wind and the Trees', on a philosophical theme, to contain numerous instances of 'there is' and 'there are'. In fact, there are just nine occurrences in the text:

> We only know that there is a wind because the trees on some distant hill suddenly go mad.
>
> We only know that there is a real revolution because all the chimney-pots suddenly go mad on the whole skyline of the city.
>
> You cannot see a wind; you can only see that there is a wind.
>
> So, also, you cannot see a revolution; you can only see that there is a revolution.
>
> And there has never been in the history of the world a real revolution, brutally active and decisive, which was not preceded by unrest and new dogma in the region of invisible things.
>
> So there must always be a battle in the sky before there is a battle on earth. (Two instances.)
>
> The truth is, of course, that there will be a social revolution the moment the thing has ceased to be purely economic.
>
> So I suppose there are still modern philosophers who will maintain that the trees make the wind.

The last of these instances is the final sentence of the essay, an appropriate gesture of dismissal ('I suppose these people actually exist') to the misguided modern philosophers. The remaining instances, some of which coincide with episodes of parisonic construction (parallels, antitheses), turn with one exception on two crucial words. One of these words is *revolution*: '(we only know that) there is a real revolution', '(you can only see that) there is a revolution', 'there never has been . . . a real revolution', 'there will be a social revolution'. These repetitions, this focusing of a word by means of a particular construction, must strike us sufficiently to suggest that *revolution* is indeed the covert theme of the essay. It is a word of Latin origin, an abstraction; its concrete Saxon counterpart, which also figures in one of the existential clauses quoted above, is, of course, *wind*. Is it too bold to claim that 'wind' and 'revolution' stand for the overt scene and the immanent theme in Chesterton's parable? The exceptional instance, incidentally, is the occurrence of *battle* in the sixth example in the list. But even there we might argue that *battle* is a hyponym of *revolution*[2] and that its occurrence sustains rather than flaws the general argument, which is that a particular type of construction – the existential clause-pattern – is closely associated with the function of periodically asserting the essay's indwelling theme.

Though these observations on the language of Chesterton's argument are readily supported from the text, some readers might reject them as fanciful or overstrained. They impute to the author, it might be said, procedures too intricate to have concerned him as he got on with the job of stating his case. But the intricacy, after all, is the crudest reflex of the intricacy of thought. When we use that word in such a context as this, we mean, presumably, something of greater import than the domestic sense represented in familiar expressions like 'I've just had a thought', and 'A happy thought', 'My thoughts are with you' and 'A penny for your thoughts'. 'Thought' in these instances signifies a brief, more or less discrete mental response to a stimulus, a kind of splash in the mind. But our business is with a current, sustained and organised flow of intellectual activity. To harness that current is certainly one of the most intricate tasks that human beings set themselves.

For a linguist, the infinite potential of language is realised in specific and observable utterances; *langue*, the abstract system, the internalised sense of language, is manifested in *parole*, the words spoken or set down on the page.[3] Analogously, for anyone setting out to argue and persuade, the manifold abstractions of argument are organised in scenes and stories; *thought* is manifested in *parables*. The function of those parables is to make the argument not only intelligible, but also acceptable; without the charm of the story-teller, many important arguments would fail for want of a mind to let them in. The dialogues of Plato and the parables of Christ are alike in this, that they create a climate of acceptance for hard sayings. Dr Johnson's celebrated rebuke to a conversational blockhead – 'I have found you an argument, but I am not obliged to find you an understanding' – seems, on reflection, a little unjust. For if we wish to be understood in a certain sense, we *are* obliged to find our hearers or our readers an understanding; to find them, that is, a coherent set of terms, drawn from our common experience, by which the meaning and force of the argument can be assessed. The understanding is bred in the appeal to experience. This is what Keats (see Buxton Foreman 1931) meant by one of his comments on philosophical language:

> Axioms in philosophy are not axioms until they are proved upon our pulses: we read fine things but never feel them to the full until we have gone the same steps as the author.

But 'proving upon our pulses' and 'going the same steps as the author' does not mean a crude commitment to the Wackford Squeers system of learning for doing. ('C-l-e-a-n, clean, verb active, to make bright, to scour. W-i-n, win, d-e-r, winder, a casement. When the boy knows this out of the book, he goes out and does it'.) That kind of primitive practicality, an educational philosophy not unknown in our own day, and in places more respectable and exalted than Dotheboys Hall, was surely far from Keats's mind. We take our imaginative steps through the knowledge of what we have observed, read and felt – through a knowledge deposited in the mind until the literary artist, the poet, or the rhetorician comes along to retrieve and reconstruct it – to give shape to the illusions of resemblance – thereby enabling us to relate the strange event to the familiar setting, the unknown idea to the knowable emotion. Of all the functions of rhetoric, this is certainly the most important; and probably the least understood.

NOTES

1 In current British police/criminal slang, the word equivalent to 'frame' is *fit up* – 'to fit up', as verb, 'a fit-up', as noun. It can be said that Chesterton 'fits up' his potential adversaries in debate, or that his argument is 'a fit-up'.

2 A hyponym is a particular name within a general notion: thus 'love', 'fear', 'hate' are hyponyms of 'emotion' (which is a *hyperonym*, a superordinate term). The relationship of *battle* to *revolution* is not strictly hyponymic, but suggests nonetheless the relation of the 'contained', or 'included', to the 'container', or 'inclusive'.

3 The *langue/parole* distinction, familiar to linguists, was formulated by Ferdinand de Saussure in his *Cours de Linguistique Générale* (based on lectures given at the University of Geneva, and published by his pupils

in 1915). For de Saussure, there is a system of language (*langue*) which we all acquire and share communally, realised in a practice of speech (*parole*) which characterises us as individuals. 'Language' and 'speech' are interconnected, as the individual life is connected with the life of the community: 'Si nous pouvions embrasser la somme des images verbales emmagasinées chez tous les individus, nous toucherions le lien social qui constitue la langue. C'est un trésor déposé par la pratique de la parole dans les sujets appartenant à une même communauté . . .' (If we were able to take in the entire sum of all verbal images stored in the minds of all individuals we could depict the social bond that is 'language'. It is a depository stocked by the usages of speech among individuals belonging to the same community . . .' (de Saussure 1955: 30, my translation). My suggestion is that in literary rhetoric there is an analogous contrast/ complement of communally accepted systems of argument and the individual management of illustration and parable.

REFERENCES

BUXTON FOREMAN, M. (ed.) *The Letters of John Keats*, Vol. 1, no. 61. Oxford University Press, 1931.

CHESTERTON, G.K. 'The Wind and the Trees', in *Tremendous Trifles*, 5th edn. London: Methuen, 1913.

DE SAUSSURE, FERDINAND. *Cours de Linguistique Générale*, cinquième édition. Paris: Payot, 1955.

Eleven

Narrative openings: Scott Fitzgerald's 'The Cut Glass Bowl'

There is a type of narrative that is 'realistic' or 'historic', and that deals essentially in the truth-to-life of dates, topographies, institutions, actions and so forth; and a counter-type that is 'mythic', appealing to the emblematic truths of symbol, of allegory, of the psychological world, or 'inner life'. Between these types (which, for all their differences, need not be mutually exclusive) formulae like *once upon a time* and *long, long ago* draw a line of interesting distinction. As to meaning, such formulae are of course not in the least like the time-indicating phrases they superficially resemble – e.g. 'once before the war', 'fifty years ago'. If there is ever any time-reference in *once upon a time,* it is no more than imaginary; what the phrase actually does is to signal the onset of a certain kind of story. It is in effect a performative device, like 'here's a good one', or 'let me tell you a tale', or the Beowulf poet's *Hwaet!,* instructing the audience to sit up and take notice.

By using it, narrators declare their intentions, and free themselves from the obligations that would normally fall on them as story-tellers. For example, they evade the ordinary requirement to set a story in a convincing temporal frame (e.g. Imperial Rome, Victorian England, America in the 1920s), and in doing so they put off one of the shackles of likelihood; if they want to write about bears they may do so without having to worry about the existence of zoos or game wardens or bear-traps at the time of their narrative. Another demand conveniently by-passed by the formula is that the story should respect the physical laws of nature; with *once upon a time* the narrator assumes the right to introduce all manner of 'unnatural' phenomena – speaking beasts, singing fountains, magically endowed objects, human beings with spectacularly superhuman powers. In short, the formula claims a mythic licence to ignore the 'reality' or verisimilitude of the everyday world, and explore *far other worlds and other seas.*

On the other hand, there are narrative laws that remain in force, formula or no formula. One of these is the law of *sequence*; even in the timelessness of once-upon-a-time there is a pattern of events implying earlier and later, act and consequence, cause and effect. In fairy tales, it is true, sequences are often repeated (ritually, three times) but this is a device with mythic force; there is no way forward from sequence into consequence until a power is broken or until the appointed figure – hero, prince, lucky suitor – arrives to propose the correct solution. (Shakespeare uses this device in the 'casket' scene of *The Merchant of Venice*, where Portia's suitors have the choice of gold or silver or lead.)

Another narrative law concerns *motive*. However arbitrary and irrational and however unmotivated events may seem to be, the reader must always feel that somewhere in the story there is a key principle that explains and sanctions all absurdities. This psychological conviction is far more important than mere physical probability. Consider, for example, the story of the Frog Prince. We are ready to accept, without demur, the superficial magic of the tale, the proposition that a human being can be turned into a frog, because this acceptance is a precondition to the essential point of the story, which is that human compassion (when the Princess kisses the frog) has power to subvert the machinations of evil. The transformation of prince to frog is merely a mythic short cut leading us to the central matter, the real story. Were one to attempt a 'historic' narrative on the theme of human goodness correcting the distortions of an afflicted life, it would be necessary to invent a biography, with much realistic and corroborative detail. There would be no short cut.

A MYTHIC/HISTORIC NARRATIVE

These reflections are prompted by a piece of modern fiction, Scott Fitzgerald's 'The Cut Glass Bowl' (Fitzgerald 1976), a story that actually depends, structurally and thematically, on a counterpoise of the 'historic' and 'mythic' types in narration. The historic element is the straightforward story of a marriage, in its downward progression, step by banal step, from romance to disaster and death. At the beginning of the tale we meet its 'heroine', Mrs Harold Piper (Evylyn), a 27-year-old woman who has been married for seven years. She is beautiful and, it would seem, reprehensibly capricious; but she has begun to realise, belatedly, that she really loves her husband – for which reason she would like to break free from the affair in which she is involved. Her attempt comes too late, however; ironically, on the very afternoon when she has summoned her lover to tell him that the affair is over, Harold Piper arrives home early and finds them together.

The relationship between husband and wife is almost irreparably damaged, but there are still the children, Donald and Julie, and there is Harold's business career. The next episode of misfortune comes when Evylyn, now 35 years old, gives a party at which the principal guest is a man with whom Harold is hoping to go into partnership; it is the chance of his lifetime. Harold, however, drinks too much and gets into a brawl, irretrievably losing the promised opportunity. On the same occasion an even worse misfortune occurs; the Pipers' 3-year-old daughter Julie scratches her hand on the punch bowl, develops blood poisoning, and is maimed for life. To the alienation of wife and husband is now added the husband's commercial failure and the crippling of a child. The final blow falls during the First World War when the son, Donald, is killed in France. Demented by this ultimate loss, Evylyn herself dies, slipping and falling down the front steps of her own home as she tries to throw out an accursed object, that cut-glass bowl, concomitant of a series of domestic catastrophes.

This history is signposted by the narrator with allusions that enable the reader to establish, with some precision, dates and intervals of time not specifically stated. Thus it appears that the Pipers were married in 1892 when Evylyn was 20 and Harold 29; that Donald was born in 1893 and Julie in 1904; that the episode in which Evylyn is caught with her lover takes place in 1899; that the drunken evening, and the accident to Julie, occur in 1907; and that the deaths of Donald and Evylyn befall in 1918. In only one instance is a date explicitly given; otherwise, any reader who may be curious about the time-scheme of the story – and it has been accurately worked out by its author – is put to the detective task of scanning back and forth, comparing data, completing equations. It is almost as though Fitzgerald wished first to establish, and then deliberately to blur, his calendar of events. The effect is to make the story's time-span of nineteen years seem like an indeterminate age – though the termini are there for us to note, if we will.

The time-indices, then, are half concealed. On the other hand, episodes in the story are very deliberately marked by a different kind of index, that is, by descriptions of Evylyn's changing and fading beauty. From episode to episode the story's titular object, the cut-glass bowl, stands coldly immutable, while the human victim of events bears the marks of time:

> . . . the beautiful Mrs Harold Piper . . .
>
> (1st episode)

> Concerning Mrs Harold Piper at thirty-five, opinion was divided – women said she was still handsome; men said she was pretty no longer.
>
> (2nd episode)

> If Evylyn's beauty had hesitated in her early thirties it came to an abrupt decision just afterwards and completely left her.
>
> (4th episode)

These descriptions, occurring at the beginning of episodes, are a measure of the passage of time more significant and poignant (note their stylistic variation, the progress through an elegantly structured irony into brutal flippancy) than any date could be; but then, they are a kind of mythic measure.

For indeed there is a strong mythic element, without which this story would be formless, and hence pointless. Evylyn's misfortunes are associated with the large cut-glass bowl given to her as a wedding present by an embittered former suitor:

> You remember young Carlton Canby? Well, he was very attentive at one time, and the night I told him I was going to marry Harold . . . he drew himself way up and said: 'Evylyn, I'm going to give you a present that's as hard as you are and as beautiful and as empty and as easy to see through.' He frightened me a little – his eyes were so black. I thought he was going to deed me a haunted house or something that would explode when you opened it. That bowl came, and of course it's beautiful. Its diameter or circumference or something is two and a half feet – or perhaps

> its three and a half. Anyway, the sideboard is really too small for it; it sticks way out.

This is the malign object of fairy-tale, ritually and (it seems) causally present at each of Evylyn's mishaps. It is the ringing sound of the bowl, accidentally struck, that frustrates the attempt of her lover to hide when her husband unexpectedly comes home. It is the sharp edge of the bowl that cuts Julie's hand, and the sheer capacity of it that tempts Harold into preparing indiscreetly large quantities of punch. Into the bowl is tossed the letter bringing news of Donald's death in action, and by its very weight the bowl causes Evylyn to lose balance and fall on the front steps, when she is intent on smashing it. The bowl keeps its glittering beauty through all the years while Evylyn is losing hers; but when the bowl is shattered, her life also ends.

This bowl, evidently, is the mythic object that provides the 'short cut' explanation. A curse has been put on Evylyn; nothing she does can alter that. Indeed, it may seem that in this story notions of personal and moral responsibility are put at a distance; if you bear a curse, you yourself have no further power in the matter. Fitzgerald, however, is not wholly satisfied with this as a myth for the twentieth century, and suggests a subtle reinterpretation. At the crisis of her tale, Evylyn feels that the bowl is speaking to her:

> It seemed to be smiling now, a very cruel smile, as if to say: 'You see, this time I didn't have to hurt you directly. I didn't bother. You know it was I who took your son away. You know how cold I am and how hard and how beautiful, because once you were just as cold and hard and beautiful.'

At this point the bowl is true to its fairy-tale function, as the magically efficacious object, the author of all calamities. But presently Evylyn hears its voice again. It no longer *seems as if* the bowl speaks. In her near-madness, she actually hears it:

> 'You see, I am fate', it shouted, 'and stronger than your puny plans; and I am how-things-turn-out and I am different from your little dreams, and I am the flight of time and the end of beauty and unfulfilled desire; all the accidents and imperceptions and the little minutes that shape the crucial hours are mine. I am the exception that provides the rules, the limits of your control, the condiment in the dish of life.'

Here the narrative status of the bowl changes. It is no longer the simply malignant fairy-tale object that does all the damage because it has a will and a life of its own. What it here represents is not that active, indwelling will, so much as a reflection of life's inexorable hostility. In this passage it is seen as the inanimate and arbitrarily elected symbol of fate – of 'how-things-turn-out' – an object tangibly representative of all the intangible wrongs and errors of a lifetime. When Evylyn makes her desperate attempt to destroy it, her action is more pathetic, more human, than the fairy-tale bid to break the power of a demonic object. The smashing of the faceted bowl means, symbolically, a revenge on all that is misshapen in her life; but the breaking of life's wrongs is indissociable from the breaking of life itself.

The 'myth' of 'The Cut Glass Bowl' is therefore rather different, in psychological essence, from the myth of its literary models, the folk-tales of magically endowed objects. In effect, Fitzgerald reverses the mythic convention; his story tells us that objects and curses do not control our lives, but that our lives, with their arbitrary circumstances and our inadequacies, may generate curses which we attach to objects – in order to have something to blame and hate. We ascribe the fault to this piece of furniture, that ornament or machine; we wish it had never come into the house. This is the real myth, displacing the illusion of the parent-myth, in which objects actually have the implanted will to harm and destroy. Yet even while we thus subvert the content of the traditional myth, we still need its *form* to serve as an explanation for our experience.

Fitzgerald's story exemplifies this. Were the history of Evylyn Piper to be related without any reference to the bowl and its fancied powers, the result would be a disjointed report of calamitous but unrelated incidents. (A relationship between parts, and hence a 'meaning' for the whole story, might of course be established – but only as a result of much authorial commentary.) To make sense of what happens to Evylyn, the mythic framework is necessary; then one incident finds its natural relationship to another, and we can begin to interpret the dossier of Mrs Piper's activities either in simple fairy-tale terms ('there is a curse on her, which in three steps destroys all she has') or in the sense, suggested above, of the 'displaced myth'. The bowl may be the agent of the curse or only the attribute of accursedness, but either way it is indispensable to the story.

THE OPENING OF 'THE CUT GLASS BOWL'

The conditions for interpreting Fitzgerald's story are implicit in its opening. He deals fairly with his readers; he warns them from the outset – not explicitly, but by virtue of certain linguistic and psychological procedures – that his narrative will be an interfusion of the historic and the mythic. The story is prefaced by two paragraphs which have no episodic relationship to the main narrative, but are in fact a kind of prelude or shadow-play. They are reproduced below, together with the first sentence of the third paragraph, the beginning of the 'history':

> There was a rough stone age and a smooth stone age and a bronze age, and many years afterward a cut-glass age. In the cut-glass age, when young ladies had persuaded young men with long, curly moustaches to marry them, they sat down several months afterward and wrote thank-you notes for all sorts of cut-glass presents – punch-bowls, finger-bowls, dinner-glasses, ice-cream dishes, bonbon dishes, decanters, and cases – for, though cut glass was nothing new in the nineties, it was then especially busy reflecting the dazzling light of fashion from the Back Bay to the fastnesses of the Middle West.
>
> After the wedding the punch-bowls were arranged on the side-board with the big bowl in the centre; the glasses were set up in the china-closet; the candlesticks were put at both ends of things – and then the struggle for existence began. The bonbon dish lost its little handle and became a pin-tray upstairs; a promenading cat knocked the little bowl off the sideboard, and the hired girl chipped the middle-sized one with the sugar-dish; then the wine-glasses succumbed to leg-fractures, and even the dinner-glasses disappeared one by one, like the ten little niggers, the last one ending up, scarred and maimed, as a toothbrush holder among shabby genteels on the bathroom shelf. But by the time all this had happened the cut-glass age was over, anyway.
>
> It was well past its first glory on the day the curious Mrs Roger Fairboalt came to see the beautiful Mrs Harold Piper.

About this opening, two things in particular are stylistically remarkable. One is the handling of a complex of time-references; and the other is a syntactic/semantic play with the notion of *agency*.

THE TIME ELEMENT

As to the treatment of time, consider the story's first sentence: 'There was a rough stone age and a smooth stone age and a bronze age, and many years afterward a cut-glass age.' By its very form this invites comparisons with fairy-tale openings like *Once upon a time there were three bears*, which similarly depend on 'existential' (*there* + *be*) statements. But we have to note that the assertion *there were three bears* is 'conditioned', as it were, by the formula *once upon a time*, and is hence assigned to the mythic domain. We accordingly treat *there were three bears* as a form of existential statement to be interpreted as openly fictive rather than as quasi-factual. Now if we compare this with Fitzgerald's opening, it will appear that in *his* existential assertions the 'fictive' or mythic, and the 'factual' or historic, are juxtaposed. To say that 'there was a stone age' or 'there was a bronze age' is to make a statement of the historic, in the sense that there were periods of culture now generally recognised as taking their character from dominant artefacts in stone or bronze; but to say *there was a cut-glass age* is merely mythic. Although Fitzgerald eventually assigns his cut-glass age to a period of 'real' time (the 1890s), it is nonetheless a product of his imagination, a private and poetic interpretation of history.

But if this opening sentence does indeed embody a 'mythic' element, where is the obligatory formula, the *once upon a time* that directs our reading? The answer is, that the phrase *many years afterward* is in this case the primer of the myth, functioning as the narrative equivalent of *once upon a time* or *long, long ago*. The point may be made with the help of a phrase-to-phrase tabulation on the model of 'Once upon a time there were three bears':

'Historic' statement	*Time formula*	*'Mythic' statement*
	Once upon a time ⟶	there were three bears
There was a rough stone age . . . and ⟶	many years afterward ⟶	[there was] a cut-glass age

Perhaps the most interesting thing about this opening is what it suggests about the perspective in which mythic time is viewed. In conventional fairy-tale narration, the era of myth is seen retrospectively, from the standpoint of the present:

'Mythic time' ←——————————× *'Now'*

'once long ago'
'once upon a time'

In Fitzgerald's opening, by contrast, 'mythic time' is seen in reverse perspective, as a projection from an actual era in the past:

Past ×——————→ *'Mythic time'* *'Now'*

stone age cut-glass age
'many years afterward'

Here is no link with present time, or the 'now' of the story. In the narrative of 'The Cut Glass Bowl', this is emotionally and psychologically significant. The events of the tale fill the gap between 'mythic time' and 'now', but the deviousness of the opening ensures that the 'cut-glass age' remains a distant, irrecoverable time, something over and done before our story really begins. Psychologically, the cut-glass age is as dim and distant as the stone age, and in that respect is different from its ostensibly 'factual' identity, *the eighteen nineties*. The contrast here between myth-time and real-time is important. Though the bowl can be no more than 26 years old when Evylyn dies, it figures in the story as an object of ancient malignancy – a magic artefact of the *cut-glass age* rather than a machined product of the 1890s.

The reversal of perspective which so interestingly marks the first sentence recurs in the second: 'In the cut-glass age, when young ladies had persuaded young men with long, curly moustaches to marry them, they sat down several months afterward and wrote thank-you notes for all sorts of cut-glass presents . . .' The point of recurrence is located in the phrase *several months afterward*, echoing the *many years afterward* of the preceding sentence. Thus, *several months afterward* stands in relationship to *in the cut-glass age, when young ladies had persuaded young men . . . to marry them*, as *many years afterward* does to *stone age*:

stone age←——→many years afterward——cut-glass age, when young ladies had persuaded←——→several months afterward

The first two sentences of the story, linked by the words *in the cut-glass age*, thus show time as a forward drift, with a perspective standpoint in the past; the cut-glass 'age' is defined from the base of a preceding age, and an event within the cut-glass age is defined from the base of a preceding event.

This is the time-perspective of the first two paragraphs, until we come to the terminus of 'by the time all this had happened the cut-glass age was over'. When the narrative proper begins, it is significant that the first time-orientation in the historic account is retrospective, looking *back* from the 'now' of the story; Evylyn refers to the year of her marriage, 'seven years ago, in ninety-two'. In the first two paragraphs, as the 'mythic' matter of the story is being foreshadowed, the pointers of time are turned forward; with the onset of 'history' they are turned back.

This retrospectiveness characterises the style of successive episodes, not only in the direct allusions to time, but also in the back-shifting use of tenses and modal auxiliaries. In this passage, for example, 'now' is in the past, looking recollectively to an earlier past:

> Her thirty-fifth birthday had been an exceptionally busy one, for they were entertaining on short notice that night, and as she stood in her bedroom window in the late afternoon she discovered that she was quite tired. Ten years before she would have laid down and slept, but now she had a feeling that things needed watching: maids were cleaning downstairs, bric-a-brac was all over the floor, and there were sure to be grocery men who had to be talked to, imperatively – and then there was a letter to write to Donald, who was fourteen and in his first year at school.

Everything in Evylyn's story, in fact, looks back to the moment when the cut-glass bowl is presented to her; everything in the preamble looks forward to the day when it takes its place on her sideboard. There is a crucial moment when 'mythic' time merges into 'historic' time.

THE ELEMENT OF AGENCY

The opening of the tale makes certain prefigurings of character and agency. In *the young ladies*, for example, and the *young men with long, curly moustaches*, there may be a typological suggestion of Evylyn, just such a young lady, and Harold, just such a young man. Possibly, too, the *hired girl* who chips the middle-sized bowl foreshadows the careless servant Hilda (who leaves the bowl on the floor for little Julie to cut herself) and the absent-minded cleaning woman Martha (who cannot recall where she has left the fatal letter). Most striking of all the players in the prefatory dumb-show, however, are the cut-glass pieces themselves, which in the second paragraph emerge as actors in a drama of accident and survival. We are all but invited to think of these dishes and glasses as objects actually presented to Evylyn and Harold, and to identify the bowl in the centre of the sideboard as Evylyn's bowl, *the* bowl. Certainly it is noticeable that the general allusions to 'young ladies' and 'young men', as well as to 'bonbon dishes' and 'dinner glasses', become, in the second paragraph, more specific in implication, through the use of the definite article: '*the* hired girl', '*the* bonbon dish', '*the* dinner glasses', etc., suggest a particular household.

In some sentences the cut-glass piece is the object/recipient (syntactically the object, in semantic role the recipient, or 'patient'): *a promenading cat knocked the little bowl off the sideboard, the hired girl chipped the middle-sized one*. The trivial act of a casual or thoughtlesss agent changes the fate of a prized piece, exiling it to the society of *shabby genteels* – a phrase which might characterise Evylyn and Harold in the last phase of their story:

> As in most families whose fortunes have gone down rather than up, she and Harold had drifted into a colourless antagonism. In repose they looked at each other with the toleration they might have felt for broken old chairs.

In other sentences the cut-glass items figure as subjects and quasi-agents (or patients): *the bonbon dish lost its handle, the wine-glasses succumbed to leg fractures, the dinner glasses disappeared one by one*. Here the impression that glass artefacts are beings with the capacity to suffer and change is even more marked. A crucial clause is *and then the struggle for existence began*. Whose existence? Is it only the existence of these cut-glass citizens in their sideboard community? Or is it by implication the existence of those human beings whose lives they prefigure – who are also vulnerable, who also lose, succumb to wounds, disappear? Once again, the mythic and the historic merge: there is a myth of the glasses which is a paradigm of 'real life' existences. The one notable absentee from this catalogue of victims and agents is the big bowl itself. There is no human image to which it can be related, no suggestion of loss, injury or frailty that can be associated with it. The big bowl of the opening paragraphs is a survivor: and Evylyn's bowl, in the story proper, declares itself as fate, whose cold, hard presence stands immutable through a history of injuries, breakages, wrecks.

'PRECONDITIONING' AS A NARRATIVE DEVICE

A good opening determines the narrative tempo and establishes points of reference; the writing of the first page of a short story governs the speed and assurance with which the author can develop plot and theme in the pages that follow. In part, this is a matter of 'planting' information, imitating the Chekhovian principle of stagecraft which says that if you have a gun on the wall in Act I, it has to go off in Act III. Every writer makes 'plants' of this kind, which at first sight seem merely decorative but which later discharge important functions. In the first part of the story of 'The Cut Glass Bowl', Fitzgerald goes to the trouble of specifying the kind of items covered by the phrase 'all sorts of cut-glass presents'. This at first glance is a mere stylistic expansion; but in the second paragraph he is able to draw selectively upon the list of cut-glass objects, in order to create the animated personnel of a drama that prefigures the story itself. It is a particular example, and a good one, of the general compositional rule that every detail in a short story should be a hook on which a theme can be hung.

The opening of a story may involve more than this, however. Some openings advise the reader of the constraints and liberties of his reading. There is 'preconditioning': so that if we are told that *there were men with teeth on their toes*, our willingness to accept an extraordinary assertion without looking into its credentials may depend on whether it is prefaced by *once upon a time*, or (let us say) *in the fifteenth century*. *Once upon a time* gives licence to myth, whose statements we do not put to rational question; *in the fifteenth century* presupposes history, and with it the rule of 'common sense' and 'natural law'. To assert – whether in opening a story or in any other context – that *in the fifteenth century there were men with teeth on their toes* is to tell a manifest lie; to begin a narrative with *Once upon a time there were men with teeth on their toes* is quite another matter. You may tell me this, and I will accept it as the precondition of a story I hope is going to be interesting and instructive.

What Fitzgerald brings off in the opening paragraphs of 'The Cut Glass Bowl' is a rather complex act of preconditioning. On the one hand he suggests *once upon a time* – that is, 'this is a myth' – and, on the other, *at the end of the last century* – meaning 'this is a real-life story'. The alert reader is forewarned that he is about to read a modern history in a mythic perspective. Whether 'forewarning' or 'preconditioning' is a general principle of story-telling, and what its variants are, is perhaps a matter for research. Intuition, that vague counsellor, suggests that some sort of preconditioner is to be found, if no more than vestigially, in the opening lines and paragraphs of any narrative; but one would no doubt go a long way to find another story as carefully preconditioned as 'The Cut Glass Bowl' – a tale which comprehends imaginatively the partnering illusions of resemblance and transcendence.

REFERENCE

FITZGERALD, F. SCOTT. 'The Cut Glass Bowl', in *The Stories of F. Scott Fitzgerald*, Vol. 1: *The Diamond as Big as the Ritz and Other Stories.* Harmondsworth: Penguin Books, 1962, repr. 1976.

Part IV

Means to an end

Twelve

The biro, the word processor, and putting pen to paper

A strange and mystic business, writing. Almost no progress has taken place since it was invented.
(John Steinbeck)

I have no other drill sergeant but chance to put order into my writings.
(Michel de Montaigne)

It is indeed a mystic business, mystic from beginning to end, but the greatest mystery is in the beginning. How to begin? is the question that torments narrators, historians, philosophers, critics, and all who live and variously prosper by the craft of writing. No one really knows how to answer this question once and for all, or how to advise others, though people have been asking and advising for a long time. Go back two thousand years, and you might find a teacher giving his students this counsel:

> At first the pen must move slowly but surely. We must make choice of what is best, and not be carried away by things that come on the spur of the moment; we must bring judgement to bear on our ideas, and if they pass muster we must present them with care. For we must indeed *choose* both ideas and words, and each choice is to be separately weighed in our minds. Then we need to work out the order of composition, bearing in mind all the rhythmical possibilities and putting the words down just as they come to us. To do this as carefully as possible, we shall often have to revise what we have just written. For apart from the fact that in this way we ensure better cohesion between what follows and what precedes, the warmth of thought, which has cooled a little during our writing is kindled afresh, and takes new impetus as though by repeating its course.

This is Quintilian, the Quintilian of the *Institutio Oratoria* (Butler 1920–21), a grand old schoolmaster and a credit to the tribe of professors. I imagine him addressing his scholars, who sit all-in-a-row in some frowsty porch or atrium (keep the big boys away from the little ones, he prudently warns), insisting on the importance of establishing discourse on a reliable base, making a safe track as one goes, leaving behind no serpents or hostages. 'At first the pen must move slowly.' Just so; think about it, he advises. Focus your inward gaze. Make a considered choice of your every word. Pay particular attention to rhythm, for rhythm is the connecting principle of the text – get the rhythm right at the beginning and you will keep control over your discourse as it expands. (Quintilian, we should not forget, was engaged in training writers to be *orators*.) Pause quite frequently for revision. Do not try to push the writing too far beyond the first impulse, for then it will become 'frigid' – that is, laboured, contrived, artificial, a form without feeling. Revision should help to rekindle the humanity of composition, restoring the inclination to compose. So one can imagine the ancient *rhetor* instructing his charges, the big boys and the little ones, on some fair Italian morning, two thousand years ago.

On the other hand, and it is another and a distant hand, here is a writer who, in the course of a long life, came to change his mind about the tedious business of starting a meaningful text:

> There seems to be a sort of fatality in my mind leading me to put at first my statement and proposition in a wrong or awkward form. Formerly I used to think about my sentences before writing them down, but for several years I have found that it saves time to scribble in a vile hand whole pages as quickly as I possibly can, contracting half the words, and then correct deliberately. Sentences thus scribbled down are often better ones than I could have written deliberately.[1]

This is Charles Darwin, in a passage from his autobiography, written late in his career, in his Grand Old Manhood (Ralling 1988). It is not the Darwin of the *Beagle* days, the young enthusiast hunched among his specimens and notebooks in that cramped and heaving cabin. If I imagine him at all now, I must see him in the comfort of his Victorian house, with its Victorian spaciousness, its well-upholstered Victorian furniture, its tidy Victorian domestics tending the generous Victorian fire and trimming the Victorian lamps – huge, frosty-globed or greenmantled – which they set down on the desk where the master sits scribbling his way through sheet after sheet of Victorian paper.

Yes, he has paper, that is a significant fact. He has plenty of it. (If not, he can send out for more.) It is one clue to his changed philosophy of composition: has paper, can scribble. He can afford to ride the long impulse, to obey the first confusing-diffusing pressure to get things down, in any order, via any convenient scheme of continuity, before he altogether loses touch with whatever it was he had some idea of saying. His revision, when it comes, is an editorial process, a tidying of the compositional surface, unlike Quintilian's, which implies a constant visiting of the depth. Quintilian has recourse to fiery metaphors of creativeness – of *warmth*, of *rekindling*; Darwin is less evidently disposed to make a mystery of it.[2]

Almost two millennia separate Darwin from Quintilian, but time in itself is not the important hiatus. I have plucked down these examples almost at random from my shelves (*almost* – I must confess to being familiar with them from other occasions); what most interestingly separates them, I would say, is their representation of extreme compositional temperaments. Quintilian's instinct, nurtured by his rhetorical designs, tells him to go slow, to lay the groundwork, to fix, from the start, the sustaining principles of a style. Darwin's mature method is to work unmethodically, loosely, rattling past the first obstacles, covering the ground at some length before pausing to assess progress. 'Stay', says the one; and 'go', says the other, 'go quickly'. Then which am I, I must ask, a stayer or a goer? Or each by turns? Are there compositional aims that call for Quintilian's judicious pauses, while others justify Darwin's headlong onset? Perhaps here, on this page, going slow is the only way to get it right, but there, on that other sheet, going fast is the only way not to lose it. To question oneself in this way is to become aware of problems that must have beset other writers, more eminent or more public, ancient classics or modern journeymen. Did Hooker, that majestic stylist and (now largely) unread theologian, deliberate his work, clause by clause? Was Edward Gibbon a stayer or a goer? Sterne, then? Virginia Woolf? The writer of yesterday's *Guardian* leader? And incidentally, could it be of any relevance to these questions that Hooker used a quill, that Virginia Woolf (I guess) used a fountain pen, and that the leader-writers of broadsheet newspapers almost certainly use a keyboard and a word-processing package?

For of course more things are attendant upon composition than compositions may reveal. I reflect upon present experience. I am trying, just now – which is the 'just now' of a fine hot winter morning in Tenerife – to compose a piece on the theme of the Biro and the Word Processor; and as I do so I find myself enquiring, intently, painfully, comically, in a mixture of tempers, into everything contingent upon this piece's gradual emergence onto the page. The fact of my being in Tenerife can be of no concern to the eventual reader, but it is of some technical importance to me, since it imposes on me a different experience of writing – a set of assumptions and practices somewhat unlike those I take for granted when I sit down at my desk in England. There, indeed, I have a desk (whereas in my Canarian fastness the breakfast table must do), a desk on which sits a word processor which I use at all times, beyond all reason, besottedly. I dare say I would use it, at need, to leave instructions for the milkman, if only the milkman were given to reading instructions. But here on this island I have no word processor. I use a biro, which is a good deal more portable, though possibly less versatile and certainly not so neat. Each has its merits and demerits. Quintilian, I think, would have recognised the biro as a *stilus* capable of rapid as well as considered inscriptions. Darwin, I am quite sure, would have revelled in the word processor, which is, when one comes to think of it, a type of Darwinian evolution.

Now, as to my ballpoint procedures, or birotechnology: I open my spiral notebook flat, and draft the running text onto the right-hand page. I reserve the left-hand sheet for revisions, for interpolations, for trying out alternative phrasings, for cryptic reminders of where I am going or what I must later do. Indeed, I divide the pages much as I might split the word processor screen; and often I carry material from the left-hand page across and into the right-hand draft, much as in word processing where I might transfer text from one 'document' to another. In this respect, the two techniques, of composing with biro or word processor, seem to be fundamentally similar, and I am led to wonder whether, in devising my clumsy biro-and-notebook method, with its flowerings of arrows and asterisks pointing me hither and yon, I am not merely aping the word-processing facility; or whether, as seems more likely, biro and word processor each realise, in particular ways, basic compositional processes, the primary mentality, as it were, of composition.

Writing, one might think, requires two adjacent levels of resource: the resource of the evolving text and the resource of some kind of storage for the impressions, reservations, anticipations, hints of hints of what might be possible, that build up as composition proceeds and increasingly support the procedure. Call the left-hand page – or the lower segment of the split screen – Quintilian's patch; call the right-hand page – or the screen's upper section – Darwin's acre. These are the *imminent* conditions of writing, meaning the immediately relevant, material provisions of a task in prospect, which is to be tackled whenever one sits down to write, whether it be with the enthusiastic anticipation of a good morning's run, or with an uncomfortable feeling of starting from cold and having to coax the machine into motion. The pen has to be put to paper, and pushed; some keystrokes have to be made; onto the paper there must be placed something that makes syntactic/semantic sense. Do you want to write? Here are the tools, says the admonitory voice within; here is a method – now get on with it.

Which is not to say that the business of writing cannot be quite substantially affected, particularly at the outset, by circumstances not so much *imminent* as *contingent*. All manner of things are contingent upon the act of composition, being not *of* it but existing *around* it, shaping the writer's attitude to the task in hand. I, fussily to the point of insistence, happen to prefer a black ballpoint for boldness (and here I am struggling along in a genteel, recessive blue); there is a brand of notebook I like and will go to some trouble to get (and just now I am making do, willy-nilly, with another, inferior sort); as to the kind of chair I sit in, that is of no consequence, though at this moment I am enduring what common parlance calls, not inaccurately, a Bad Back.

The particular 'Badness' of it is that I cannot comfortably sit or stand or lie in one position for very long, but must be forever on the move, leaving one activity for the relieving postures of another. I write, I read, I walk, I shave (the last desperate resort of *homo scribens*), but always with a keen sense of the temporal limitations of my condition. Thus I know, with peculiar certainty, that the drafting of this essay was begun at 10.20 a.m. on Valentine's Day 19--, and that a form of the first page and a half, from 'It is indeed a mystic business' down to 'some fair Italian morning, two thousand years ago' was laid out by 11.55 a.m., after which I made coffee and took a turn round my living room. Orthopaedic accident thus appears to have forced upon me a way of framing my composition – nothing less than a system of topics, paragraphing, sectioning. If there is any pattern in this text, or any structure for the reader to find, it may be that it all comes from a maladjusted pelvic joint.

Ah, but what an absurdity! All this business of ballpoints and backaches – what has this to do with the real matter of composition? Little enough, if the 'real matter' is the will to drive the pen along, making well-formed sentences, ordering a text. That is writing as a job to be done; but writing makes additional levies upon the writer, accidentally, irrationally, circumstantially. Though done in isolation, in a solitude constructed behind defences of closed doors and unplugged telephones, writing can never be an end wholly isolable from the interminable experience of being merely human, of itching and scratching and yearning to be elsewhere, even as one yawns and scowls and concentrates on being only here, doing this and trying to do it well. The aches and pains, the preferences and superstitions, are contingent powers, drawing out lines of inclination and perception which converge upon the writing, touching it with greater or lesser effect. There is a network of variously powerful connections, physical and psychological, leading away, trailing back, beyond and behind this hour, this day, this season, invoking and catching at the long unending etcetera of experiences, insights, fantasies and transient emotions.

But the sense that writing is thus ordinarily placed among the events of living – an episode in the common round – offends and unsettles writers, driving them to claim for it an elevated, near-magical status, as an activity which must be honoured with adequate preparations, routines ritual and placatory. So, there are those who dislike any but a black ballpoint; who before they begin must have a pot of pencils, Faber HB, new-sharpened and fragrant on the desk before them; who must wash or change into a clean shirt; who thrive on the scent of coffee or fresh flowers, or who keep pieces of orange peel in the desk drawer – anything to mark a frontier and at the same time ease its crossing. A strange and mystic business, writing. Scholarly commentators may well dismiss such stuff as 'anecdotal' – interesting, perhaps, but not relevant to the making of the text. Yet scholarship might moderate its scepticism a little; more can go into a text than the text will eventually show.

The phrase 'putting pen to paper' – still in common use though often no more than symbolic – embraces the sense of writing as a concrete, palpable, *artisanal* process. Certain materials are available to the artisan – basically, a writing instrument and a working surface – and their limitations in use, the conditions they impose upon writing as *inscription*, shape in ways more or less discernible the processes of writing as *composition*. The Roman student of rhetoric worked with a *stilus* and a small tablet of wax. The Victorian sage, on the other hand, enjoyed a supply of modern ink, a steel nib designed to control and direct its flow and, most important, a generous supply of paper. The paper is in a sense a key to the style, or the philosophy of style, inasmuch as it determines the role of memory in composition. The Roman student would be obliged to cultivate a certain kind of compositional memory, a type of *pre-storage*, forming each construction in his head, using techniques demonstrated to him by his teacher, before inscribing it on his wax tablet. By contrast, one consequence – happy or otherwise – of having paper to blot, scrawl on, annotate, crumple, eventually waste, is that there is no demand on the writer to complete the internal forming of the sentence. The only pressure on the writer playing the Darwinian game is the impulse to get the sense of it down and visible before it is smudged out of recall by the continual tumbling and diffuse patter of mental and physical impressions. Memory plays a part in both kinds of composition, but there is a great difference between *rehearsing* – and so 'memorising' before writing begins – and *recording*, that is, providing evidence for the memory to check *after* writing. 'Let me write it down before I forget it', the impulse to make a running record, is a common enough piece of self-admonition. Less often do we note the impulse to rehearse, 'Let me first memorise this thoroughly, so that I may then write it down'.

The availability of writing materials becomes (the point must be obvious) a measure of their value. The less paper we have, for example, the more circumspectly do we use it; a respect for the material is engendered, which may in the first instance be no more than a matter of simple economy, the need to avoid waste. As a boy at elementary school, in days when beating children was an approved pedagogic practice, I was more than once punished for blotting my allotted sheet of exercise paper; through mischief or ineptitude I had wasted some of the school's meagre resources. But the respect may be of a much higher kind, an ennobling of the material, and consequently an ennobling of the message it bears.

There is a story by Robert Graves (Graves 1971), about a country in which poets are allowed periodically to absent themselves from the duties they share with other citizens, in order to retire into some solitary place where they may meditate their compositions. They are each supplied with twenty writing tablets, not of wax or any degradable substance, but of silver. When a poet is satisfied, after much contemplation, that he has created something durable and fit to be recorded as a 'true' poem, then – and only then – is it inscribed upon the silver, in the knowledge that each inscribed poem depletes the available material. There will be one silver tablet less, and when all the silver tablets have been used, there will be no further possibility of 'writing'. The twenty silver tablets will be assumed to represent the definitive *oeuvre*, as our critics might say, or the best and clearest episodes of the poet's communings with the Muse, as Graves himself might have put it.

This fable in fact reflects Graves's own frequently declared views on poetic composition – ironically, perhaps, since Graves in his time used a great deal more than the paper equivalent of twenty silver tablets; the published revisions of his *Collected Poems* present continual problems to the critic and bibliographer. In spirit, however, the story is a special case of something commonly felt: that some writings are of such inherent value that they should be committed to a durable, or 'ennobled' surface. There is a letter to be kept for the best paper, a document that must be copied onto parchment, a royal decree or an ecclesiastical chronicle deserving of nothing less than the indestructible nobility of vellum. Such feelings, first awakened in ceremonial times, are in our day generally reduced to a simple conviction of the value of *the book*. All methods of composition have value only as preparations for the book; the printed page is the noble surface which (every struggling author must hope) ennobles the message.

Each age has its technology, absorbing or cancelling earlier technologies, offering to the writer materials which in various ways promote and impede the process of writing. The classic *stilus* must often have moved sluggishly in the wax; the steel nib scraped awkwardly on my boyhood's exercise paper; not without effort were the keys of that ancient Underwood, my old postgraduate companion, thumped and battered. A strange and mystic business, writing. It can be hard on the fingers, the wrists, the forearms, even. 'Writer's Cramp' is a known malady; even the operators of computer keyboards, surely the lightest, least resistant of instruments, are allegedly prone to a fatigue resonantly called Repetitive Strain Injury (which is but old writer's cramp writ technologically large).

But the resistance of the material, like its availability, like, even, its 'nobility', is a factor that helps to shape a mode of composition, to produce a style. I think of the peculiar instance of the writer devising a text for a mason to carve in stone or marble – indeed an 'ennobled' and 'ennobling' material. Consider: there is no scribbling in marble, no easy cancelling, no prompt correcting, little room for talkativeness. The writer of the proposed inscription must accede to the conventions of a style adapted to carving in stone. By and by, the style migrates out of marble and on to paper. There are writers who occasionally affect this stonecarver style, which is called 'lapidary'. This is an apparently singular instance in the lexicon of descriptive labels. We do not hear of the wax tablet style (*stiloceramic*?), or the fountain pen style (*pennifontane*?), or the microchip style (*silicophoric*?), yet one feels nevertheless that there are styles which are ultimately the product of tools and conditions of labour. The very word 'style' derives from the name of a tool; the ages of style are the successive ages of the toolmaker.

'There was a rough stone age and a smooth stone age and a bronze age', Scott Fitzgerald begins his story 'The Cut Glass Bowl', 'and many years afterward a cut glass age.' So of writing: there was an age of the *stilus*, and a long age of the quill, and after that the first age of the nib, followed by the second age (the fountain pen age), leading in due course to the age of the ballpoint and the felt tip; while in the meantime the ages of the keyboard had begun, first with the typewriter and then with the word processor. Throughout these eras there have been corresponding changes of surface: wax, wood-shavings, parchment, paper of various kinds, and at length the 'surface' of the word processor, which is hardly a surface at all, or perhaps a displaced surface.[3]

The writer at the computer keyboard may assume that the writing surface is the screen – the so-called Visual Display Unit – but the screen is only a monitor recording a process of enregistration onto a disk within the machine, from which, at need, the text may be retrieved as 'hard copy' – the final, deferred, *tactile* product of the writer's labour. Between pen and paper, the scratchily resistant, awkward paper, there is the relationship of immediate touch, representing the contact between the writer and the writer's words. Between the keyboard and the disk, monitored by the VDU, there is no resistance, no sense of working on a present surface; what there is, is a feeling of authoritative distance, the distance that allows and promotes critical assessments of an almost objective kind. Staring at the monitor, I can make quite firm decisions about the wording and cohesion of my text; the word processor is an excellent editorial instrument. What I do not feel, and often wish to feel, is the weight and substance of the text, its reality under my thumb, in my fist. I cannot feel how the composition struggles into being. The writing flows before my eyes, or is dismissed at a touch of the 'delete' key. It is almost too easy; yet, truly, that is the very point upon which manufacturers of word processors construct the appeal of their products – the ease of a writing system which puts no moment of obstruction in the writer's way, and therefore compels no (possibly beneficial) moments of deliberation.

One might think, after reading Quintilian, that some writings are inherently 'slow', though Darwin might suggest that there is something to be said for making them 'fast'. These perceptions of tempo shadow a distinction amounting almost to a principle in the history of style: a distinction between *rhetoricity* and *visibility*. 'Rhetoricity' characterises the ages of the *stilus* and the quill; the writer's frequent pauses, compelled by the resistance or limited availability of materials, the management of sentence-structure via figures and schemes which express an organisation of memory, the development, in consequence, of certain patterns of punctuation – these are features suggesting that the role of rhetoric in written discourse may be, as much as anything, 'instructive', enabling the writer to understand and *possess* the composition as it goes along. Rhetoricity is audibility. As we write, we hear the phrases, build the rhythms, in some internal chamber of repetition; and the very awkwardness of inscription, its retardation, occasionally helps us in our listening to the beat of the text.

'Visibility', on the other hand, assumes increasing importance in this age of the keyboard, our century of rapid mechanical inscription. The typewriter (old style) disgorges its prim sheets of black and white; only the cumulative fatigue of key-shift and carriage return, or the pauses to fumble with a new ribbon or clean the type, interrupt the process of instantly visible production. But the mechanical typewriter is already a thing of the past, a quaint old resource, for now we have the word processor which *shows* what is happening moment by moment; will *retrieve*, at a few keystrokes, the story of what has already happened; will *allow* deletions and transpositions without the labour of rewriting the whole page and without the mess of scissoring, pasting, or daubing with correction fluid; and will, above all, *disburden* the memory. Why should I need to rehearse (as in fact I regularly do) the structure of a long sentence when I have the silicone chip to do the memorising for me? And why, furthermore, should I be too fussily concerned with the organising power of punctuation, which presents me with the frame of my discourse, when I can easily run through it afterwards and put in a few commas at need? There are questions of rhetoricity, a discipline of the ear; but modern inventions allow us to rejoice in visibility, the privilege of the eye.

My ingenious friend the word processor makes all things rapid, fluent, readily visible. I can shuffle the text, I can construct and store passages to be retrieved at will into other passages, I can devise commands that will show me, at the touch of a finger, things filed away for recurrent use. 'Visibility!', as Humpty Dumpty might have put it, 'that's what *I* say!' Yet that visibility, that wondrous summoning for inspection and reference, has its limitations. The compilers of word-processing manuals stress the virtues of instant retrieval and consultation, but their examples and exercises suggest a preoccupation with official letters and reports in general and the documentations of commerce. They make no more than glancing reference, seemingly, to the problems of embarking upon and sustaining a long text, narrative or discursive, during the composition of which a command of the total structure is something provisionally 'filed' in the writer's own brain, not in the machine. It is a great thing that the screen can instantly display for me the look of a page, and yet it is not enough. I must have the feel of the text, all the time; I must hear it in my head. I must even – at the risk of seeming absurd – hear it in advance.

Dryden, I think, could hear his text; he had no word processor, no typewriter, no fountain pen, but only a quill, rhetoricity's allotted instrument. And here the quill depicts a stately progress:

> It was that memorable day, in the first summer of the late war, when our navy engaged the Dutch – a day wherein the two most mighty and best appointed fleets which any age had ever seen, disputed the command of the greater half of the globe, the commerce of nations, and the riches of the universe. While these vast

> floating bodies, on either side, moved against each other in parallel lines, and our countrymen, under the happy conduct of his royal highness, went breaking, by little and little, into the line of the enemies; the noise of the cannon from both navies reached our ears about the city, so that all men being alarmed with it, and in a dreadful suspense of the event, which they knew was then deciding, every one went following the sound as his fancy led him; and leaving the town almost empty, some took towards the park, some cross the river, others down it; all seeking the noise in the depth of the silence.

The date is 1688, and that is the opening of his *An Essay of Dramatic Poesy* (Dryden 1962), surely one of the most engaging specimens of English vernacular eloquence. It makes an entrance, unhurriedly, serenely, like some grave, sonorous *praeludium* by Purcell or Dr Blow. It is all phrasing; and every phrase must be heard and relished. The sense of voice – the acoustic illusion – is what matters; 'visibility' is of no great account. No one with any feeling for style is in a hurry to get to the end of Dryden's paragraph; no one scans ahead (as I do with dishwasher service contracts and even, I am afraid, some passages of deconstructionist criticism). It is enough to savour it clause by clause, *in the mind's ear.* And this remarkable writing suggests that indeed there has been no progress in the craft, no great technical advance, in the nearly seventeen hundred years separating Quintilian and John Dryden. The quill moves slowly; it articulates segments of speech; it assigns marks of punctuation, to which we readers learn to attribute values akin to those of the dynamic markings in music. The quill moves slowly, to the inkhorn, to the paper, back to the inkhorn, with perhaps a momentary suspension while the writer contemplates the turn of his next phrase.

There is a tempo to this prose, *andante sostenuto*, a tempo appropriate to the pen transcribing rhetorical cadences. And so it remains throughout the *Essay*. The work is conceived as a civil dialogue, calmly conducted by gentlemen of parts and learning, while offstage a war rudely bombinates. Their exchanges are orderly, sustained, the account of their talk keeps its composure and regular timing, with no mimesis of such abrupt changes of pace as occur in 'natural' conversation, no imitation of the intrusive event (e.g. 'suddenly a fragment of shell whizzed past our ears'),[4] no stammerings, no hums, fewer ha's, and no irruptions into the decent course of debate. Dryden is one of the great classical *prosateurs* who, in their writings, keep a personal tempo, deliberate, measured and governed by traditional principles of rhetorical structure.

It is with the emergence of the art, or mimetic *arts*, of the novel, with the author's surrender of one *persona*, his own, to a diversity of *personae* in diverse situations, thinking, speaking, responding, reacting, that frequent variations in prose tempo become apparent to the reader. But there is no such attempt at changing narrative tempi in *An Essay of Dramatic Poesy*. For all the noise of modern warfare in the offing and rumours of citizens vacating the streets of a capital city, this world of discursive language is strangely tranquil. Its characters speak like senators in some profoundly civilised assembly. Here no voice is raised above a polite level, here are no irrelevant alarms; various topics are all related to one topic, the contesting minds are of one mind, and it is the mind of John Dryden as he sits at his desk, dips the pen, pauses, listening to the voice in his head, writes a little until the scant uptake of ink runs out of the quill, and pauses again. Slowly the quill moves; slowly but surely it dictates – or perhaps accommodates – a style.

Imagine Dryden at his desk; see the quill; then infer the relationship between an instrument and a way of writing. That kind of imaginative inference occurs not uncommonly when writers meditate on their own craft. There is an example of it in Michael Ondaatje's novel *The English Patient* (1992: 94). The novel's eponymous principal (who happens to be Hungarian) listens restively while his Canadian nurse reads to him, too quickly it seems, and without respect for an author's phrasing. He breaks in:

> Read him slowly, dear girl, you must read Kipling slowly. Watch carefully where the commas fall, so you can discover the natural pauses. He is a writer who used pen and ink. He looked up from the page a lot, I believe, stared through the window and listened to birds, as most writers who are alone do. Some do not know the names of birds, though he did. Your eye is too quick and North American. Think about the speed of his pen. What an appalling, barnacled old first paragraph it is otherwise.

It is a charming vignette, though a fiction-within-a-fiction – a picture of Kipling at work, bound by the functional disciplines of pen and ink, pausing to gaze out of the window, over and beyond the immediate frontiers of composition, listening to the birds, watching their flight, and then recalling his mind to the notation of his text. Here is the artist, actually profiting from the *imminent* use of his tools, unconsciously responding to the *contingent* circumstances of his work: 'He is a writer who used pen and ink. He looked up from the page a lot, I believe. . . .'

But what is it, this text that the Canadian nurse begins to read – slowly, dear girl – to the English Patient? Why, it is *Kim*. The 'barnacled' opening sentences read:

> He sat, in defiance of municipal orders, astride the gun Zam-Zammah on her brick platform opposite the old Ajaib-Gher – the Wonder House, as the natives called the Lahore Museum. Who hold Zam-Zammah, that 'fire-breathing dragon', hold the Punjab; for that great, green-bronze piece is always the first of the conqueror's loot.

This is the passage which, for the English Patient (and, we may perhaps assume, for Ondaatje, his creator) typifies Kipling's 'slow' composition.

At first the pen moves slowly. Its pauses – as imagined by Ondaatje – are like the intervals of birdsong, like the spasms of flight, evoking a natural, and, as it were, 'irrational' rhythm. Thus one writer finds metaphors for the quality of another's writing. How different, this happy metaphoric view of Kipling at work, from the figurative judgement pronounced by the brothers Fowler (1939: 34) in *The King's English*, where the complaint is that 'he (Kipling) and his school are americanising us':

> His style exhibits a sort of remorseless and scientific efficiency . . . that suggests the application of coloured photograph to description; the camera is superseding the human hand.

The Fowlers detect in Kipling a mechanical efficiency, the efficiency of the camera. (In 1906 the camera was still quite a recent invention, and an emblem of modern technology.) For them, his prose is a recording lens – he sees with an automatic eye. For Ondaatje it is still a human eye, a natural eye that registers the stillness and vitality of nature, and transmutes these registrations into compositional movement. Each of these views is fanciful, each plausible. They do not tell us exactly how Kipling went to work, but they suggest the feel of the work; they are attempts to find metaphors for the *accidental* properties of writing.

For the grammarian, the commentator, the linguistic stylistician (a child of our time, like the beautician and the mortician), metaphor will not do. These judges will look at a text and hear nothing of birds, of inkwells, of what time of day it was, and whether the light came over the right or the left shoulder. For them there is only the evidence of what appears on the page; the subjectivities of 'slow' and 'rapid', if they are allowed to exist, are to be related to the explicit and exclusive evidence of the text. We look again at the opening sentences of *Kim*, and, still following the English Patient's advice, take note of where the commas fall, so that we can 'discover the natural pauses'. And yes, the pauses do appear to be 'natural'; but the commas can be explained in another way. There are six commas in the cited extract, three in the first sentence and three in the second. Further marks of punctuation are the dash in the first sentence, and the semi-colon in the second.

What is the purport of these marks? Do they, after all, denote 'natural pauses'? The question is whether they are instructions to the reader, as dynamics for a reading (this is more or less the English Patient's view), or whether they speak of the writer's instructions to himself, his processing of the text as it develops. If we distinguish – and here I use *ad hoc* terms – between *stem text* (the basic, irreducible, indispensable message) and *branch text* (the additions, interpolations, afterthoughts), it appears that those marks of punctuation, and particularly the commas, encapsulate pieces of branch text. Let the extract be written without its branches, or 'barnacles', and this emerges:

> He sat astride the gun Zam-Zammah on her brick platform opposite the old Ajaib-Gher. Who hold Zam-Zammah hold the Punjab.

That tells the story in a laconic way, but its omissions are crucial. It does not expand or explain. It does not tell us what 'Zam-Zammah' and 'Ajaib-Gher' *mean*. It does not hint that sitting on the cannon is a prohibited act and hence, most probably, a boyish prank. And dropping the semi-colon in the second sentence means cancelling the explanatory comment of the final clause.

It is the branch text that here creates for the stem narrative a setting and a commentary. But how, by what compositional method (other than by filling his pen and noting the flight of birds) did Kipling meld or marry or ingraft branch and stem? Did he first write the stem text and then expand it, putting in the necessary branches – in something like Darwin's way? Or did he write stem text and branch text together, fitting phrase into phrase as he went along – following Quintilian's counsel? Certainly, the text is cunningly fashioned ('barnacled' is surely the wrong word), answering or possibly prompting the reader's questions, yielding up information bit by bit, cleverly releasing the implications attendant upon a burgeoning tale. Simply as an impressionistic label, the word 'slow' seems appropriate to the compositional method. But those touches of information, those inferences and clarifications, might have been conveyed in a different syle, and to different effect, by relocating the pieces of branch text. Thus:

> In defiance of municipal orders he sat astride the gun Zam-Zammah on her brick platform opposite the Lahore Museum, known to the natives as Ajaib-Gher, the Wonder House. Since the great green-bronze piece is the first of the conqueror's loot, whoever holds 'the fire-breathing dragon', Zam-Zammah, holds the Punjab.

That redrafting contains all that the original contains, with very few changes of wording. It gets the information onto the page, quickly; but it is beyond a doubt inferior in style and narrative technique to the text – the 'barnacled old first paragraph' – that Kipling has given us. The pattern of prominences has changed. Branches precede stems, instead of interrupting or following them; explanations come before assertions. It has lost its tension as narrative prose, and has turned into something much more dull and functional, a matter of stylistic packaging in which constructions are placed in a way least likely to interfere with the transactional monotone of the text.

The pen moves slowly. Yes. It is remarkable how firmly this word 'pen' is fixed in the tribal consciousness as a primary symbol of the practice and profession of writing, of inscription, of composition, and of the dignity of authorship. I 'take up my pen'; I 'put pen to paper'; 'the pen', I say, 'is mightier than the sword'; 'they come as a boon and a blessing to men', memory prompts me, 'the Pickwick, the Owl, and the Waverley pen'; also, 'thus far, with rough and all unable pen, our bending author hath pursued his story', etc. Will we ever – deep as we now are into the age of Keyboard Man – use the word 'typewriter' in quite the same symbolic-honorific-metonymic fashion? 'One of the finest stories to have come from Mr Updike's typewriter'? 'Ms Rubens' gifted keyboard continues to beguile us'? It is curious. I have used a typewriter day by day (or 'on a daily basis', as our journalists are given to saying) ever since I could afford to lay out four pounds ten shillings for that elderly, bolt-upright, cast-iron Underwood, the pride of my youth, and yet I still 'put pen to paper', acknowledge 'slips of the pen', or think of myself, in the pomp of Latinity, as writing *currente calamo*, as though the keyboard had never replaced the quill. And yet the keyboard, no less than the pen, moves in mysterious ways.

A passage in Anne Tyler's comic novel, *The Accidental Tourist* (Tyler 1986: 12), tells of a man and his typewriter. Look at him, the poor hack; one Macon Leary, a writer of travel guides for bewildered businesspersons, positively relishing the physical effort of his two-fingered labours:

> He spent pleasurable hours dithering over questions of punctuation. Righteously, mercilessly, he weeded out the passive voice. The effort of typing made the corners of his mouth turn down, so that no one could have guessed how much he was enjoying himself. *I am happy to say*, he pecked out, but his face remained glum and intense. *I am happy to say that it's possible now to buy Kentucky Fried Chicken in Stockholm.*

It is hardly necessary to explain that the comedy of this dwells in the mismatch between the trivial message – that it is possible to buy Kentucky Fried Chicken in Stockholm – and the elaboration of Macon's earnest, concentrated activity. He is obsessed with the immediate task of prose-making. He is impervious to his surroundings, sees no birds, feels no backache. No such contributory distractions or heuristic afflictions for him. His righteousness is the intense commitment of a man embarking on some great, glowing work of *belles lettres*. It is absurd – yet Tyler's description is nevertheless a convincing account of the writer absorbed in the toil of writing, enjoying the effort, taking something like pleasure from the resistance of the material – in this case, the resistance that typing offers.

We laugh and nod, because we have known it. Having to 'peck out' the message – the labour of inscription – somewhat retards the compositional process, obliging Macon to consider questions of pointing ('dithering over punctuation', although there is no interior pointing in the sentence quoted), and involves him in a patrolling of his own style ('weeding out the passive' – although this does not 'weed out' the impersonal construction 'it is possible to buy', which a true passive-hater might have replaced with the forthright declarative 'you can now buy'). Placing ourselves in imagination before that strenuous machine, with its ponderous touch, its half-moon of flailing type, its shift key that hoists the platen in preparation for the K (bump), then the F (bump), then the C (bump – oh, how in Underwood days one learned to detest CAPS) – we might attempt to construct the 'natural pauses' of a two-finger typist.

What are the probabilities of Macon's phrasing as he effortfully hammers out his piece on the qwerty keyboard of his mechanical typewriter? This, perhaps?:

> I'm happy to say
> that it's possible now
> to buy Kentucky Fried Chicken
> in Stockholm

But that, as a possible segmentation of the typist's effort, is one that lies discernibly close to the divisions of a syntactic structure. The divisions run thus:

1. A 'reporting' construction, 'I'm happy to say'.
2. The 'reported' clause, 'that it's possible now'.
3. An infinitive clause dependent on the reported clause, 'to buy Kentucky Fried Chicken'.
4. An adverbial adjunct, 'in Stockholm' – placed at the end of the sentence because Macon has left himself nowhere else to place it.

These, however, were not Macon's only syntactic options. He might have written, for example, 'I'm happy to say that in Stockholm it's now possible to buy Kentucky Fried Chicken'; or, more adventurously, 'In Stockholm, I'm happy to say, it's now possible to buy Kentucky Fried Chicken'; or yet more flexibly – but this breaks his embargo on the passive – 'Kentucky Fried Chicken may now be bought in Stockholm, I'm happy to say'; which further yields 'Kentucky Fried Chicken, I'm happy to say, may now be bought in Stockholm'. These alternatives are increasingly 'marked', as some linguists would put it – that is, are significant departures from an assumed norm of word-order[5]; and Macon is a normative writer, a dullish, unimaginative man beating out his text on a well-beaten typewriter. Anne Tyler presents a convincing picture of this inexpert typist, the corners of his mouth turned down, grimly telling his routine tale. He goes slow, but not as Kipling goes slow; in Macon's case it is because the typewriter and his ordinariness will not allow him to go fast.

Many begin slowly, for many reasons. See there, Dryden with his quill, slowly, surely, building up a sovereign tempo; see there, Kipling with his pen, creating a narrative movement; and see here, the fictional, typewriter-toughened Mr Leary, thumping it out, as the rest of us do, for the copy-editor and the printer, getting it right if he can, as we all try to do, because that is what the publisher pays for, and because Macon, in his fictional role, is a fatally fussy man whose compositional labours are an emblem of his character.

Many begin slowly, but sometimes the entry is fast, as in Thomas Keneally's beginning of a skilful tale, *Woman of the Inland Sea* (1993):

> A woman in her early thirties, one traveller, the handsome but slightly frowning Kate Gaffney-Kozinski, running across the rain-glossed pavement in Potts Pour, she saw from a poster in front of the closed newsagent's that her defrocked uncle had given another interview to one of those smooth-paged magazines.
>
> She stopped in front of the poster. As an artefact she found it sad and hard to believe in. Her hand sought – beneath the neck of her dress – the scar tissue behind her left shoulder. She had no time – the delicatessen was about to close and she had no coffee for Murray – but she stopped, shuddered, let her breath go in large gasps of steam, and began to weep.

This is by any account an extraordinary opening. Particularly remarkable, for its impression of tumbling haste, is that first sentence, which is also the novel's first paragraph. Here indeed is rapid movement. The commas arrange the text in a quite distracted way, making an odd turbulence in the first half of the sentence. From its mid-point onwards, from the Subject–Verb group *she saw*, to the ending in *one of those smooth-paged magazines*, the construction seems straightforward. This is the stem text. Everything before it is "branching", in the sense outlined earlier.

The peculiarity of this branch text is that its constituent phrases, *a woman in her early thirties*, followed by *one traveller* (but why *one*? why not *a*?), followed by *the handsome but slightly frowning Kate*

Gaffney-Kozinski, followed by *running across the rain-glossed pavement at Potts Pour*, might without apparent loss of meaning, and with no obvious damage to any notion of logical sequence, be set down in almost any order that ingenious permutation might contrive. The order could be this:

> The handsome but slightly frowning Kate Gaffney-Kozinski, one traveller, a woman in her early thirties, running across the rain-glossed pavement in Potts Pour . . .

Or, equally, this:

> One traveller, a woman in her early thirties, the handsome but slightly frowning Kate Gaffney-Kozinski, running across the rain-glossed pavement in Potts Pour . . .

Or this:

> Running across the rain-glossed pavement in Potts Pour, a woman in her early thirties, one traveller, the handsome but slightly frowning Kate Gaffney-Kozinski . . .

These are all acceptable syntactically. The order chosen by Keneally can, however, be interpreted as the logical or semantically sensible pattern, which is:

1. General identification:	'A woman in her early thirties'
apposition:	'one traveller'
2. Specific identification:	'the handsome but slightly frowning Kate Gaffney-Kozinski'
3. Action:	'running across the . . . pavement in Potts Pour'

That is a descriptive tracing of a movement from the general to the particular, and one that would suggest a careful authorial control of the wording. Nevertheless, the impression persists of rapidity and randomness in this opening.

That impression, perhaps not well captured in the traditional grammatical labellings of Subject and Predicate, may be better accounted for in terms of *information structure*, or *thematic structure*; specifically, with reference to the concepts of *Theme* and *Rheme*. The Theme of a sentence is its informational starting point, the announcement of something to be talked about; and the 'something' may be expressed as a noun, a noun phrase, an adverbial phrase, a clause, or, indeed, any category of grammatical form. The Rheme, accordingly, is what is said about the Theme, and its grammatical realisations are also diverse. (For example, in 'Our Charlie keeps ferrets', the Theme/Rheme division corresponds to the Subject/Predicate structure; in 'Our Charlie, he keeps ferrets', the Rheme is a predication following a 'topic', *he*; in 'Our Charlie, what a man!' the Rheme is an interjection, or 'exclamative' clause.)[6]

In Keneally's opening sentence/paragraph (a paragraph consisting of one sentence containing forty-seven words), the Rheme – or rheme-complex – is 'she saw from a poster', etc. All that precedes that – our 'branch text' – is thematic. It is, however, a complex of Themes, most of them rather less simple than 'Our Charlie', though the pattern is basically that of 'Our Charlie, he keeps ferrets'. The Theme is 'A woman in her early thirties'. It is also 'one traveller'. It is 'The handsome but slightly frowning Kate Gaffney-Kozynski'; it is also 'running across the rain-glossed pavement in Potts Pour'; and these distinct Themes converge on the topic 'she'. The movement is rapid, almost confusing, because it is at first difficult for the reader, plunging into the story with a push from the author, to grade this thematic material, to decide what needs to be known, first and foremost, at this initial point of contact with a character who is evidently the story's central figure. There is almost an excess of information to be ordered and stored; what the websurfers and internetters call an 'infoglut'.

With the second paragraph the writer draws breath and tempers the pace. Sentence length – and with it, the density of thematic structure – is for the moment reduced. A simple sentence of seven words is followed by another simple sentence – though thematically more complex – of twelve words. But the rhythm begins to pick up again in the next sentence, sixteen words long, with a parenthetical comment on the stem text; and in the sentence following, thirty-four words in length, with a long 'commentary' parenthesis and a complex Theme/Rheme structure, the rapid stride of the narrative is resumed. The novel has begun at a canter, paused for a moment, and then settled to a loping pace – a seemingly restive but masterfully controlled opening.

How, though, are these changes of tempo detected by the reader? (That is, if the reader can take the trouble to observe them – for it is not obligatory, or indispensable to the enjoyment of the novel – to take conscious note of such stylistic tremors, or to seek enlightenment in grammatical theory.) Is it by attributing particular significance to the emblematic role of punctuation, as the English Patient would have us do? Is it by always insisting on the rhetoricity of the text, its implied representation of a voice, speaking? Is it by assigning values to variations in sentence structure, having some notion of the diverse syntactic resources our language offers to us?[7] Behind the look of the page, that shining, superficial presence, do we – can we – discern evidences of what was actually going on in the writer's mind, perhaps in the writer's environment, as the composition developed?

The English Patient, taking a passage by Kipling, and knowing for a virtual certainty that Kipling wrote with pen and ink, makes that knowledge a point of assured reference for his observations on compositional tempo. (Note: He *knows* about the pen and ink; he only 'believes in' the contingent circumstances of musing and bird-watching.) We read a piece of Dryden's prose, secure in the certainty that his instrument was a quill, and readily relate those quill-movements to the essentially vocal rhythmic/syntactic schemes of formal oration. We are told about a man 'pecking out' his text on an old-fashioned typewriter, and we assume a relationship between the labour of typing and the shape of the text. But, looking at Thomas Keneally's introduction to *Woman of the Inland Sea*, who can say, by way of diagnosis, whether those interesting fluctuations of pace were worked out with a pencil, with a biro and notebook, with a portable typewriter, or with the latest word-processing package? Be sure, no analyst will now come along and say, with the utter confidence of one who knows that there can be no two ways about it, 'watch carefully where the commas fall . . . he is a writer who uses a fountain pen / a biro / a Smith-Corona / a MS-DOS PC with word-processing software'. Because we know that any and all of these instruments are available to the modern author, we dare not diagnose so assuredly. Who is ever totally confident of what can be checked by referring to a living informant? (One could write to Mr Keneally and ask, but apart from the fact that such an intrusive act might call for a little nerve, there is the dreadful possibility of finding that one's suppositions have been wrong.)

It is a significant property of modern composition that it can be worked out and worked over with a fairly wide range of executive instruments and materials. I can avail myself, in varying moods and circumstances, of the biro and/or the word processor (and/or, if I so wish, a fountain pen, and/or a pencil, in which case let it not be too soft, nor yet too hard). As the materials of writing become more complex, more convenient for divers purposes, so the links between style as composition and style as a process of inscription become obscure. We can ask each other 'What do you use for writing?', knowing that this is not a question our forebears would have had much, if any, occasion to ask. We are a long way from Quintilian, and almost as far, technologically speaking, from Darwin. The time is probably not very distant when we will compose with the aid of instruments that make our personal computers look as quaint as old fountain pens. But writing remains a mystic business. The elaboration of instruments and inscriptional methods only complicates the endless compositional etcetera, which I may try to represent here in my essay, but which I can never fully grasp, still less explain.

There comes a point in any process of composition at which the writing begins to quit the writer; it liberates itself from its lugubriously human begetter, starts to mind its own business, and gives increasingly the impression of taking on an independent existence. So my essay on the Biro and the Word Processor is now beginning to go away from me. I think that I may have resolved certain tensions – as, when to go fast and when to go slow, when to favour rhetoricity or when to promote visibility, when to restrict my attention to the imminent business of writing and when to muse, daydream or fret among contingent circumstances. I have reconciled myself to the blue biro and persevered with the wrong kind of notebook. The accursed Bad Back has, over a period of weeks, become the Tolerably Impertinent Back, the Companionate Back, *my* Back – an almost acceptable sacroiliac reminder of mortality and the passage of time. I have put pen to paper and I have set a few things in place since the Back drove me to writing.

So the work moves away from me, away from its representative status as a piece of me, my flesh, my nervous system, the fretful commotion of my impressions, whims, prejudices. It is time for me to make a fair copy, to unravel skeins of text, to make choice among alternatives sketched out on the left-hand pages of my notebook. I shall revise, perhaps more than a little, here adding a sentence or two, there taking away an otiose paragraph (not always knowing quite why it is otiose, but trusting the instinct of the moment). Presently, restored to my computer, I shall put this text onto disk; the monitor, and, eventually, the print-out, will make it visible, distanced, in the semblance of a book, a text objectively separated from the personal history of its making.

I may then even revise a little more, changing a word here or there, or altering the position of a phrase – but this will be editorial work, a final preparation of the piece for its public ennoblement on the printed page. And there on the page it will stand at last, wholly visible, at times revealing to my privileged though wistful eye the places where error and dubious judgement still lurk, but generally responding to my scrutiny with the blank indifferent stare that will lead me to wonder if I really wrote this piece, and how I ever came to put pen to paper on such an errand. I will never know. It seems, when all is said and done, that I have no other drill sergeant but chance to put order into my writings.

NOTES

1 This passage is quoted from Darwin's Autobiography, written during the last five years of his life, when he and his wife were living in settled, comfortable circumstances at Down House, in Kent, about 16 miles from London. A picture of Darwin's study at Down House is reproduced in Moorehead (1971: 202). I came upon this after I had composed my fanciful description of the Victorian sage in his study, and I am gratified to note that the distance between fancy and illustrated fact is not very great.

2 But Darwin seems to have been in two minds about his own compositional procedures. On the one hand we find him claiming to have changed his former habit and now to 'scribble in a vile hand whole pages as quickly as I possibly can'. On the other he states, in the paragraph preceding the quoted extract, that 'I have as much difficulty as ever in expressing myself clearly and concisely', and consoles himself with the reflection that this difficulty 'has had the compensating advantage of forcing me to think long and intently about every sentence . . .'. Thus even the scribbling Darwin would appear to have known his Quintilianesque moments. A strange and mystic business, writing.

3 Wood shavings? Certainly. Recent excavations of a Roman fort on Hadrian's Wall (at Chesterholm, known to the Romans as Vindolanda) have turned up a remarkable collection of tablets containing administrative records of the Batavian garrison which occupied the fort at the end of the first century AD. These writing tablets are in the form of wide shavings of wood.

4 But one of the loveliest short passages in the *Essay* describes the boating party straining their ears to catch the sound of those non-whizzing shells:

> and then, every one favouring his own curiosity with a strict silence, it was not long ere they perceived the air to break about them like the noise of distant thunder, or of swallows in a chimney – those little undulations of sound, though almost vanishing before they reached them, yet still seeming to retain somewhat of their first horror, which they had betwixt the fleets.

Rarely can cannon-shot have been described with such careful composure.

5 This might be thought a rather free interpretation of the marked/unmarked distinction as widely understood among linguists; see however, Quirk *et al.* (1985: sect. 2.35n). The authors note that this distinction is 'realised morphologically by the presence and absence of an inflection', but go on to say that 'it is common to extend the use of "marked" and "unmarked" to grammatical contrasts which are formally or semantically unequal'. Such an extension would include a labelling of the construction 'In Stockholm it's now possible to get fried chicken' (the phrase 'in Stockholm' being emphatically *fronted*) as 'marked', by contrast with 'It's now possible to get fried chicken in Stockholm'.

6 The terms Theme and Rheme have their origin in the work of grammarians associated with the Linguistic Circle of Prague. My comments are necessarily brief and general; for fuller information the reader is referred to Halliday (1985: Ch. 3).

7 For instance, such resources as are examined by M.A.K. Halliday under the heading 'elaborating, extending, enhancing'. See Halliday (1985: 202ff). The structure of the opening sentence of Keneally's *Woman of the Inland Sea* (Keneally 1993) seems to correspond to the Hallidayan concept of 'enhancement', whereby one part of a complex construction supplements the reading of another part with which it is juxtaposed, though not necessarily in a clear logical relationship.

REFERENCES

BUTLER, H.R. (ed.). *Quintilian: Institutio Oratoria*. London: Loeb Classics Library, 4 vols, 1920–21; X.iii.5.

DRYDEN, JOHN. *An Essay of Dramatick Poesie*, in G. Watson (ed.) *Of Dramatick Poesie and Other Essays*. London: Everyman, 1962.

FOWLER, H.W. and FOWLER, F.G. *The King's English*. Oxford University Press, 1936; repr. 1939.

GRAVES, ROBERT. *Seven Days in New Crete*. Bath: Cedric Chivers, 1971.

HALLIDAY, M.A.K. *An Introduction to Functional Grammar*. London: Arnold, 1985.

KENEALLY, THOMAS. *Woman of the Inland Sea.* London: Sceptre Books, rev. edn, 1993.

MOORHEAD, ALAN. *Darwin and the Beagle.* London: Penguin Books, 1971.

ONDAATJE, MICHAEL. *The English Patient.* London: Picador, 1992.

QUIRK, RANDOLPH *et al. A Comprehensive Grammar of the English Language.* London: Longman, 1985.

RALLING, CHRISTOPHER (sel. and arr.). *The Voyage of Charles Darwin; His Autobiographical Writings.* London: British Broadcasting Corporation, 1988; p. 75.

TYLER, ANN. *The Accidental Tourist.* London: Chatto & Windus, 1985; repr. Penguin Books, 1986.

Part V

Appendices

Appendix I

Thomas Gray: 'Elegy written in a Country Churchyard'

The following is the text used in Chapter 5 (ed. Roger Lonsdale, Longman's Annotated English Poets). In several not unimportant points of punctuation the modern text differs from that of the 1751 edition (see Chapter 1, pp. 16–19); the latter, however, is not readily accessible, and to have used it might have seemed perverse. To help the reader follow the analysis on pp. 84–99, the proposed 'sectioning' of the poem is indicated here, and the stanzas are numbered.

The churchyard at nightfall

The curfew tolls the knell of parting day, 1
The lowing herd wind slowly o'er the lea,
The ploughman homeward plods his weary way,
And leaves the world to darkness and to me.

Now fades the glimmering landscape on the sight, 2
And all the air a solemn stillness holds,
Save where the beetle wheels his droning flight,
And drowsy tinklings lull the distant folds;

Save that from yonder ivy-mantled tower 3
The moping owl does to the moon complain
Of such as, wandering near her secret bower,
Molest her ancient solitary reign.

The rustic dead: their simple, useful lives

Beneath those rugged elms, that yew-tree's shade, 4
Where heaves the turf in many a mouldering heap,
Each in his narrow cell for ever laid,
The rude forefathers of the hamlet sleep.

The breezy call of incense-breathing morn, 5
The swallow twittering from the straw-built shed,
The cock's shrill clarion or the echoing horn
No more shall rouse them from their lowly bed.

For them no more the blazing hearth shall burn, 6
Or busy housewife ply her evening care:
No children run to lisp their sire's return,
Or climb his knees the envied kiss to share.

Oft did the harvest to their sickle yield, 7
Their furrow oft the stubborn glebe has broke;
How jocund did they drive their team afield!
How bowed the woods beneath their sturdy stroke!

The vanity of ambition and pomp

Let not Ambition mock their useful toil, 8
Their homely joys and destiny obscure;
Nor Grandeur hear, with a disdainful smile,
The short and simple annals of the poor.

The boast of heraldry, the pomp of power, 9
And all that beauty, all that wealth e'er gave,
Await(s) alike the inevitable hour.
The paths of glory lead but to the grave.

[but on *await(s)* see note 10, p. 101]

Nor you, ye Proud, impute to these the fault, 10
If Memory o'er their tomb no trophies raise,
Where through the long-drawn aisle and fretted vault
The pealing anthem swells the note of praise.

Can storied urn or animated bust 11
Back to its mansion call the fleeting breath?

Can Honour's voice provoke the silent dust,
Or Flattery soothe the dull cold ear of Death?

Hidden talent, buried gifts

Perhaps in this neglected spot is laid 12
Some heart once pregnant with celestial fire;
Hands that the rod of empire might have swayed,
Or waked to ecstasy the living lyre.

But Knowledge to their eyes her ample page 13
Rich with the spoils of time did ne'er unroll;
Chill Penury repressed their noble rage,
And froze the genial current of the soul.

Full many a gem of purest ray serene 14
The dark unfathomed caves of ocean bear:
Full many a flower is born to blush unseen
And waste its sweetness on the desert air.

Some village Hampden that with dauntless breast 15
The little tyrant of his fields withstood;
Some mute inglorious Milton here may rest,
Some Cromwell guiltless of his country's blood.

The virtue of obscurity

The applause of listening senates to command, 16
The threats of pain and ruin to despise,
To scatter plenty o'er a smiling land,
And read their history in a nation's eyes,

Their lot forbade: nor circumscribed alone 17
Their growing virtues, but their crimes confined;
Forbade to wade through slaughter to a throne,
And shut the gates of mercy on mankind.

The struggling pangs of conscious truth to hide, 18
To quench the blushes of ingenuous shame,
Or heap the shrine of Luxury and Pride
With incense kindled at the Muse's flame.

Far from the madding crowd's ignoble strife 19
Their sober wishes never learned to stray;
Along the cool sequestered vale of life
They kept the noiseless tenor of their way.

Our need to be remembered

Yet even these bones from insult to protect 20
Some frail memorial still erected nigh,
With uncouth rhymes and shapeless sculpture decked,
Implores the passing tribute of a sigh.

Their name, their years, spelt by the unlettered muse, 21
The place of fame and elegy supply:
And many a holy text around she strews,
That teach the rustic moralist to die.

For who to dumb Forgetfulness a prey, 22
This pleasing anxious being e'er resigned,
Left the warm precincts of the cheerful day,
Nor cast one longing lingering look behind?

On some fond breast the parting soul relies, 23
Some pious drops the closing eye requires;
Ev'n from the tomb the voice of nature cries,
Ev'n in our ashes live their wonted fires.

A death foretold

For thee who, mindful of the unhonoured dead, 24
Dost in these lines their artless tale relate;
If chance, by lonely Contemplation led,
Some kindred spirit shall inquire thy fate,

Haply some hoary-headed swain may say, 25
'Oft have we seen him at the peep of dawn
'Brushing with hasty steps the dews away
'To meet the sun upon the upland lawn.

'There at the foot of younger nodding beech 26
'That wreathes its old fantastic roots so high,

'His listless length at noontide would he stretch,
'And pore upon the brook that babbles by.

'Hard by yon wood, now smiling as in scorn, 27
'Muttering his wayward fancies he would rove,
'Now drooping, woeful wan, like one forlorn,
'Or crazed with care, or crossed in hopeless love.

'One morn I missed him on the customed hill, 28
'Along the heath and near his favourite tree;
'Another came; nor yet beside the rill,
'Nor up the lawn, nor at the wood was he;

'The next with dirges due in sad array 29
'Slow through the church-way path we saw him borne.
'Approach and read (for thou can'st read) the lay,
'Graved on the stone beneath yon aged thorn.'

The Epitaph

Here rests his head upon the lap of earth 30
A youth to fortune and to fame unknown.
Fair Science frowned not on his humble birth,
And Melancholy marked him for her own.

Large was his bounty and his soul sincere, 31
Heaven did a recompense as largely send;
He gave to Misery all he had, a tear,
He gained from Heaven ('twas all he wished) a friend.

No farther seek his merits to disclose, 32
Or draw his frailties from their dread abode,
(There they alike in trembling hope repose)
The bosom of his Father and his God.

Appendix II

'The Prelude', Bk I, the 'boat' episode

The 1850 version of this passage is presented in full in Chapter 6, where the 1805 version is sporadically quoted. Here, for extended comparison's sake, are both versions. (The edition is that of J.C. Maxwell, *William Wordsworth, The Prelude. A Parallel Text.* Harmondsworth: Penguin Books, 1971, repr. 1975).

(A) Book I, 372–427 (1805)

One evening (surely I was led by her)
I went alone into a shepherd's boat,
A skiff that to a willow tree was tied
Within a rocky cave, its usual home.
'Twas by the shores of Patterdale, a vale
Wherein I was a stranger, thither come
A schoolboy traveller, at the holidays.
Forth rambled from the village inn alone,
No sooner had I sight of this small skiff,
Discovered thus by unexpected chance,
Than I unloosed her tether and embarked.
The moon was up, the lake was shining clear
Among the hoary mountains; from the shore
I pushed, and struck the oars and struck again
In cadence, and my little boat moved on,
Even like a man who walks with stately step,

Though bent on speed. It was an act of stealth
And troubled pleasure, nor without the voice
Of mountain-echoes did my boat move on;
Leaving behind her still, on either side,
Small circles glittering idly in the moon,
Until they melted all into one track
Of sparkling light. A rocky steep uprose
Above the cavern of the willow tree,
And now, as suited one who proudly rowed
With his best skill, I fixed a steady view
Upon the top of that same craggy ridge,
The bound of the horizon, for behind
Was nothing but the stars and the grey sky.
She was an elfin pinnace; lustily
I dipped my oars into the silent lake,
And, as I rose upon the stroke, my boat
Went heaving through the water like a swan;
When, from behind that craggy steep till then
The bound of the horizon, a huge cliff,
As if with voluntary power instinct,
Upreared its head. I struck and struck again,
And growing still in stature the huge cliff
Rose up between me and the stars, and still,
With measured motion, like a living thing,
Strode after me. With trembling hands I turned,
And through the silent water stole my way
Back to the cavern of the willow tree;
There in her mooring-place I left my bark, –
And through the meadows homeward went, with grave
And serious thoughts; and after I had seen
That spectacle, for many days, my brain
Worked with a dim and undetermined sense
Of unknown modes of being; in my thoughts
There was a darkness, call it solitude
Or blank desertion. No familiar shapes
Of hourly objects, images of trees,
Of sea or sky, no colours of green fields;
But huge and mighty forms, that do not live
Like living men, moved slowly through my mind
By day, and were the trouble of my dreams.

(B) Book I, 357–400 (1850)

One summer evening (led by her) I found
A little boat tied to a willow tree
Within a rocky cave, its usual home.
Straight I unloosed her chain, and stepping in
Pushed from the shore. It was an act of stealth
And troubled pleasure, nor without the voice
Of mountain-echoes did my boat move on;
Leaving behind her still, on either side,
Small circles glittering idly in the moon,
Until they melted all into one track
Of sparkling light. But now, like one who rows,
Proud of his skill, to reach a chosen point
With an unswerving line, I fixed my view
Upon the summit of a craggy ridge,
The horizon's utmost boundary, for above
Was nothing but the stars and the grey sky.
She was an elfin pinnace; lustily
I dipped my oars into the silent lake,
And, as I rose upon the stroke, my boat
Went heaving through the water like a swan;
When, from behind that craggy steep till then
The horizon's bound, a huge peak, black and huge,
As if with voluntary power instinct
Upreared its head. I struck and struck again,
And growing still in stature the grim shape
Towered up between me and the stars, and still,
For so it seemed, with purpose of its own
And measured motion like a living thing
Strode after me. With trembling oars I turned,
And through the silent water stole my way
Back to the covert of the willow tree;
There in her mooring-place I left my bark, –
And through the meadows homeward went, in grave
And serious mood; but after I had seen
That spectacle, for many days, my brain
Worked with a dim and undetermined sense
Of unknown modes of being; o'er my thoughts
There hung a darkness, call it solitude

Or blank desertion. No familiar shapes
Remained, no pleasant images of trees,
Of sea or sky, no colours of green fields;
But huge and mighty forms that do not live
Like living men, moved slowly through the mind
By day, and were a trouble to my dreams.

Index